"In his latest work, *The Muslim Majority*, Robin Hadaway
folk Islam, which represents the beliefs and practices of the majority of
Muslims, is expressed in the main branches of Islam. Sufficiently academic
but refreshingly practical, Hadaway provides specific instruction on how
contextualization can be used to effectively communicate the gospel cross-
culturally in evangelizing folk Muslims. *The Muslim Majority* should not be
overlooked by anyone who desires a genuine understanding of Islam and
is mandatory reading for those who desire to reach folk Muslims with the
good news of Jesus Christ."

— Paul Chitwood, president, International Mission Board

"In *The Muslim Majority*, professor Hadaway engages with the challenge
of bringing the message of salvation to folk Muslims. This innovative
book draws on years of experience to offer creative solutions to the long-
standing challenge of reaching Muslims for Christ. Hadaway reports that
conventional gospel presentations in terms of a guilt/innocence worldview, supplemented by doctrinal apologetics, will not answer the felt
spiritual needs of the 70 percent majority of Muslims. Instead, he calls
for creative approaches to reach these people, who see life through a fear/
power worldview (folk Muslims), or through an existential/transcendent
worldview (Sufis). This is a vital contribution to the greatest missional
challenge facing the church today."

— Mark Durie, senior research fellow, Arthur Jeffery
Centre for the Study of Islam, Melbourne, Australia

"This is a useful introduction to folk Islam in African contexts. Hadaway
provides a balance between contextual explanations and his personal experiences. He also points helpfully to redemptive analogies as effective means to
introduce gospel truth."

— Ant Greenham, associate professor of Missions and Islamic
Studies, Southeastern Baptist Theological Seminary

"Dr. Robin Hadaway takes you deep into the heart of the vast majority of Muslims. He digs deep beneath the veneer of formal Islam that informs most of the current approaches that largely address matters of theology and culture. Then he presents us with a more effective approach that addresses the 'real' worldview of the majority of Muslims, folk Islam, which is a mixture of religious beliefs, mysticism, and superstitious practices. This approach can trigger a revolutionary method that promises to multiply the fruit of missionary labor. This book is not only to be read but also to be shared for maximum exposure."

—Georges Houssney, founder and president, Horizons International

"Robin Hadaway writes out of costly service, personal experience, and serious missiological reflection concerning what it would take for ordinary Muslims amongst the Beja people to find most sympathetically that Jesus Christ desires to be their Savior and Lord. On the author's heart, especially, are folk Muslims and Sufi folk Muslims. He evaluates various historic and contemporary approaches to Christian sharing of the gospel with Muslims and proposes some contextualized missional approaches meaningful within the worldview of the Beja. I am pleased to commend his helpful contribution."

—Bill Musk, retired Anglican Bishop of North Africa

"Dr. Hadaway, writing from his perspective as an academician, has compiled excellent insights into the, at times, esoteric world of folk Islam. His research on Sufism and African Traditional Religions are of particular note. Hadaway has refuted the common-held belief that Islam is monolithic and exclusively doctrinal. His sharing of practical insights are worth the price of this relevant book."

—Phil Parshall, missionary, SIM International

"Robin Hadaway gets to the heart of what leads to an effective witness to Muslims when he proposes that it must be contextualized according to worldview. As he develops this argument the various chapters provide useful insight into how to approach each Muslim context according to the real-life circumstances of those who live there. For those who would go beyond general references to the world of Islam to a level that seeks to personally encounter a Muslim in their context with the gospel, this book is a must-read."

—Dean Sieberhagen, associate professor of Islamic studies and director, Islamic Studies Program, Southwestern Baptist Theological Seminary

"Robin Hadaway in *The Muslim Majority* exposes the fallacy of the widely held notion that most Muslims adhere to Islamic orthodoxy in both faith and practice. The result is that most strategies for reaching Muslims fail because they are not designed to understand the actual folk Islam which often prevails in the lives of the majority of Muslims in the world. Not since Phil Parshall's *Bridges to Islam*, published in 1983, has a book come along which so helpfully addresses the particular challenges posed by folk Islam. May this book be widely read by those serving the nearly 2 billion Muslims who still await the fulfillment of their deepest hopes."

—Timothy C. Tennent, president and professor of world Christianity, Asbury Theological Seminary

THE
MUSLIM
MAJORITY

ROBIN DALE HADAWAY

THE
MUSLIM
MAJORITY

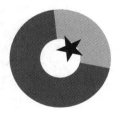

FOLK ISLAM
AND THE
SEVENTY PERCENT

B&H
ACADEMIC
NASHVILLE, TENNESSEE

I dedicate this book to my wife, Kathy,
who lived with me in remote, poor, and dangerous places
to take the gospel of Christ to the ends of the earth.

CONTENTS

PREFACE

This book is the result of a long journey. Although raised in a Christian family, I decided I was an atheist by the age of thirteen. I honed this skeptical worldview through college as a philosophy minor and political science major. I accepted Christ as a senior at the University of Memphis after a near-fatal aircraft incident, radically changing my worldview. After four years in the United States Air Force, I resigned my commission as an officer and began seminary. At Dallas Theological Seminary and later, Southwestern Baptist Theological Seminary, I internalized a biblical worldview. After graduating with a master of divinity degree and working a short stint in business, I moved to the Los Angeles area to pastor a church in Monterey Park, the first Chinese majority city in America. While pastoring this multi-ethnic congregation, I thought I was sufficiently involved in missions. In 1980, however, my wife, Kathy, and I journeyed with some youth to the Glorieta Baptist Conference Center in New Mexico for Foreign Missions Week. There we met a group of missionaries who had planted one hundred churches the previous year. Within four years, our family moved to Tanzania to help Don and Mary Alice Dolifka, Gene and Jane Roach, and Charles and Cheri Orange start urban churches, beginning our career in missions.

The International Mission Board (IMB) of the Southern Baptist Convention (SBC), our sending agency, trained us for eight weeks at their rented facility in Callaway Gardens, Georgia, in early 1984. While this orientation to life on the mission field featured excellent courses, the fields of missionary anthropology and worldview studies were just beginning. When we arrived in Tanzania, it was the second poorest country in the world. We had to shoot wild game in the hunting area for meat and raise many of our vegetables. I also noticed that African Traditional Religion (ATR) had quite a hold on the Sukuma tribe in Mwanza, Tanzania, where we worked. As I shared the gospel with these fine African people, I observed that, although they were courteous, many of my arguments did not resonate with them. We lost a child at birth during Swahili language school, and our next child was born with a disability. Therefore, after just four years on the mission field, we returned to the United States to pastor again. After two years of shepherding a church in the Phoenix, Arizona, area, our daughter's developmental doctors at UCLA told us that Joy could return overseas.

Within six months we resigned our church and were asked by the IMB to begin the first work among the Beja people of North Africa. During a year's study of Arabic before leaving the States, the IMB allowed me to enroll in two courses at Fuller Theological Seminary in Pasadena, California. A course taught by Paul Hiebert on folk religion answered many of the questions that had surfaced in Tanzania. When we arrived in North Africa in March 1991, we discovered that there were only twenty other Christian workers affiliated with any agency in the country. As we planted churches in this closed, limited-access country, I noticed the worldview of the Beja people was similar to that of the Sukuma tribe of Tanzania. Furthermore, the folk or popular Islam of the Beja people of North Africa mirrored the traditional religion of the Sukuma of Tanzania. My understanding of that connection has crystallized over the last seventeen years as I have taught missions courses at Midwestern Baptist Theological Seminary in Kansas City, Missouri. I have discovered that folk Islam is the *real* Muslim majority.

ACKNOWLEDGMENTS

I must pay tribute to those who have contributed to this book. First, my wife, Kathy, and my children—Bethany, Seth, and Joy—co-labored with me in our ministry among the Beja people of North Africa. Second, the late Paul Hiebert introduced me to the field of missionary anthropology and folk religion in 1990. Third, the late Willem Saayman of the University of South Africa and Keith Eitel of Southwestern Baptist Theological Seminary greatly supported me during my research and writing for this book. Fourth, I owe a great debt to my ministry partners, Pastor Philemoni of Tanzania, and Jonadab, 'Isa, and Faruk of Sudan, for their assistance in understanding their cultures. I know of no finer believers anywhere.

ABBREVIATIONS

African Traditional Religion(s) (ATR)
International Mission Board (IMB)
Christian Standard Bible (CSB)
Muslim Background Believer (MBB)
Southern Baptist Convention (SBC)
Sudan Notes and Records (SNR)

GLOSSARY

Ababda: One of the five major Beja subdivisions. They live in southern Egypt and are largely monolingual in Arabic.

African Traditional Religion(s) (ATR): Traditional religions on the continent of Africa. ATRs generally hold to a belief in a Supreme Being, spirits, and a life after death. Many practice ancestor veneration, while their religious personnel perform beneficial magic or malevolent witchcraft.

Amarar: One of the five major Beja subdivisions. They live in eastern Sudan and speak Beja, though some are bilingual in Arabic.

Andot: Beja board game similar to backgammon but played with camel dung. *Andot* means "camel pellets" in Beja.

animism: Older, outdated (and pejorative) term for traditional religion and ATR (African Traditional Religion).

Ansar Mahdi: "Helpers of the *Mahdi*." Some Beja still revere the memory of the Sudanese *Mahdi* of the late eighteenth century, Muhammad Ahmed. This small political group is called the *Ansar Mahdi* (more political than religious).

'Arif: Gnostic, mystical knowledge in Sufi Islam. The term comes from the Arabic word *'arafa* (to know). The word also can mean "expert" or "master." *Ma'arifa* (knowledge) and *'irfan* (*gnosis*) are derivatives of *'arafa*.

Ashraf: A small Beja subgroup who claim to be of the bloodline and lineage of the Prophet Muhammad.

ATR: *See* African Traditional Religion.

*ayatollah*s: Living *Imams* (Shia Islamic clergy). Means "sign of God." They rule in place of the coming *Mahdi*.

bafumu (*mfumu*): Plural of *mfumu*, shaman in Sukuma ATR. *Bafumu* are believed to dispense good magic.

balogi: Plural of *nogi*, evil sorcerers or witches who dispense evil magic in Sukuma ATR.

Bantu: A term coined in 1856 to describe more than 400 African tribes that speak cognate languages that utilize *ntu* and *batu* (or a variation) for man and men respectively. The first Bantu originated in central Africa and spread to eastern and southern Africa from the Red Sea to the Indian Ocean and to the Cape. Sukuma and Swahili are Bantu languages (see appendix 2).

baqa: Subsistence. "New life in God" in Sufism that is similar to the "born again" concept in Christianity.

baraka (*baraqa*): Spiritual power, blessing, divine grace.

basir (pl., *busara*): A traditional healer and spiritual diagnostician reputed to be able to "see the unseen" in Beja folk Islam.

batemi: Plural of *ntemi*. Chiefs in Sukuma ATR.

Beja (*Bega, Bedawiet, Bija*): Arabic term for a Cushitic tribe of 1.3 million people who live in eastern Sudan, southern Egypt, and northern Eritrea. Also, the name for the language of *To-Bedawie* spoken by a majority of the tribe. See appendix 1 for a map of their location.

Beni-Amer: One of the five major Beja subdivisions. Most live in Eritrea, but many also live in eastern Sudan. Most speak *Tigre*, but some are bilingual in Beja.

Bisharin (*Bishariin*): One of the five major Beja subdivisions. Most live in eastern Sudan while a few reside in southern Egypt. Many are bilingual in Beja and Arabic.

bufumu: The good or helpful magic and divination of the *bafumu* (*mfumu*) in Sukuma ATR.

bulogi: Witchcraft, sorcery, the evil magic of a *nogi* in Sukuma ATR.

busara: Plural of *basir*. Diviners who can see the unseen.

Busharia: Egyptian Arabic name for the *Ababda* subdivision of the Beja who live in southern Egypt.

caliph: One chosen to lead the nation of Islam after Muhammad's death. The Prophet's successor is the meaning of *caliph*.

contagious magic: "Materials or substances once in contact with the intended victim are used in the magical attack."[1]

contextualization: "making concepts or ideals relevant in a given situation."[2]

Deim: Arabic word meaning "neighborhood" or "native dwelling area."

dervish: Persian word (from *darwish*) that means "poor man" and "traveler of the Sufi path."

dhikr: Remembrance. Sufi ritualistic repetition of the ninety-nine names of God. The practice is mandatory in Sufi Islam.

---

[1] Arthur C. Lehmann and James E. Myers, eds., *Magic, Witchcraft, and Religion: An Anthropological Study of the Supernatural*, 2nd ed. (Mountain View, CA: Mayfield, 1989), 256–57.

[2] Byang Kato, in David J. Hesselgrave and Edward Rommen, *Contextualization: Meanings, Methods, and Models* (Pasadena, CA: William Carey Library, 2000), 33.

Dinka: The largest tribe in Southern Sudan.

'Eid al-Adha: The festivity (*eid*) of sacrifice concludes the Hajj (pilgrimage to Mecca).

'Eid al-Fatr: The feast (*eid*) of fast-breaking concludes a month's fasting during Ramadan.

faki (*faqir, fiki, fagir*): Poor man (see *dervish*), or traveler on the Sufi path. The feminine is *fakira*. In Beja folk Islam, a traditional healer is called a *faki* (plural, *fugara*).

fana: In Sufism, dying to self or self-extinction.

Fateha: The opening verses of the Quran, which read: "In the name of God the Compassionate, the Merciful. Praise be to God, Lord of the universe, the Compassionate, the Merciful, Sovereign of the Day of Judgment!"[3]

fiki: Another transliterated spelling of *faki*.

flaw of the excluded middle: Thesis of the late Paul Hiebert that claims Westerners use science to explain everyday experiences and relegate other-worldly matters to religious speculation and a future afterlife. The "flaw of the excluded middle" unnaturally separates the supernatural from the world of sensory perception. The purview of folk religion is to explain the middle-level problems and fears with supernatural explanations that identify the causes and recommend the cures.

folk Islam (popular Islam): Mixture of traditional religious beliefs and practices with orthodox Islam. Also known as popular, informal, low, and common Islam.

---

[3] N. J. Dawood, trans. *The Koran: With Parallel Arabic Text* (London: Penguin Books, 1990), xvii.

folk religion: The religious beliefs, faith, rituals, and practices of ordinary mankind. Also known as popular religion or low religion.

fugara: Plural form of *faki*.

Hadendoa (Hadendowa): The largest of the five major Beja subdivisions. Most live in eastern Sudan, but a few dwell in Eritrea and are called the *Hedareb*. Many are bilingual in Beja and Arabic.

Hadith: A compilation of stories about Muhammad and words attributed to him. *Hadith* is the common Arabic word for tale, narrative, report, story, or interview.

Hajj: Pilgrimage to Mecca. One of Islam's five pillars.

Hedareb: The *Hadendoa* Beja living in Eritrea.

Heequal: Beja word for the spiritual essence of luck-bringing. This quality is prized by healers and diviners.

Hillmen: A nickname for the Beja of the Red Sea hills, given to them by the Egyptians in the third century AD.

homeopathic magic: "Homeopathic principles of medicine . . . are based on Analogic magic [or 'Imitative magic'], wherein it is assumed that the external similarity rests on what would seem to be an apparent internal connection and a basic inner unity and dependence."[4]

imam: A senior official in charge of a large mosque. This title is also given to the descendants of Caliph Ali in Shia Islam.

Insider Movements: A movement that advocates that Muslims who become believers in Christ should remain Muslims in both name and cultural identity.

irenic (approach): Peaceful and nonconfrontational.

---

[4] Wayland C. Hand, "Folk Medical Magic and Symbolism in the West," in Lehmann and Myers, eds., *Magic, Witchcraft, and Religion*, 193.

'Isa (*Eisa*): Quranic Arabic name for Jesus the Messiah.

Isma'ilis: *See* Seveners. The Isma'ilis are led by the Aga Khan and are the wealthiest Muslims.

Ithna Ashariya (*ithna asharah*): "Twelve" in Arabic. The Twelvers, the majority subsect of Shia Islam, recognize twelve imams. They believe the Twelfth Imam is in hiding (Muhammad al-Mumtazzar) and will return at a later date.

Jacobites: "In the Byzantine world, the Jacobites were known as Monophysites—those that believed Christ possessed only the divine nature and lacked humanity."[5] In the Muslim world they were called Jacobites, named for Jagoub el Baradai, who formulated their doctrinal canon.

jihad: Arabic for "struggle" or "strive." Greater jihad is one's personal struggle against sin. Lesser jihad is the holy war against the enemies of the faith.

jinn (*jinns*): spiritual beings in Islam. They are usually evil but sometimes capricious.

Ka'ba: The place where Muslims believe God commanded Abraham and Ishmael to build upon the original worship site of Adam. Stone cube in the sacred mosque in Mecca. The black stone is in the southeast corner of the *Ka'ba*.

karai: Beja word for *werehyena* (see *werehyenas*).

karama: In folk Islam, a *karama* is a sacrificial offering to God to cause something positive to happen. The word means "nobility, generosity, and token of esteem" (Arabic).

---

[5] Vali Abdi, "Jacobite Explanation of the Trinity in the Context of Mu'tazilite Theology: Abu Ra'itah al-Takriti," *Religious Inquiries* 8, no. 16 (December 2019): 7, http://ri.urd.ac.ir/article_100711._f9ed7a438dc1f4f0cb748dc4543d907a.pdf.

Karijites: Seceders. This small Islamic sect rejects both the Sunni and Shia positions regarding the succession question in Islam.

kashf: Arabic word meaning "remove," but Sufis use the term for the "unveiling" concept of the mystic Sufi quest.

Khalifa: The Sudanese Arabic name for *caliph*, or successor of the *Mahdi*. After Muhammad Ahmed, the Sudanese *Mahdi*, died in 1885, *Khalifa* Abdullah ruled Sudan until 1898.

kulogwa: The act of casting spells by the *balogi* (evil sorcerers/witches) in Sukuma ATR.

Liwelelo: The high god of Sukuma ATR.

Maasai: A Nilotic tribe in northern Tanzania and southern Kenya.

Mahdi (Mahdia): Second great prophet who will come to deliver Islam during a time of shame and trouble. Sunnis, Shiites, and Sufis all have versions of the Mahdi. Muhammad Ahmed bin Abdallah proclaimed himself the Mahdi and expelled the British from Sudan in 1885 but died the same year. The Mahdia is the Mahdi's government.

manga: Spirit-possessed medium in Sukuma ATR.

marabout: West African Sufi holy man similar to a sheikh or a *pir*.

ma'rifa: Arabic for *gnosis* or mystic knowledge in Sufism.

masamva: The ancestors in Sukuma ATR.

middle-level: *See* flaw of the excluded middle.

mingay: Beja word for a malady that strikes children, called "left aloneness."

mirguay: Beja word for "fright sickness."

mfumu (pl. *bafumu*): The medicine man (or woman) and diviner in Sukuma ATR who heals by magic or homeopathic medicine. Second in importance only to the *ntemi* (chief).

Milad al-Nabi: Birthday of the Prophet. Muhammad's birthday is increasingly celebrated as the third *'eid* (feast).

mystical Muslims: Arthur J. Arberry defines mysticism as a "constant and underlying phenomenon of the universal yearning of the human spirit for personal communion with God"[6] Sufis are considered the mystics of Islam. Folk Muslims and much of popular Islam fit within this category.

Nabatab: Beja Cushitic nobility who subjugated the *Tigre*. They adopted the customs and *Tigre* language of the conquered people. The *Tigre* and the *Nabatab* together compose the *Beni-Amer* Beja. The *Nabatab* make up 10 percent of the total.

Neo-Pentecostalism: *See* third wave Pentecostalism *and* Power Encounter.

Nestorians: Followers of Nestorius, bishop of Constantinople, whose heretical views were condemned in AD 431. He held that Christ was really two people loosely divided into the divine and the human, although Nestorius never subscribed strictly to the views he was condemned for.

ngemi wa mbula: Assistant to the chief (*ntemi*) in charge of making rain in Sukuma ATR.

Ngoma ya bufuma: Magic drum dance in Sukuma ATR.

Night of Power: The twenty-seventh night of the month of Ramadan. Folk Muslims believe prayers and devotion offered on this night can alter destiny.

Nogi (pl. *balogi*): Sorcerer or witch in Sukuma ATR practicing evil magic. *Balogi* keep their identities secret and are often executed if discovered.

---

[6] Quoted in Phil Parshall, *Bridges to Islam: A Christian Perspective on Folk Islam* (Downers Grove, IL: InterVarsity Press, 2006), 10.

Ntemi (pl. *batemi*): Sukuma chief. *Batemi* are believed to have the magical power to bring rain in Sukuma ATR.

Nubians: Descendants of the Egyptians of the upper Nile. The Nubians adopted Christianity and held out against Islam until about AD 1400. Today, they number about one million and live in equal numbers in southern (Upper) Egypt and northern Sudan.

Nyamwezi: A *Bantu* people in Tanzania ethnically and linguistically related to the Sukuma tribe.

orthodox Islam: The doctrinal Islam of the Quran. Also called formal, official, high, and ideal Islam.

pir: Persian word for *sheikh*.

polemics: Argumentative discussion by disputation.

popular Islam: *See* folk Islam.

popular religion: *See* folk religion.

power encounter: According to David Hesselgrave, a power encounter was originally understood as "a visible, practical demonstration that Jesus Christ is more powerful than the false gods or spirits worshipped or feared by a given society or people group." The term has been expanded by third wave Pentecostalism to include not only speaking in and interpreting tongues but exorcising demons and territorial spirits, raising the dead, slaying in the spirit, spiritual mapping, and prayer walking.[7]

Qadiriyya: Important Sufi order founded by Abd al-Qadir al-Jilani in the twelfth century. *Qadiriyya* Sufis are the "whirling dervishes" who gather each Friday at sundown at the tomb of Hamad al-Nil, who led the Sudanese

---

[7] David J. Hesselgrave, *Paradigms in Conflict: 15 Key Questions in Christian Missions Today*, 2nd ed. (Grand Rapids: Kregel, 2018), 157–58.

segment of the order in the nineteenth century. Fifty percent of Beja Sufis follow this order. They are also known as the Jiladiyya.

Quran (Koran, Qu'ran): Islam's holy book.

Rashaida: A tribe originally from Arabia that moved during the nineteenth century to the Red Sea coast of Africa. They number about 150,000 in Eritrea and half that in Sudan.

redemptive analogy: Concept in a host culture that can be used to illustrate the Christian gospel message.

Salif: Beja tribal traditional law (trumps Islamic law).

sama': The Arabic word for "listen" or "hear." For Sufis, the word means to listen to the heart through listening to chanted or recited poetry.

Seveners: Shiite subsect who acknowledge only seven of the first twelve imams recognized by the majority *Ithna Ashariya* (Twelvers) Shia Muslim sect.

Shahada: The first pillar of Islam is the repetition of the phrase "There is no god but God, and Muhammad is His prophet."

Shaitan (*Shawatin*, plural): Satan, devil, demon.

Sharia (Shari'a): Islamic law. The Quran plus the Prophet's Sunna as recorded in the hadiths as interpreted by the Muslim jurists came to be called the *Sharia*.

sheikh (*Shaykh*): The leader of a Sufi order. There are three grades of sheikhs. Only the highest grade possesses spiritual authority. The lowest grade of sheikh teaches or leads an Islamic school (*Khalwa*). Often an honorary title as well.

Shia (Shiites, partisans of Ali—from *Shi'at 'Ali* or party of Ali): The minority Muslim sect (15 percent of Islam), who believe the leader of Islam should be a descendant of Ali. They live mostly in Iran, Iraq, Pakistan, India, Afghanistan and Yemen.

siir: A Beja word for illness caused by the evil eye.

Sufis (Sufism): The ascetic and mystical sect of Islam. Sufis are not a division of Islam, as Sufis follow either Sunni or Shia Islam. The term may come from the woolen garments (*suf* means wool) worn by early followers or from *suffa* (Arabic, meaning "bench"), or "people of the bench." Carl Ernst, in the *Shambhala Guide to Sufism,* says the term may be linked to the Arabic word for "bench" or *sofa,* literally, 'People of the Bench.'[8] See the first block quote on page 43. This is a minority view.

Sukuma: A Bantu people who are the largest tribe in Tanzania and the second largest in East Africa. *Kisukuma* is the language, *Wasukuma* the people, and *Usukuma* the land (see appendix 3).

Sungusungu: An independent, generally nonreligious, informal association of vigilantes in Tanzania.

Sunna: A beaten path in the desert, or well-worn instruments. Acquired the meaning "well trusted and reliable" and came to mean the living, practical Islamic tradition.

Sunni: The majority sect (about 85 percent) in Islam. Sunnis believe the community of Islam should choose its leader.

sura (pl. suras): A chapter in the Quran.

sympathetic magic: "Items associated with or symbolic of the intended victim are used to identify and carry out the spell."[9]

---

[8] Carl W. Ernst, *The Shambhala Guide to Sufism* (Boston: Shambhala Publications, 1997), 22.

[9] Arthur C. Lehmann, "Demons, Exorcism, Divination, and Magic," in Lehmann and Myers, eds., *Magic, Witchcraft, and Religion,* 257.

syncretism: The combination, blending or reconciliation of differing or conflicting beliefs in religion.

Tahlil **formula**: "*La ilaha il-la Allah*: There is no deity but God." This is said ritually by most Muslims, but especially by Sufis.

tariq (*tariqa, tarik, tarika*): Arabic word for "road," "way," or "path." A derivative term that means "manner," "procedure," "Sufi religious order," "creed," "faith," "religion," or "method."

tasawwuf: The process of taking up the "way [path] of Sufism."

tawil: Arabic word for "long," "tall," or "high" but signifies "deeper or greater meaning" in Sufi Islam.

Third Wave Pentecostalism: Synonymous with Neo-Pentecostalism. Includes groups that have gone beyond what most evangelicals consider orthodox. *See* power encounter.

tiffa: The male Beja hairstyle known as "fuzzy-wuzzy," whichs hangs in ringlets down the back and along the side of the face. The Beja believe the *tiffa* posseses magical powers.

Tigre: A Semitic language spoken by the *Beni-Amer* Beja of Eritrea. In Eritrea, the *Beni-Amer* are known as the *Tigre* tribe. However, historically the *Tigre* people (the serfs) were subjugated by the *Nabatab* nobility and together became the *Beni-Amer* tribe as it is known today.

To-Bedawie: The formal name for the Beja language.

toodip: Beja word for epilepsy. Believed to be caused by evil spirits. The Arabic word is *sara'a*.

traditional religion: Aboriginal beliefs, practices, rituals, and doctrines native and indigenous to a culture.

Twelvers: See *Ithna Ashariya*.

ulama: A clergy and scholarly class in Islam. The term comes from *alim*, the Arabic word for "scholar."

ummah (umah): Community of Islam (Arabic).

Wahhabi (Wahhabism): The puritanical Islamic movement originating in Arabia at the end of the eighteenth century. The followers of Abd al-Wahhab (1703–1787) insist on a literal interpretation of the Quran. *Wahhabism* has become the orthodox Islamic school of thought.

werehyenas (*karai*): Mythological creatures (in Beja thought) that can transform from human to hyena and vice versa.

witchcraft: I prefer the broad definition given by John Mbiti in *African Religions and Philosophy*: "Witchcraft is a term used more popularly and broadly, to describe all sorts of evil employment of mystical power, generally in a secret fashion."[10]

worldview: The presuppositions a culture or ethnic group possesses about reality and the nature of things. The mental map a society uses in perceiving the world.

Zaidis: The Shia subsect that believes any descendant of Caliph Ali can become the imam (religious leader). Ali was the fourth caliph of Sunni Islam and the first imam of Shia Islam.

zar: A "non-Muslim" evil spirit that possesses Muslim men and women and is especially prevalent among the Beja people.

---

[10] John Mbiti, *African Religions and Philosophy*, 2nd ed. (Oxford: Heinemann Books, 1989), 196–97.

INTRODUCTION

Introducing Folk (or Popular) Islam

An article in the *Kansas City Star* emphasizes the sway popular Islam holds over many Muslims today.

> For more than two years, Ali Hussain Sibat of Lebanon has been imprisoned in Saudi Arabia, convicted of sorcery and sentenced to death. . . . His crimes: manipulating spirits, predicting the future, concocting potions and conjuring spells on a call-in TV show called "The Hidden" on a Lebanese channel, Scheherazade. It was, in effect a Middle Eastern psychic hot line. . . . Sibat was jailed after agreeing to give a woman a potion so that her husband would divorce his second wife. "Most of my treatments were with honey and seeds," he said. "You would put the charm in the honey and drink from it."[1]

This event illustrates how profoundly folk Islam differs from its more orthodox expression. Popular Islam often confronts life's problems through magic while orthodoxy worships Allah in submission, faith, and ritual.

---

[1] "'Sorcerer' Awaits Beheading by Saudi Officials," *Kansas City Star*, April 25, 2010, A26.

Muslims number slightly more than 1.8 billion persons worldwide, making Islam the world's second-largest religion.[2] Folk Islam mixes "pristine Islam with the ancient religious traditions and practices of ordinary people."[3] Estimates indicate that 70 percent of Muslims follow popular Islam.[4] Speaking about the religious beliefs of the common people, the late Paul Hiebert states, "The failure to understand folk religions[5] has been a major blind spot in missions."[6] A full 40 percent of the world holds to popular religion.[7]

Most methods for reaching Muslims have concentrated on one of two broad approaches, with a third blending the first two methods. The apologetics approach seeks to establish that Christianity is more valid or reasonable than Islam. Various contextualized "bridge" approaches seek common ground between Christianity and Islam.

Apologetic arguments have not been very effective with folk Muslims because arguments fail to answer the "why" questions posed by popular Islam. Examples of these questions include, "Why did my child die?" and "Why was there no rain for my crops this year?" Popular religion demands answers to such inquiries. For instance, when we were missionaries in

---

[2] See Paul Marshall, Roberta Green, and Lela Gilbert, *Islam at the Crossroads: Understanding Its Beliefs, History, and Conflicts* (Grand Rapids: Baker, 2002), 73.

[3] William J. Saal, *Reaching Muslims for Christ* (Chicago: Moody Press, 1991), 51.

[4] See Phil Parshall, *Bridges to Islam: A Christian Perspective on Folk Islam* (Downers Grove, IL: InterVarsity Press, 2006), 2.

[5] The terms *popular Islam* and *folk Islam* are similar. The former are the practices and beliefs that stand apart from the norms and behavior sanctioned by the "'*ulama*' [religious authorities]" (Stewart), while the latter is "a mixture of pristine Islam with the ancient religious traditions and practices of ordinary people" (Saal). Musk uses the terms *folk, popular, low, non-official,* and *informal* to differentiate between traditional forms and the high, formal, official, ideal, and theological forms of the faith. See Charles C. Stewart, "Introduction: Popular Islam in Twentieth-Century Africa," in *'Popular Islam' South of the Sahara,* ed. J. D. Y. Peel and Charles C. Stewart (Manchester: Manchester University Press, 1985), 365; Saal, *Reaching Muslims for Christ,* 51; and Bill Musk, "Popular Islam: An Investigation into the Phenomenology and Ethnotheological Bases of Popular Islamic Belief and Practice" (PhD diss., University of South Africa, 1984), 20–21.

[6] Paul G. Hiebert, R. Daniel Shaw, and Tite Tienou, *Understanding Folk Religion: A Christian Response to Popular Beliefs and Practices* (Grand Rapids: Baker, 1999), 29, 74.

[7] See David J. Hesselgrave, *Communicating Christ Cross-Culturally,* 2nd ed. (Grand Rapids: Zondervan, 1991), 223.

Africa, we lost a child at birth. The women from our Kenyan church came and sat in silence with my wife. The unspoken question was, How could this happen? The opening illustration in this chapter of a woman seeking to prevent her husband from remaining married to a second wife serves as an example of this. Also, the Muslim religious leaders of the Berti of Northern Darfur in Sudan "are known for the efficacy of their medicines which consist of Koranic verses written, then washed off slates and drunk by their clients."[8] According to Phil Parshall, one of the major felt needs in folk Islam is healing:

> The folk Muslims reaction to illness is often of a more mystical nature. He will go to his *pir* [Muslim holy man] so that the *pir* may breathe upon his body. Holy water will be drunk. Amulets with Quranic verses of healing potency will be worn. Magical formulas will be repeated. Promises of donations to a special saint will be made. Fervent prayer will be offered in the name of a departed *pir*.[9]

Another reason for the ineffectiveness of apologetic arguments is that folk Islam lacks sufficient theological content to participate in an argument or discussion about doctrine. Popular religionists often have to first be taught the beliefs of their own creed in order to be shown it is less viable than Christianity.[10] Imagine a missionary teaching the doctrine of Islam's five pillars to a Muslim so the Christian worker can refute it.

Most contextualized methods also miss the mark with folk Muslims, who rarely attend Islamic worship, observe the five pillars of Islam, or read the Quran. Rather than arguing about doctrine, they try to discover common ground between Islam and Christianity. This may include adaptation to dress, custom, and religious terminology.

The more controversial contextualized methods present some unique problems. Certain national believers and missionaries, for example, promote

---

[8] Stewart, "Introduction: Popular Islam in Twentieth-Century Africa," 365.

[9] Parshall, *Bridges to Islam*, 114.

[10] See Hiebert, Shaw, and Tienou, *Understanding Folk Religion*, 9.

"insider movements."[11] They encourage national converts from Islam to remain Muslims in identity, avoiding the name Christian. Insider movement proponent (and my friend) Kevin Higgins describes the phenomenon thusly:

> [Insider movements are] a growing number of families, individuals, clans, and/or friendship-webs becoming faithful disciples of Jesus within the culture of their people group, *including their religious culture*. This faithful discipleship will express itself in culturally appropriate communities of believers who will also continue to live in as much of their culture, including the religious life of the culture, as is biblically faithful.[12]

A few, including me, have proposed a fourth approach for reaching Muslims—contextualizing according to worldview. This book explains the differences between popular Islam and official Islam and then explores the best approaches for evangelizing these folk Muslims. Definitions of popular and orthodox Islam appear in the glossary and in footnote 5, but Bill Musk succinctly summarizes the designations. He writes, "Various terms may be used to describe the official aspect of a particular faith. They include the ascriptions 'formal', 'high', 'ideal' or 'theological.' That formal form contrasts with the 'popular', 'informal', 'low', or 'folk' aspect of religious expression."[13] Musk says that official religion deals with the meaning of life, possesses complex institutions, and provides ethical guidance. Popular religion, however, is pragmatic, amoral, and deals with the problems of everyday life.[14] I advocate

---

[11] For a better understanding of insider movements from their perspective, see *Understanding Insider Movements: Disciples of Jesus Within Diverse Religious Communities*, ed. Harley Talman and John Jay Travis (Pasadena, CA: William Carey Library, 2015), 7–8, 91. For insights from perspectives both for and against (but largely a critique), see *Muslim Conversions to Christ: A Critique of Insider Movements in Islamic Contexts*, ed. Ayman S. Ibrahim and Ant Greenham (New York: Peter Lang, 2018).

[12] Kevin Higgins, "The Biblical Basis for Insider Movements: Asking the Right Question, in the Right Way," in Ibrahim and Greenham, *Muslim Conversions to Christ*, 212 (italics in the original).

[13] Bill Musk, *The Unseen Face of Islam: Sharing the Gospel with Ordinary Muslims at Street Level*, rev. ed. (London: Monarch Books, 2003), 180.

[14] Musk, 180–81.

a contextualized approach to popular Islam, addressing its unique character, which differs significantly from its orthodox counterpart.

Two major streams flow into popular Islam:

1. Some Muslim folk practices originate from within Islam itself, as the Quran and the Hadith (الحديث) provide rich material for the development of nonorthodox beliefs. In addition, the major Muslim groups—Sunnis, Shiites, and Sufis—exhibit practices that can only be called folk Islam.

2. Much of popular Islam in the Muslim world is derived from the preexisting religions of the peoples who embraced Islam many years ago. Rather than abandon their traditional (animistic) practices, these groups have simply mixed or added Islam to them. For instance, a folk Muslim may consult spirits or cast spells in order to influence the supernatural.

Generally speaking, most Westerners hold to a guilt/innocence worldview and craft their gospel presentations accordingly.[15] Apologetics-based gospel presentations, which rely on propositional truths and guilt/innocence reasoning (right/wrong, good/bad), often fall on deaf ears in the Islamic world because most Muslims hold a different worldview.[16]

Roland Muller says that "in the Muslim cultures of the Middle East, which are primarily shame-based, the church has struggled to communicate the gospel in an effective manner."[17] Muller points out that all cultures, including Islamic ones, are blends of differing kinds of societies.[18] That is, no culture reflects only one view. A shame/honor society holds relationships, reputation, and honor above other values. For example, the shame/honor worldview esteems saving face over forthrightness. On the other hand, the existential/transcendent worldview exalts religious experience. For instance,

---

[15] See Roland Muller, *Honor & Shame: Unlocking the Door* (Bloomington, IN: Xlibris, 2000), 36.

[16] See Muller, 12–13.

[17] Muller, 20.

[18] See Muller, 20.

most Sufis value the religious feelings produced from their ecstatic dances or counting the ninety-nine names of God. Sufis consider these activities to be more important than praying five times a day.

In the second stream of folk Islam, the fear/power worldview is the most widely held perspective by those from traditional, or animistic, backgrounds. Fear of evil spirits and dark forces categorizes this worldview. Popular religion in general, and popular Islam in particular, uses spells, potions, and prayers to prevent misfortune and ward off evil.

Each group, therefore, requires a different evangelistic approach. This book shows how popular Islam differs from orthodox Islam and how such differences render these Muslims more reachable for the gospel.

Folk (Popular) Religion

Popular Islam is a subset of popular religion. Hiebert defines folk religion as "the religious beliefs of the common people."[19] As might be expected, popular religion is not confined only to Islam. There are folk Hindus, folk Buddhists, and even folk Christians.[20] Whereas high religion ponders the questions of eternity and cosmology, the issues of everyday life trouble the followers of popular religion.[21] Hiebert compares and contrasts the two:

> On the formal level, philosophical religions, such as Confucianism, Buddhism, Hinduism and Christianity, deal with ultimate questions and claim ultimate truth. In contrast, the everyday life of most villagers is dominated by folk religions that deal with everyday questions and rely on local earthbound spirits, ancestors, witchcraft, magic, evil eye, and other unseen powers to explain and respond to human dilemmas.[22]

---

[19] Hiebert, Shaw, and Tienou, *Understanding Folk Religion*, 74.
[20] See Hiebert, Shaw, and Tienou, 77.
[21] See Musk, "Popular Islam," 21.
[22] Paul G. Hiebert, *Transforming Worldviews: An Anthropological Understanding of How People Change* (Grand Rapids: Baker Academic, 2008), 131.

Although both official and folk religions ask "why" questions concerning unexplained events, the latter focus their attention on ameliorating their effects. High religions for the most part accept the unexplainable but are more preoccupied with the theoretical and theological doctrines of the afterlife. For instance, official religion explains how to attain the afterlife. Folk religions focus on life on earth and attempt to influence the supernatural. The orthodox versions of religions offer explanations for paranormal activity, while their popular religions desire power over the spirit world. Hiebert underlines this point, writing, "Folk religions are not interested in an academic understanding of metaphysics and truth, but in procuring a good, meaningful life and guarding against evils that disturb it."[23]

Not surprisingly, the popular beliefs and practices of folk religion are also present in the West. Many Americans, and American companies, believe the number thirteen is unlucky. For example, most buildings in the United States lack a thirteenth floor. Numerous airlines in America omit the thirteenth row on their aircraft. It is reported that the late United States Senator John McCain and his staff routinely "knocked on wood" in order not to incur bad fortune during his 2008 United States presidential campaign.[24] Additionally, athletes throughout the world often observe folk practices to bring good luck during sporting events.

Folk religious practices, even by those who claim to belong to a high religion, are common occurrences. Often many people in societies characterized by high religions do not actually know much about their faiths. Instead, people seem more concerned with their folk practices in order to live as comfortably as possible.[25]

---

[23] Hiebert, *Transforming Worldviews*, 84.

[24] "Extra, Extra, McCain Staffers Knock KC," *Kansas City Star*, April 20, 2008, A2.

[25] See Paul G. Hiebert, *Anthropological Insights for Missionaries* (Grand Rapids: Baker, 1985), 222.

Islamic Influences upon Folk Islam

Islam seems to be particularly suited for the development of folk religion.[26] One researcher says that in no other religious community is there such a difference between orthodoxy and folk beliefs.[27] George Braswell depicts folk Islam this way:

> Quranic Islam follows the formal teachings and letter of the law embedded in the Quran. Folk Islam tends to combine Quranic Islam with other beliefs and practices of a particular culture . . . Folk Islam may include power encounters with the spirit world, especially in health and healing and life decision concerns . . . *Sufism* is considered the mystical arm of Islam. It stresses the love of God, the closeness of God, and feelings about God.[28]

Two principal streams feed into popular Islam. These are (1) Islamic influences (especially Sufism) from within the religion itself, and (2) traditional religious practices, which include African Traditional Religion (ATR), Arabian traditional religion, American traditional religion, and Asian traditional religion, which often predates the advent of Islam.[29] In speaking about the dissimilarities between orthodox and popular Islam, Musk notes great differences in almost every facet of their expression.[30] The contrasts involve theology, practices, speech, politics, structures, ethics, and emotions. He writes:

> The two worlds are essentially different in the sense that they cohere around alternative views of reality. They may coincide, or co-exist at

---

[26] See Musk, "Popular Islam," 229.

[27] See Musk, 20.

[28] George W. Braswell Jr., *Islam: Its Prophet, Peoples, Politics and Power* (Nashville: B&H, 1996), 286.

[29] I have taken the liberty of listing other instances of traditional religion, such as Asian traditional religion, American traditional religion, and Arabian traditional religion. All three exist but are not commonly referred to as ATR.

[30] Musk, "Popular Islam," 25.

various points along the way but the constructs of the universes are different, even largely opposed to each other. They are built on distinct paradigms . . . Their protagonists are traveling different roads.[31]

Conclusion

Folk religions receive less attention than their orthodox counterparts for several reasons. First, folk religions are difficult to study because they largely consist of cultural practices rather than doctrinal declarations. Second, folk religions do not seek affirmation from nor attempt to argue with their detractors. Instead, they are intent on pursuing rituals to alleviate suffering and achieve a better life.

Folk Islam conforms to the same pattern as other folk religions. Although followers of this brand of Islam identify strongly as Muslims, their practices indicate otherwise. Folk Islam includes Sufi mysticism and tribal beliefs inherited from a pre-Islamic past.

In this book we will travel down the roads of both orthodoxy and nonorthodoxy, observing how each kind of Muslim thinks and feels. Along this journey we will discover how to reach folk Muslims for Christ. First, we will examine Islamic orthodoxy.

---

[31] Musk, 25.

Folk Islam *AND*
Islamic Orthodoxy

When my wife and I arrived in Nairobi, Kenya in 1984 to study Swahili in preparation for serving as missionaries in Tanzania, part of our training included visiting different mosques. I soon learned there were Sunni, Shia, Sufi, and Aga Khan mosques represented in our city. Furthermore, I noticed that Muslims of Indian descent frequented some of the mosques, while others were populated largely by Somalis. I had no idea there were so many different sects within Islam.

Introduction

The subject of Islam is so vast that a complete study of the religion represents a daunting challenge. One researcher suggests that Muslims fall into one of nine classifications. Although not exhaustive, Joshua Massey divides Islam into the following categories:

1. **Nominal Muslims**: Muslims in name only, who only go to the mosque on eid (a major Islamic holiday) once or twice a year.[1]

---

[1] There are two major festivals in Islam: *'Eid al-fitr* (fast-breaking feast) at the conclusion of a month's fasting during Ramadan, and *'Eid al-adha* (festivity of sacrifice)

2. **Fringe Muslims**: These Muslims, often urban youth, are infatuated with Western culture . . . Some are disappointed with their religious leaders, who, they believe, are living in the past and not taking advantage of all that modernity offers.

3. **Liberal left-wing Muslims**: These are open-minded Muslims who are not intimidated by conservative Islamic fundamentalists. They are often well educated and financially well off.

4. **Conservative right-wing Muslims**:[2] [These tend to support dictatorial military rulers as well as strict Islam]. . . .

5. **Ultra-orthodox Muslims**: Islamic reformist movements, like the Wahhabis (called "the Protestants of Islam"), frown on what has become of Islam throughout the world today: a mix of Qur'anic observance with superstitions, sacred shrines, richly ornamented tombs, divination, omens, and excessive reverence of Muhammad.

6. **Modern Muslims**: These have successfully integrated Western technology with Islamic devotion and are proud to be part of a global Islamic community.

7. **Mystical[3] Muslims**: Sufis and folk Muslims who, according to Wahhabis and conservative right-wing Muslims, are desperately in need of serious reform.

8. **Communistic Muslims**: In some parts of Central Asia and other former communist lands, Islamic identity has been almost completely stripped away.

---

concluding the Hajj. Increasingly, a third 'eid is being celebrated called *Milad al-Nabi* (birthday of the Prophet) in honor of Muhammad, according to Akbar S. Ahmed in *Islam Today: A Short Introduction to the Muslim World* (London: I. B. Tauris, 1999, 2001), 39–41.

[2] Don Petterson calls this category "political Islam" and states, "Neither political Islam nor Islamic fundamentalism should be equated with extremism, for although some Islamists are extremists, most of course are not." Whereas conservative right-wing Muslims tend to support dictatorial military rulers as well as strict Islam, liberal left-wing Muslims often embrace limited democracy and secularism to an extent. Petterson, *Inside Sudan: Political Islam, Conflict, and Catastrophe* (Boulder, CO: Westview Press, 1999), 191.

[3] Arthur J. Arberry defines mysticism as a "constant and underlying phenomenon of the universal yearning of the human spirit for personal communion with God." Quoted in Parshall, *Bridges to Islam*, 10 (see intro., n. 4).

9. **Rice Muslims**: Some poor animistic tribes of sub-Saharan Africa or low Hindu castes of South Asia convert to Islam for material benefit or economic convenience.[4]

This book concentrates on the folk Islam described in category 7 on Massey's list. Folk Islam represents the beliefs and practices of the majority[5] of Muslims in the world today.[6] Massey places both Sufis (Islamic mystics) and folk Muslims (those who practice superstitions, divination, etc.) under the category of "mystical Muslims." I suggest that folk Muslims should be the broader classification, and Sufis a subset. While many Sufis are folk Muslims, not all folk Muslims can be termed mystical. Of course, some Sufis are not mystical either but consider themselves Sufis by heritage and not by practice. Many folk Muslims have more in common with traditional religions than mysticism. Sufism will be examined more closely in chapter 3.

There are two principle adherents to popular Islam: (1) Sufi folk Muslims and (2) traditional religion folk Muslims.[7] Folk Islam and theological (orthodox) Islam differ substantially. Aside from the obvious unorthodox practices, folk Muslims appear to possess a totally different mindset from their orthodox counterparts.

Orthodox, Official, or High Islam

A baseline for orthodoxy must be established in order to understand how far popular Islam has deviated from the traditional orthodox Muslim

---

[4] Joshua Massey, "His Ways Are Not Our Ways," *Evangelical Missions Quarterly* (*EMQ*) 35, no. 2 (1999): 198, https://missionexus.org/his-ways-are-not-our-ways/.

[5] As noted earlier, Parshall in *Bridges to Islam*, 2, estimates the number of folk Muslims to be about 70 percent of Islam. Almost 100 years ago, Samuel M. Zwemer, in *The Influence of Animism on Islam* (New York: Macmillan, 1920, viii), placed the practitioners of popular Islam at 94 percent of the total. There have been no studies on why this percentage is lower than 100 years ago. I believe that higher education and exposure to other cultures has changed this percentage. Most likely the number of folk Muslims will drop further in coming years.

[6] See Parshall, *Bridges to Islam*, 2.

[7] Parshall, 4. Parshall calls Sufism "a fairly well-defined influence within folk Islam."

religion. As the custodians of the holy cities and places of worship, many Muslims believe the Saudi religious authorities reflect the faith's orthodox form.[8]

The Beliefs of Orthodox Islam

The Islamic Affairs Department of the Embassy of Saudi Arabia in Washington, DC. published a book that explains the Muslim faith to English speakers in North America, titled *Understanding Islam and the Muslims*. The book summarizes Islamic orthodoxy from the official Sunni Saudi perspective:

> What do Muslims believe? Muslims believe in One, Unique, Incomparable God; in the Angels created by Him; in the prophets through whom His revelations were brought to mankind; in the Day of Judgment and individual accountability for actions; in God's complete authority over human destiny and in life after death.
>
> Muslims believe in a chain of prophets starting with Adam and including Noah, Abraham, Ishmael, Isaac, Jacob, Joseph, Job, Moses, Aaron, David, Solomon, Elias, Jonah, John the Baptist, and Jesus, peace be upon them. But God's final message to man, a reconfirmation of the eternal message and a summing-up of all that has gone before was revealed to the Prophet Muhammad, peace be upon him, through Gabriel.
>
> How does someone become a Muslim? Simply by saying "there is no god apart from God, and Muhammad is the Messenger of God." By this declaration the believer announces his or her faith in *all* God's messengers, and the scriptures they brought.

---

[8] See Parshall, 3.

What does "Islam" mean? The Arabic word "Islam" simply means "submission," and derives from a word meaning "peace." In a religious context it means complete submission to the will of God.[9]

Muslims believe every person is originally born a Muslim.[10] If someone is an unbeliever it is because the unbeliever's parents influenced them to leave Islam and embrace a false faith.[11] There are many beliefs and practices important to Muslims, but *Understanding Islam* summarizes the core principles of orthodox Islam as the Five Pillars of Islam:

> What are the "Five Pillars" of Islam? They are the framework of the Muslim life: faith, prayer, concern for the needy, self-purification, and the pilgrimage to Makkah for those who are able.[12]
>
> 1. FAITH. There is no god worthy of worship except God and Muhammad is His messenger. This declaration of faith is called the *Shahada*, a simple formula which all the faithful pronounce. . . .
>
> 2. PRAYER. *Salat* is the name for the obligatory prayers which are performed five times a day, and are a direct link between the worshipper and God. There is no hierarchical authority in Islam, and no priests, so the prayers are led by a learned person who knows the Quran, chosen by the congregation. . . .
>
> 3. THE "ZAKAT." . . . The word *zakat* means both "purification" and "growth." . . .[13]

---

[9] *Understanding Islam and the Muslims*, Islamic Affairs Department (Washington, DC: Embassy of Saudi Arabia, 1989), 5–7.

[10] See Hammudah Abdalati *Islam in Focus*, 2nd ed. (Indianapolis: American Trust Publications, n.d.), 14.

[11] See Georges Houssney, *Engaging Islam* (Boulder, CO: Treeline Publications, 2010), 106.

[12] Due to differences in transliteration schemes, the Saudis spell Mecca, *Makkah*. Transliteration differences also account for the various differences in spelling Quran (e.g., *Qu'ran* and *Koran*).

[13] Georges Houssney, author of *Engaging Islam*, says, the first pillar, Faith, is better called "Creed." because Faith is a Christian concept. Furthermore, Houssney, a native Arabic speaker, says that *zakat* means "personal growth" and "purification." Email to the author, January 29, 2021.

Each Muslim calculates his or her own *zakat* [offering] individually. For most purposes this involves the payment each year of two and a half percent of one's capital. . . .

4. THE FAST. Every year in the month of Ramadan, all Muslims fast from first light until sundown, abstaining from food, drink, and sexual relations. . . .

    Although the fast is most beneficial to the health, it is regarded primarily as a method of self-purification. . . .

5. PILGRIMAGE (Hajj). The annual pilgrimage to Makkah—the Hajj—is an obligation only for those who are physically and financially able to perform it. . . .

The rites of the Hajj, which are of Abrahamic origin, include circling the *Ka'ba* seven times, and going seven times between the mountains of Safa and Marwa as did Hagar during her search for water.[14]

The importance Muslims place upon their writings, particularly the Quran, impacts popular Islam. Zwemer comments about folk practices related to the Quran: "Not only do we find bibliolatry, i.e., worship of the Book, but also bibliomancy, i.e., the use of the Quran for magical or superstitious purposes."[15] Muslims believe the Quran represents the exact word of God.[16] The official Saudi discourse concerning the Quran and the Hadith is enlightening:

What is the Quran? The Quran is a record of the exact words revealed by God through the Angel Gabriel to the Prophet Muhammad, peace be upon him. It was memorized by Muhammad, peace be upon him, and then dictated to his Companions, and written down by scribes, who cross-checked it during his lifetime. Not one of its 114 chapters, *Suras*, has been changed over the centuries, so that the Quran is in every detail the unique and miraculous text which

---

[14] *Understanding Islam and the Muslims*, 13, 16–17, 20.
[15] Zwemer, *The Influence of Animism on Islam*, 23.
[16] See Abdalati, *Islam in Focus*, 187.

was revealed to Muhammad, peace be upon him, fourteen centuries ago.

What is the Quran about? The Quran, the last revealed Word of God, is the prime source of every Muslim's faith and practice. It deals with all the subjects which concern us as human beings: wisdom, doctrine, worship, and law, but its basic theme is the relationship between God and His creatures. At the same time it provides guidelines for a just society, proper human conduct and an equitable economic system.

Are there any other sacred sources? Yes, the *sunna*, the practice and example of the Prophet, peace be upon him, is the second authority for Muslims. A *hadith* is a reliably transmitted report of what the Prophet, peace be upon him, said, did, or approved. Belief in the *sunna* is part of the Islamic faith.[17]

The second most important book for Muslims is the Hadith [الحديث.]. George Braswell says the Hadith is "a collection of stories about Muhammad and sayings attributed to him."[18] *Hadith* is also the common word for "tale," "narrative," "story," or "interview" in Arabic. Hans Wehr's *Arabic-English Dictionary* says the word can mean "speech; chat, chitchat; small talk; conversation, talk, discussion; interview; prattle, gossip; report, account, tale, narrative; Prophetic tradition, Hadith, narrative relating deeds and utterances of the Prophet and his Companions."[19]

The topic of Muhammad frequently arises when speaking with Muslims, both folk and otherwise. Born in Mecca about the year 570, Muhammad was orphaned early in life and was raised by his uncle Abu Talib.[20] As a young man, his honesty and integrity brought him to the

---

[17] *Understanding Islam and the Muslims*, 12.

[18] Braswell, *Islam*, 11 (see intro., n. 28).

[19] Hans Wehr, *Arabic-English Dictionary: A Dictionary of Modern Written Arabic*, 3rd ed., J. Milton Cowan, ed. (Ithaca, NY: Spoken Language Services, 1976), 161.

[20] See John L. Esposito, *Islam: The Straight Path*, 5th ed., upd. (New York: Oxford University Press, 2016), 6.

attention of an older wealthy widow who operated commercial caravans. Muhammad's marriage to Khadija produced six children, four of whom (all girls) attained adulthood. Upon reaching the age of forty, Muhammad began receiving visions during retreats to the cave of Hira outside of Mecca. These revelations, received over a twenty-two-year period, would be written down or memorized in the Quran, the "recitation."[21] Muslims believe the Quran is "literally the word of God, God's own eternal speech."[22] The significance of the person of Muhammad cannot be overemphasized. Islam holds that no person can match the virtue of Muhammad.[23] Every Muslim attempts to emulate the example of the life of Islam's Prophet.[24]

Muslims also believe Muhammad was the last, or "seal" of the prophets of Judaism and Christianity.[25]

In addition to the five pillars of Islam, orthodox Islam has at least five primary beliefs. These include (1) a belief in one God, (2) a belief in the existence of angelic messengers (both good and evil), (3) a belief in the holy Scriptures (Quran, Torah, Ingil, or Gospel, and Zabur or Psalms), (4) a belief in the Prophet-Messengers (Muhammad, Adam, Noah, Abraham, Ishmael, Isaac, Jacob, Joseph, David, Solomon, Moses, Aaron, Job, Jonah, John the Baptist, and Jesus), and (5) a belief in a hereafter, including a divine judgment and heaven and hell.[26]

---

[21] Esposito, 7–8.

[22] Fred M. Donner, "Muhammad and the Caliphate," in the *Oxford History of Islam*, ed. John L. Esposito (New York: Oxford University Press, 1999), 6–7.

[23] See Gabriel Said Reynolds, *The Emergence of Islam: Classical Traditions in Contemporary Perspective* (Minneapolis: Fortress, 2012), 39.

[24] See Andrew Rippin, *Muslims: Their Religious Beliefs and Practices*, 3rd ed. (New York: Routledge, 2005), 50.

[25] See I. A. Ibrahim, *A Brief Illustrated Guide to Understanding Islam*, 2nd ed. (Houston: Darussalam, 1997), 48.

[26] See Faisal Abdul Rauf, *What's Right with Islam: A New Vision for Muslims and the West* (New York: HarperCollins, 2004), 55–58.

Other Islamic Influences upon Folk Islam

One area of difficulty involves discerning the scope of the influence of popular religion upon orthodox Islam. A number of folk practices within Islam seem to come from pre-Islamic sources. Bill Musk observes folk religion within the pages of the Quran itself: "In many respects, the formal religion couches within its own codifications and condoned practices, elements of folk Islam."[27] Zwemer also advocates this position, writing, "Even in Arabia the stern monotheism of the Wahhabi Reformers was unable to eradicate the pagan superstitions of Islam because they are embedded in the Koran and were not altogether rejected by Mohammad [*sic*] himself, much less by his companions."[28]

One of these practices, worshiping at the *Ka'ba*, is important in both orthodox and folk Islam. *Understanding Islam* explains its significance:

> What is the *Ka'ba*? The *Ka'ba* is the place of worship which God commanded Abraham and Ishmael to build over four thousand years ago. The building was constructed of stone on what many believe was the original site of a sanctuary established by Adam. God commanded Abraham to summon all mankind to visit this place, and when pilgrims go there today they say, "At Thy Service, O Lord," in response to Abraham's summons.[29]

Muslims today circle the *Ka'ba* seven times during the Hajj. Muslim author Tanja Al-Hariri-Wendel acknowledges the ritual's pagan origins:

> Pagan Arabs regarded the idols *Manah*, *al-Lat* and *al-Uzza* as daughters of Allah. The Arabs placed more emphasis on these three female divinities than on the five idols given to them by 'Amer Ibn Luhaij in Noah's time. For example, the Quraysh, the tribe to which the Prophet Muhammad belonged, used to circle the *Ka'bah*

---

[27] Musk, "Popular Islam: An Investigation," 229 (see intro., n. 5).
[28] Zwemer, *The Influence of Animism on Islam*, 4.
[29] *Understanding Islam and the Muslims*, 8.

saying, "In the name of *al-Lat*, in the name of *al-ʿUzza*, and *Manah*
the third, the different ones! They are the highest of all swans, and
one may hope for their intercession with God!" The idols *Manah*,
al-Lat, and *al-ʿUzza* were regarded as mediators with God. They
were compared to cranes flying high in the sky.[30]

Al-Manah, *al-Lat*, and *al-ʿUzza* reappear in the Quran when
Muhammad first identifies them as deities. The Prophet's later rejection of
his earlier teaching is the subject matter for *The Satanic Verses* by Salman
Rushdie, which explores some of these discrepancies.[31] The Iranian government called for the author's death even though Rushdie is a Muslim himself.

The subject of folk Islam's influence upon orthodox Islam is complex.
The seamless combining of Quranic, pre-Quranic Arabian, and other
sources by Muslims over the years increases the difficulty in discovering
the origin of many customs in Islam. Stewart captures the complexity of
the problem:

> The genius of Islam lies in part in its receptivity and ability to incor-
> porate diverse esoteric practices during the process of Islamization.
> This is readily apparent in Sub-Saharan Africa where Islam in this
> century has spread more rapidly than in any comparable time in
> the past. Yet therein also lies an inherent tension that has made the
> problem of defining a Muslim central to the concerns of Islamic
> scholars and reformers throughout the history of Islam. This ten-
> sion surfaces in matters as diverse as theology (classically, the uses
> and abuses of *Sufism* and the *Sufi*), art and music.[32]

I have felt this same tension in attempting to separate the Muslim influences upon popular Islam from the practices attributable to traditional

---

[30] Tanja Al-Hariri-Wendel, *Symbols of Islam* (New York: Sterling, 2002), 43.
[31] See Salman Rushdie, *The Satanic Verses* (New York: Viking Penguin, 1988), 123.
[32] Stewart, "Introduction: Popular Islam in Twentieth-Century Africa," 365 (see intro., n. 5).

religion, which includes African, Arabian, American, and Asian traditional religion. Sometimes a distinction is not clear.

Subdivisions and Major Sects in Islam

Orthodoxy deemphasizes the divisions within Islam and portrays Muslims as part of a unified family, *ummah,* or Community of Islam, in the world.[33] Despite this assertion, there are many groups and subgroups within the faith. Khalid Duran counts seventy-three different sects within Islam,[34] reflecting a hadith where Muhammad gives this number. Although it is impossible to cover every faction, a description of the major subdivisions is important to understanding popular Islam. Marshall, Green, and Gilbert say, "Beyond the previously mentioned Five Pillars of Islam and six principles,[35] no single Islamic belief system is adhered to by all Muslims. Thus, it is impossible to state categorically what all Muslims believe."[36] There are two main divisions of Islam. In addition to these two branches there are other minor visions that have emerged. The next three chapters will look at the subgroups of Islam.

Conclusion

Orthodox Islam presents as the version of the religion most Westerners recognize. The outside world sees Muslims praying at the mosque daily, circling the *Ka'ba* during the Hajj, and fasting during the month of Ramadan. They think, *This is Islam.* There is another Islam, however, hiding in the shadows, concealed from most outsiders. It is this Islam we will explore.

---

[33] See Seyyed H. Nasr, *Islam: Religion, History, and Civilization* (New York: Harper Collins, 2003), 14–15.

[34] Khalid Duran in Marshall, Green, and Gilbert, *Islam at the Crossroads*, 27 (see intro., n. 2).

[35] Although not named the "six principles," these fundamental principles are summarized by the Saudi Arabian officials in the section "What Do Muslims Believe?" of *Understanding Islam and the Muslims.*

[36] Marshall, Green, and Gilbert, *Islam at the Crossroads*, 27.

2

Folk Islam *AND* Sunni Muslims

In 1979 Juhayman al-'Utaybi (1943-1979), a strict Wahhabi [Sunni] who was disillusioned by the profligate lifestyle of the Saudi royal family, attempted to revolt against the Saudi regime in the name of Muhammad ibn 'Abdallah al-Qahtani, a student at the Islamic University in Riyadh, believed to be the Mahdi.[1] Qahtani's mahdi status had been revealed in dreams to his wife and sister. He fulfilled many of the predictions about the Mahdi which occur in the *Hadith*: the Mahdi would appear at the *Ka'ba* at the turn of the Islamic century (1979 overlapped with the year 1400 in the Islamic calendar), and was to have the same name as the Prophet and similar physical characteristics. Juhayman and his followers believed that after a long period of deviation from true Islam, the Mahdi would appear and put an end to corrupt, tyrannical regimes. They seized the Grand Mosque in Mecca but

---

[1] This refers to the second great prophet who will come to deliver Islam during a time of shame and trouble. Sunnis, Shiites, and Sufis all have versions of the Mahdi. Aziz Chaudhry says, "All this happened as foretold by the Prophet. The function of the Mahdi and the Messiah was reformation of Muslims and revival of Islam." Aziz Ahmad Chaudhry, *The Promised Messiah and Mahdi* (Islamabad: Islam International Publications, 1996), 25.

were eventually dislodged by the Saudi security forces after a violent siege.[2]

Sunni Islam

As the largest Islamic group, Sunni [سُنِّي] Muslims see themselves as the most orthodox division in Islam and, as the name suggests, see themselves as the followers of the Sunna [سُنَّة]. Braswell places their number at 90 percent of all Muslims,[3] while other writers put the estimate anywhere from 80 to 85 percent.[4] Montgomery Watt says, "The Quran contains liturgical and legal or social prescriptions for the life of the community of Muslims. These rules were greatly elaborated by Muslim jurists in later times to constitute what is now known as 'Islamic law' or 'Shari'a.'"[5] Malise Ruthven says, "[Sharia,] in non-religious terms means the road or way to a watering-place, the well-trodden path which must always be followed."[6] The ninth-century Muslim theologian Shafi'i and others before and after him developed what is now known as Shari'a (شريعة).

Shafi'i established the Islamic hermeneutic (interpretation) that stands today for determining Sunni orthodoxy in Islam. Shafi'i wrote, "The Quran does not contradict the hadiths, but the hadiths explain the Quran."[7] In Sunni Islam the Quran does not stand alone as the sole source of Muslim law. Shafi'i held that "it was not the Quran alone, but the Quran plus the

---

[2] Patrick Sookhdeo, *Global Jihad* (McClain, VA: Isaac, 2007), 277. Also see Yaroslav Trofimov, *The Siege of Mecca: The Forgotten Uprising in Islam's Holiest Shrine and the Birth of Al Qaeda* (New York: Anchor Books, 2007).

[3] Braswell, *Islam: Its Prophet, Peoples, Politics and Power*, 90 (see intro., n. 28).

[4] See John L. Esposito and Dalia Mogahed, *Who Speaks for Islam? What a Billion Muslims Really Think* (New York: Gallup, 2007), 2; Marshall, Green, and Gilbert, *Islam at the Crossroads*, 27; and Patrick Sookhdeo, *Global Jihad*, 216, who has the lowest figure, placing Sunnis at about 80 percent of Muslims.

[5] Montgomery Watt, *Bell's Introduction to the Quran* (Edinburgh: University of Edinburgh Press, 1970), 162.

[6] Malise Ruthven, *Islam in the World*, 3rd ed. (New York: Oxford University Press, 2006), 135.

[7] Shafi'i in Ruthven, 135.

Prophet's Sunna, as recorded in hadiths, that must guide the Muslims."[8] Sunni people are called *ahl-al-Sunna* or "People of the *Sunna*."[9] Marshall Hodgson believes the term *Sunni* to be too general and inadequate. He prefers to call these Muslims by the hyphenated term *Jama'i-Sunni* (*Jama'i* means "community"). These Muslims did not side with the Shiites and Kharijites who rejected the majority Muslim community.[10]

There are subsects and legal schools within Sunni Islam. Montgomery Watt says that there are four Sunnite schools that still exist. These are the Hanafites, Hanbalites, Malikites and Shafi'ites.[11] One Sunni group, however, warrants special attention. This group emerged victorious from conflicts within Sunni Islam to become the pure standard by which Islam is now judged.[12] *Wahhabism* is a puritanical Islamic vision within the Hanbali school of thought founded in Arabia at the end of the eighteenth century.[13] Wahhabis and Salafi Sunnis seek a return to the doctrine and practice of the early founders of Islam. Condemning idolatry and the worship of saints, Wahhabis (and most other Islamic groups) despise Sufism, insisting on a literal interpretation of the Quran.[14] Sookhdeo reflects on this Sunni subsect:

> Al-Wahhab considered Muslim society at the time to be little bet-
> ter than paganism and he revived the *Khariji* practice of *takfir*,[15]

---

[8] Shafi'i in Ruthven, 134.

[9] "In its original pre-Islamic meaning, Sunna had been applied to ancestral custom: the word has associations with a beaten path in the desert, advancing age, sharpened teeth and well-honed implements. Employed by the legists of the so-called ancient schools, it means the living 'practical' tradition, assumed to be based on the general practice and authority of the Prophet and his companions." Ruthven, 134.

[10] Marshall G. S. Hodgson, *The Venture of Islam: Conscience and History in a World Civilization* (Chicago: University of Chicago Press, 1961, 1974), 276–79.

[11] W. Montgomery Watt *Islamic Philosophy and Theology* (Edinburgh: Edinburgh University Press, 1985), 57. See also Braswell, *Islam*, 85.

[12] See Ruthven, *Islam in the World*, 368–69.

[13] See Daniel Byman, *Al Qaeda, the Islamic State, and the Global Jihadist Movement: What Everyone Needs to Know* (New York: Oxford University Press, 2015), 70–76.

[14] See Braswell, *Islam*, 98–99.

[15] The *Kharijites* represent a sect that disagrees with both Sunnis and Shi'ites.

i.e., condemning all Muslims he disagreed with as apostates in order to justify *jihad* against them. The strictly puritanical *Wahhabism* remains today the predominant Islamic movement within Saudi Arabia.[16]

The Wahhabi Sunnis, with their strict interpretation of the Quran, Hadith, and enforcement of Sharia, have become the face of official Islam.[17] According to John Esposito, "Wahhabi Islam's ultraconservative interpretation of Islam—literalist, puritanical, exclusivist, and intolerant—is based on the belief that they follow the pristine, pure, unadulterated message of the Prophet. Their brand of Islam is not shared by many other Sunni or Shia Muslims, whom many Wahhabis would condemn as unbelievers or religious hypocrites."[18] The Saudi government, however, has moderated the most militant form of Wahhabism and its emphasis on militaristic *jihad* in recent years.[19] *Jihad* is an Arabic word meaning "struggle" or "strive."[20] In Islam this can involve one's personal struggle for holiness against sin, known as greater *jihad*, or it references "holy war" on God's behalf against the enemies of the faith, known as lesser *jihad*. Some refer to *jihad* as the sixth pillar of Islam.[21]

Extremism does exist within many of the subdivisions and theological schools of Islam. This element is estimated at between 2 and 15 percent of all Muslims.[22] Esposito and Mogahed place the percentage of "politically radicalized" Muslims at about 7 percent.[23] Of course, those who would actually carry out extremist acts would be fewer in number.

The 7 percent figure comes from a Gallup Poll survey conducted in the ten most populous Muslim countries, making up 80 percent of Islam

---

[16] Sookhdeo, *Global Jihad*, 277.

[17] See Marshall, Green, and Gilbert, *Islam at the Crossroads*, 97 (see intro., n. 2).

[18] Esposito, *Islam*, 223 (see chap. 1, n. 19).

[19] See Braswell, *Islam*, 99.

[20] See John J. Donohue and John L. Esposito, eds., *Islam in Transition: Muslim Perspectives*, 2nd ed. (New York: Oxford University Press, 2006), 393.

[21] See Braswell, *Islam*, 71.

[22] See Marshall, Green, and Gilbert, *Islam at the Crossroads*, 109.

[23] Esposito and Mogahed, *Who Speaks for Islam?*, 70.

worldwide: Egypt, Indonesia, Jordan, Saudi Arabia, Turkey, Lebanon, Pakistan, Morocco, Iran, and Bangladesh.[24] The question defining the politically radicalized Muslim, translated into the local language, involved whether the respondent thought the September 11, 2001 attacks on the World Trade Center in New York City were "'completely' justified" or not.[25] The random surveys were conducted in personal interviews lasting about an hour in countries where 80 percent of the population did not possess landline telephones. The survey was administered among persons who were all above the age of fifteen, of both sexes, and in rural and urban areas.[26] This survey represents one of the most accurate scientific estimates of Muslim extremism.

Sunni Islam and Popular Islam

Charles Stewart says Sunni popular Islam has two manifestations. He believes some folk practices emerge from a distortion or embellishment of Sunni orthodox Islam.[27] For instance, whereas orthodox Islam respects Muhammad,[28] some Sunni folk Muslims worship him and pray at his grave for power. Orthodox Islam condemns folk religious practices such as praying at Muhammad's grave. Wahhabi Sunnis have attempted to completely eradicate folk religious practices.[29]

Stewart categorizes the other expression of Sunni popular Islam as political protest and reform movements.[30] One example of this expression of Sunni popular Islam is Mahdism.[31] Sunni Islam is especially vulnerable to this second

---

[24] Esposito and Mogahed, 193.

[25] Esposito and Mogahed, 69.

[26] Esposito and Mogahed, 169.

[27] Stewart, "Introduction," 365 (see intro., n. 5).

[28] *Orthodox Islam*, *High Islam*, and *Official Islam* are interchangeable terms, just as *folk Islam*, *low Islam*, and *popular Islam* are interchangeable expressions representing the other extreme.

[29] See Braswell, *Islam: Its Prophet, Peoples, Politics and Power*, 77.

[30] Stewart, "Introduction," 365.

[31] Mahdism constitutes part of the belief system of Shiites and Sufis as well. This will be explained later.

manifestation of folk Islam. Although Sunnis represent official Islam, the fervent Wahhabis in their midst sometimes stray into folk practices as illustrated by the article quoted at the beginning of this chapter. Who are the populist factions within Sunni Islam intent on restoring spiritual purity to the faith?

While the Wahhabis of Islam sought a return to a more historic and traditional Islam, the Muslim Brotherhood movement of Egypt's Hassan al-Banna (1904–1949) ignited a resurgence of political Islam in the twentieth century.[32] It would be a mistake to categorize all those in the Muslim Brotherhood movement as political radicals. Their writings clearly reveal a hunger for a deeper faith. Musk comments on a letter al-Banna wrote to King Faruq of Eygpt:[33]

> The pure Islam towards which al-Banna urged Faruq was the Islam of the Muslim Brotherhood. Their Islam was not limited to worship and ritual or mere "spirituality." It was a robust Islam, touching on all the affairs of people in this world and in the hereafter. Their Islam included the virtues of all other systems and was sufficient in itself for the rebirth of Egypt. Twentieth-century Muslims needed to return to the Islamic principles of the first Muslims.[34]

Many Muslim reformers desired only cultural and spiritual renewal, and so renounced violence and pledged to respect the political process where others, like Sayyid Qutb, advocated violent jihad. However, the Muslim Brotherhood spawned more radical splinter movements that did not share this view of nonviolence.[35] These factions include the late Hassan al-Turabi's National Islamic Front (NIF) based in Sudan, the late Osama bin Laden's al Qaeda,[36] the Taliban in Afghanistan, al-Shabab in Somalia, Boko Haram in Nigeria, and the Islamic State in Iraq and Syria (ISIS).

---

[32] See Braswell, *Islam*, 39.
[33] Faruq would later hang al-Banna, executing him for his faith.
[34] Musk, *The Unseen Face of Islam*, 126 (see intro., n. 13).
[35] See Sookhdeo, *Global Jihad*, 280.
[36] See Marshall, Green, and Gilbert, *Islam at the Crossroads*, 103.

Stewart defines one aspect of popular Islam as political protest and reform movements such as appeared in millennial *Mahdism*.[37] I do not, however, consider most Muslim protest factions to be expressions of popular Islam. Addressing fanatical eschatological Islam, Sookhdeo explains:

> This mindset also results in abundant conspiracy theories. They view Muslim history as a prelude to the End and the various battles as End-Time battles or at least dress rehearsals for them. They perceive a series of cycles of victory and defeat, and are therefore not dismayed by defeat as this is only to be expected periodically, while ultimately God will bring them victory. This final victory, achieved by God himself when the Muslims face overwhelming odds, will be superior to the victories which the Muslims themselves have gained in the past by their own strength.[38]

Conclusion

As Sunnis make up the overwhelming majority of Muslim sects, many people consider all Sunnis to be orthodox. This chapter has demonstrated that, in fact, folk practices invade many Sunni rituals and customs. The Sunni influence upon folk Islam has more to do with degree than substance. Muhammad ibn Abd al-Wahhab, the founder of the Wahhabis "was appalled by many of its [Arabia's] popular religious practices, such as the veneration of saints, their tombs, and sacred rocks and trees, which he condemned as pagan supersititions and idolatry (shirk), the worst of sins in Islam."[39] Historian Andrew Wheatcroft links the ascetic practices of the Wahhabi Sunnis to folk Islam.[40] Other Sunni Muslims stray into popular Islam when their zealousness causes them to embrace the very mysticism they despise in Sufism. This is evident in some of the folk practices we will examine later.

---

[37] Stewart, "Introduction," 365.
[38] Sookhdeo, *Global Jihad*, 289–90.
[39] Esposito, *Islam*, 151.
[40] Andrew Wheatcroft, *Infidels: A History of the Conflict Between Christendom and Islam* (New York: Random House, 2004), 358.

Folk Islam AND
Shiite Muslims

T he minority Shia branch of Islam is numerous enough to be considered a valid expression of the Muslim faith, but one often disparaged
by the majority Sunnis. The divide between Shias and Sunnis occurred over
the issue of succession to the Prophet Muhammad.[1] Theological and practical disputes developed later.

After Muhammad died in 632, a succession of four caliphs was chosen
from the Quraysh tribe in Arabia to lead the movement during its fragile
early days.[2] The word *caliph* means the successor of the Messenger of God.[3]
During the reigns of the four "rightly guided caliphs," there were internal
disagreements, but Islam remained united. Abu Bakr, the first caliph (632–
634), was Muhammad's father-in-law and the father of his favorite wife,
Aisha. Umar (634–644) was from one of the ten clans of the Quraysh tribe,

---

[1] See Hamid Dabashi, *Shi'ism: A Religion of Protest* (Cambridge, MA: Belknap Press
of Harvard University Press, 2011), 59.

[2] See Braswell, *Islam*, 90 (see intro., n. 28).

[3] Vali Nasr, *The Shia Revival: How Conflicts within Islam Will Shape the Future*
(New York: W. W. Norton, 2006), 35.

but not the clan of Muhammad.[4] The third caliph, Uthman (644–656) was one of Muhammad's sons-in-law and married his daughter Ruaqayya.[5] Ali, the fourth caliph and last united leader of Islam (656–661), was another son-in-law of the Prophet, his cousin, and the husband of his sole surviving child, Fatima. The first four caliphs are called the "rightly guided" caliphs because they lived close to Muhammad in the first Muslim community.[6] These caliphs ruled from Medina in Arabia when Islam had not yet been divided into factions.[7] The first four successors to the Prophet are accepted by all but a very few. Islam divided into Shiites and Sunnis over the question of who should succeed Ali, the fourth caliph.[8] The meaning of *Shiite* is "partisan to Ali."[9] Hamid Dabashi says, "It took decades, if not centuries, for the theological positions of the Sunnis and Shias to coagulate and contradistinguish themselves. But the seeds of their discord were sown early in Islamic history."[10]

Shiites believe Ali inherited the Prophet's infallibility in leadership and interpretation of the Quran. These beliefs, coupled with his blood kinship with Muhammad, cause Shiites to regard Ali as the first *imam*. As Muhammad's cousin and father of his grandchildren, Ali was both the fourth caliph of the Sunnis (and all of united Islam) and the first imam of the Shiites. As such, he is claimed by both groups.[11]

Although both Shiites and Sunnis revere Ali, Shia Islam rejects the Sunni caliphate. Shiites believe Islamic spiritual authority instead is invested in their imams. The doctrine of a hereditary imamate advocates that these qualities were passed down through Muhammad's grandsons Hassan and

---

[4] Heinz Halim, *Shi'ism*, 2nd ed., trans. Janet Watson and Marian Hill (New York: Columbia University Press, 2004), 6.

[5] See Marshall, Green, and Gilbert, *Islam at the Crossroads*, 47 (see intro., n. 2).

[6] See Braswell, *Islam*, 90.

[7] See Robert Payne, *The History of Islam* (New York: Dorset, 1959, 1987), 89.

[8] See Dabashi, *Shi'ism*, 59.

[9] Braswell, *Islam*, 90. Vali Nasr says that Shiite means "partisan group of Ali." The Shia Revival, 38.

[10] Dabashi, *Shi'ism*, 43–44.

[11] See Dabashi, 91.

Hussein and to their descendants.[12] The martyrdoms of Ali (661), Hassan (680), and Hussein (680) established a permanent schism in Islam that continues to embitter Shiites to this day.[13]

I would like to briefly mention the subgroups within Shia Islam that are also important to popular Islam. Ninety percent of Shiites belong to the *Ithna Ashariya* sect, or Twelvers.[14] Iranians compose almost 90 percent of this majority Shia subgroup. The Twelvers believe in a series of twelve imams who descended from Ali, Muhammad's son-in-law. In the year 878 the twelfth imam after Ali, Muhammad al-Mumtazzar, was born and proclaimed to be the expected Mahdi. Muslims believe the Mahdi will be a messiah-like figure that returns at a time of tumult and corruption to bring tranquility and justice to the world.[15] When Muhammad al-Mumtazzar disappeared at the age of nine, Twelvers developed the doctrine of the "hidden Imam," which holds that Muhammad al-Mumtazzar remains in hiding and will return at a later date. Presently his followers are spiritually led by a series of ayatollahs, or living imams, who guide the faithful during the absence of the Twelfth Imam.[16] Sunnis, Shiites, and Sufis all embrace the doctrine of a coming Mahdi, and this messianic concept plays a significant role in popular Islam. Shiites believe he will return to Kufa, Iraq, while Sunnis hold that the Mahdi will move the Ka'ba from Mecca to Jerusalem and rule from there. These are not the only differences between the Sunni and Shia versions of the Mahdi.[17]

There are geographical distinctions as well. Hadhrat Mirza Ghulam Ahmad of India founded the Ahmadiyya Movement in 1889. He declared himself the Mahdi, claiming to have come in the spirit and power of Jesus to

---

[12] See Dabashi, 90–91

[13] See Sookhdeo, *Global Jihad*, 131–32 (see chap. 2, n. 2).

[14] *Ithna asher* is the Arabic term for the number twelve. *Ithna Ashariya* is the plural form, or "twelvers."

[15] See Ruthven, *Islam in the World*, 9 (see chap. 2, n. 6).

[16] See Braswell, *Islam*, 95.

[17] See Sookhdeo, 138–39.

unite Islam under his banner.[18] Though Ahmad died in 1908, his followers have not been dissuaded. A half a world away, at about the same time, another Muslim, a Sunni Sufi, proclaimed himself to be the expected Mahdi. In 1881 Mohammed Ahmed of the Sudan rebelled against the British and Egyptian governments and won independence by 1883.[19] Unfortunately, this messiah died only five months after his victory, never achieving his vision of uniting Islam and conquering the world.[20]

The remaining 10 percent of Shiites are divided between the *Seveners* and the *Zaidis*. The Zaidis believe any descendant of Ali can become the imam, not just the descendants of Ali and Fatima, Muhammad's daughter. The Zaidis dominate in areas of Yemen and around the Caspian Sea.[21] The Seveners acknowledge only seven of the twelve imams recognized by the *Ithna Ashariyas*, or Twelvers.[22] The Seveners are also known as the *Isma'ilis*. They are famous for founding the great Islamic Al-Azhar University in Cairo more than 1,000 years ago.[23]

Isma'ilis, although composing less than 1 percent of all Muslims, have greater influence than their number would suggest due to the sway of their leader, the Aga Khan.[24] Most major cities in Africa, the Middle East, central Asia, and South Asia have at least one Isma'ili mosque. They are widely scattered throughout the Muslim world, particularly in Pakistan and India.[25] Originating in India, the *Nizari* Isma'ilis are led by the Aga Khan IV. Their adherents now live in India, Pakistan, China, Syria, East Africa, Europe, and North America. Outside of the oil-producing families, the Isma'ilis are some

---

[18] See Chaudhry, *The Promised Messiah and Mahdi*, 11 (see chap. 2, n. 1).

[19] See Winston Spencer Churchill, *The River War* (London: NEL Books, 1899, 1985), 23, 31–32, 35, 37.

[20] See Churchill, 71.

[21] See Ahmed, *Islam Today*, 48 (see chap. 1, n. 1).

[22] See Farhad Daftary, "Introduction" in *A Modern History of the Ismailis: Continuity and Change in a Muslim Community*, ed. Farhad Daftary (London: I. B. Tauris, 2011), 1.

[23] Al-Azhar University long ago abandoned Isma'ili Sufism and is now "a bastion of *Sunnism*." Ruthven, *Islam in the World*, 207.

[24] See Ahmed, *Islam Today*, 48.

[25] See Nasr, *Islam*, 13 (see chap. 1, n. 32).

of the wealthiest Muslims.[26] The Aga Khan claims descent from a Nizari Isma'ili, a leader deposed by the Mongols in the 1250s.[27]

Shia Muslims and Popular Islam

The insistence of many Shiites on venerating the descendants of the Prophet Muhammad has led this branch of Islam down a path conducive to adopting many popular Islamic beliefs. Ruthven sheds considerable light on the reason Shia Islam observes so many folk practices:

> Unlike the *ahl al-sunna* [people of the *Sunna*], the *Shi'a* found in the doctrine of the *Imamate* a device which enabled them to erect a quasi-sacerdotal structure within the framework of Islam. . . . The *Shi'ite* idea of *nass* (designation) contains a notion of spiritual succession broadly comparable to the apostolic succession in the Catholic priesthood. . . . The idea of *nass* was closely associated with another aspect of *Shi'a'ism*, namely that the Quran contains esoteric meanings that can only be properly interpreted by the *Imams*.[28]

Shiites and Sunnis broke ranks over the question of succession to the Prophet.[29] Their name comes from *Shi'at 'Ali*, meaning party, partisans or faction of 'Ali, which was shortened to Shia.[30] Shiites believe the descendants of 'Ali are the rightful rulers of Islam.[31] In a sense the Shiites can be called the royalists of Islam, since they place the highest importance on the Prophet's lineage in determining leadership. Conversely, the Sunnis can be seen as parliamentary Islam, since leadership is determined by consensus

---

[26] See Ruthven, *Islam in the World*, 209.

[27] Ruthven, 209.

[28] Ruthven, 196.

[29] See Louis Hamada, *Understanding the Arab World* (Nashville: Thomas Nelson, 1990), 117.

[30] Andrew Wheatcroft holds the view that the name comes from the daughter (Fatima) from whom the Shia line claims descent. Wheatcroft, *Infidels*, 158 (see chap. 2, n. 40).

[31] See Sookhdeo, *Global Jihad*, 271.

or voting of the community (*ummah*). Of course, Sufis do not care about either one. Sufis are more concerned with the spiritual aspect of their faith than with its leadership.

It is Shiites belief concerning the priestly or sacerdotal role of the leader in Islam that leads many Shiites away from orthodoxy.[32] Seyyed Hossein Nasr, a Muslim writer and professor emeritus at George Washington University, expresses this critical difference between Sunnis and Shiites well:

> The problem was, however, more profound than one of personalities. It also concerned the **function** of the person who was to succeed the Prophet. The *Sunnis* believed that the function of such a person should be to protect the Divine Law, act as judge, and rule over the community, preserving public order and the borders of the Islamic world. The *Shi'ites* believed that such a person should also be able to **interpret the Quran** and the Law and in fact **possess inward knowledge**. Therefore, he had to be chosen by God and the Prophet, not by the community. Such a figure was called *Imam*.[33] Although such a person did not share in the Prophet's prophetic function (*nubuwwah*), he did receive the **inner spiritual power** of the Prophet (*walayah/wilayah*).[34]

The personality cult surrounding Ali and his successors has opened the door to many beliefs and practices that are not acceptable within orthodox Islam. Shiites believe in the doctrine of the "divine light," or *nur*, that passes from imam to imam, rendering him sinless and infallible.[35] Unlike Sunnis, Shiites also believe that Muhammad was sinless and this spiritual state was

---

[32] *Sacerdotal* is defined as "excessive reliance on a priesthood." *Webster's New World Dictionary of the American Language*, 2nd College ed., David B. Guralnik, ed. (New York: World, 1970), 1251.

[33] Ahmed writes, "An *Imam* is a senior figure often in charge of a large mosque. The title of *Imam* is also given to highly respected spiritual figures directly descended from the Prophet who are the basis for twelve *Imam Shi'ism*." *Islam Today*, 9.

[34] Nasr, *Islam*, 11–12, bold mine.

[35] See Braswell, *Islam*, 92.

passed down through Ali to today's imams.[36] Shrines to departed holy men have been erected with accompanying pilgrimages similar to the Hajj to Mecca. A theology of persecution and martyrdom permeates Shiism to the extent that extreme mourning and self-flagellation often occur during pilgrimages to Shia shrines.[37]

Another belief shared among most subgroups of the Shiites is the belief in the return of the hidden Imam, as we have noted previously. This term refers to a Shia version of the Mahdi, or Muslim messiah. Ninety percent of Shiites are Twelvers. They believe the Twelfth Imam is in hiding but will return to take over his rightful place of leading the world of Islam. Until that time living imams, or ayatollahs,[38] rule in his place.[39] This belief causes most Shiites to reject the religious and secular authority of non-Shia Islam.[40] Many problems have surfaced, and even violence has erupted, over these differences in places where Shiites and Sunnis reside together.[41] Recent wars in Iraq, Afghanistan, and Yemen are more about religious variances between Sunnis and Shias than about politics.

Sookhdeo observes, "Shi'a Islam touches on the emotions much more than does Sunni Islam; self-denial and martyrdom are strongly emphasized."[42] This emphasis often leads Shiites into various folk practices. Shia adherents visit local shrines and rely on their religious leaders for direction.[43] Folk religious beliefs and practices often flow from this desire for guidance and feeling. Akbar Ahmed, another Muslim writer, and one the word's foremost authorities on modern Islam, further explains the differences between the two sides:

---

[36] See Nasr, *The Shia Revival*, 39.

[37] See Sookhdeo, *Global Jihad*, 271.

[38] Ayatollah means "sign of God" and represents the highest category of the *ulama* (religious figures) in Shia Islam. Ahmed, *Islam Today*, 9.

[39] See Braswell, *Islam*, 95.

[40] See Nasr, *Islam*, 12.

[41] See Ahmed, *Islam Today*, 47.

[42] Sookhdeo, *Global Jihad*, 44.

[43] See Braswell, *Islam*, 94.

Another difference between *Sunnis* and *Shias* rests in their belief regarding folk or cultural practices around tombs of saints. *Sunnis* are ambivalent about this, and the orthodox strongly reject these practices as un-Islamic. The *Shi'as* incorporated these as part of their custom. . . . Belief in shrines and saints was often viewed by the *Sunni* orthodox as heretical and even dangerous deviation from the true and singular worship of God (*bida*). By contrast, the *Shi'as* believe that intercession is an integral part of the divine plan for salvation. Ali and the other main Imams were divinely inspired people who because of their spirituality were intermediaries between God and the believers.[44]

Conclusion

Unfortunately, many in the West consider Shiites to be the most radical Muslims, since the majority of Shiites live in Iran, and that country is associated with Islamic extremism. Indeed, there are many fanatical Muslims living in Iran. In reality, however, there are more radicals among the Sunnis, because there are almost ten times more Sunnis than Shiites in the world. In fact, the Muslim Brotherhood (Egypt and Sudan), the Taliban (Afghanistan), al Qaeda (Afghanistan and Pakistan), Boko Haram (Nigeria), and al-Shabab (Yemen and Kenya) are all radical Sunni groups. Of the extremist Muslim groups, only the Hezbollah and the Iranian religious leadership are Shiites. In addition, most intra-Islamic wars are due to the Sunni–Shia split that dates back to the eighth century.

---

[44] Ahmed, *Islam Today*, 46.

Sufi Islam *AND* Folk Islam

To enter the *Qadiriyya* Sufi brotherhood in Sudan, the neophyte must sit facing Mecca along with his guide, who holds his right thumb. Once he repents of his past sins and repeats the *Shahada*,[1] he is ready to become a Sufi. Ali Karrar recounts this unique ritual within Sufi Islam:

> The *shaykh* would then ask the aspirant to close his eyes and open "the eyes of his heart" and concentrate on the litanies which he was about to dictate to him (*yulaqin*). Having received the litanies, the aspirant would declare his acceptance of the act of initiation by saying, "I have accepted Allah as my God, Islam as my religion, Muhammad as the Prophet and Messenger and our *shaykh* as a guide." He then would recite the *ayat al-mubaya'a* (Quran 48:10) and kiss the *shaykh's* hand. The initiation would conclude with a joint recital of the *Fatiha* by the *shaykh* and his *murid*; the aspirant had now become an adherent.[2]

---

[1] "There is no God but Allah and Muhammad is his Prophet."

[2] Ali Salih Karrar, *The Sufi Brotherhoods in the Sudan* (London: C. Hurst, 1992), 152.

Sufism represents a template or overlay upon Islam, as well as a sub-division of the faith. Reza Aslan writes, "*Sufism*, like *Shi'ism*, was a reaction-ary movement against both the Imperial Islam of the Muslim Dynasties and the rigid formalism of Islam's 'orthodox' learned class, the *Ulama*."[3] Some Muslims see Sufism as outside of Islam altogether; others view it as an integral part and the religion's most vibrant manifestation.[4] Many Muslims within orthodoxy see Sufi customs as medieval superstition perverting true Islam.[5] Sufis themselves, however, claim to be within the great "animating spirit of the Islamic tradition."[6] Despite the opposition to Sufism by ortho-dox Islam, Carl Ernst estimates that about half of all Muslims today practice a form of Sufism.[7] Karrar observes the manner in which Sufis self-identify in Sudan as follows:

> The *Sufi* orders in Sudan, as in the rest of the Muslim world, never constituted a world of their own. In the view of most *Sufi shaykhs* and followers,[8] *Sufism* and *Sharia*[9] were entirely interlocking mani-festations of faith.[10]

---

[3] Reza Aslan, *No god but God: The Origins, Evolution, and Future of Islam* (New York: Random House, 2006), 200.

[4] See William C. Chittick, *Sufism: A Short Introduction* (Oxford: Oneworld, 2000), 3; Carl W. Ernst, *The Shambhala Guide to Sufism* (Boston: Shambhala, 1997), xi.

[5] See Ernst, *The Shambhala Guide to Sufism*, xvii.

[6] Chittick, *Sufism*, 3.

[7] Ernst, *The Shambhala Guide to Sufism*, xiii.

[8] The leader of a Sufi order is called a sheikh. *Shaykh* is an alternative spelling due to differences in transliterating Arabic. Individual Sufis are often called *fakirs* or *dervishes*. Chittick writes, "Both *fakir* (Arabic *faqir*) and *dervish* (Persian *darwish*) mean 'poor man,' that is, a traveler of the *Sufi* path. The term is taken from the Koran, espe-cially the verse, 'O people, you are the poor toward God; and God—He is the Wealthy, the Praiseworthy' (35:15)." *Sufism*, 70.

[9] Islamic law. Sookhdeo writes, "Not only does *Shari'a* (Islamic law) cover the per-sonal, family and devotional life of an individual Muslim but also it lays down how an Islamic state should be governed." *Global Jihad*, 70 (see chap. 2, n. 2).

[10] Karrar, *The Sufi Brotherhoods in the Sudan*, 2.

In my experience, most Sufis do not recognize the term "Sufi" but rather are identified by their order, such as *Qadiriyya* (from *Qadris*) or *Jilaniyya* (from *Junaid*).[11] In fact, *Sufi* is a recent term coined from the German language in 1821.[12] Sufis are often called the mystics of Islam and come from both the Sunni and Shia sects.[13] In other words, a Sufi can be either a Sunni or a Shiite. In fact, one of the Sufi orders, the *Ni'matullahi*, has existed in both the Sunni and Shia worlds.[14] Although Shiism and Sufism share a belief in the extra-Quranic inspiration of their leaders and departed saints, these sects differ significantly. Sufism does not have a Sharia while Shiism does. Sufism sees Christ as the universal "seal of sanctity," where Shiites see Ali and the Mahdi as filling this role.[15]

I believe Sufis can be viewed as the "charismatics" of Islam. Sufis introduced mysticism to their religion, stressing feelings and emotions.[16] Just as charismatic beliefs can be found within most branches of Christianity, so Sufism is present within most of the Muslim subdivisions, including Shiites and Sunnis.

There are two principal kinds of Sufis: (1) the drunken, or God-intoxicated, and (2) the contemplative, or ascetic.[17] The drunken are associated with ecstatic behavior and would be considered more of a representative of folk Muslim mysticism. Contemplative Sufis are sober, by

---

[11] According to Ali Salih Karrar, the Quadiriyya Sufi order, also known as the Jilaniyya, "was the most popular and widespread tariqa in the Muslim world. It is named after Abd al-Qadir al-Jilani, who was born in Persia in 1077 and died and was buried at Baghdad in 1166." Many Sudanese Sufis are Quadiriyya (Jilaniyya). Once I was travelling in Senegal (W. Africa) and met a Quadiriyya Sufi sheikh who shortly would be traveling to Khartoum, Sudan, for the Eid. Karrar *The Sufi Brotherhoods in the Sudan* (London: C. Hurst, 1992), 21.

[12] See Idries Shah, *The Way of the Sufi* (London: Penguin Books, 1968), 13.

[13] See Marshall, Green, and Gilbert, *Islam at the Crossroads*, 28 (see intro., n. 2); Braswell, *Islam: Its Prophet, Peoples, Politics and Power*, 97 (see intro., n. 28); Sookhdeo, *Global Jihad*, 45.

[14] See Seyyed Hossein Nasr, *Sufi Essays* (Chicago: ABC International Group, 1999), 107.

[15] See Nasr, 108.

[16] See Braswell, *Islam,* 97.

[17] See Chittick, *Sufism,* 29.

contrast, and expend effort pondering the inner life. These quieter, more ascetic Sufis, emphasizing the value of a devotional life, can be categorized as Islamic mystics.

Sufism probably developed partially in reaction to a perceived sterility and formality in high Islam. Ruthven writes, "They inject a warmth into Islam which is lacking in the legalistic observance advocated by Sunni *ulama*[18] or in the fanatical loyalty of the Shiites to the tragic memories of their Imams."[19] Due to Sufism's uniqueness, and the influence it continues to project upon Islam, the movement will be treated separately from the other major divisions of the faith. Parshall claims folk Islam cannot be understood without a comprehension of Sufism.[20]

Sufism developed early in Islam through teachers such as Harith al-Muhasibi (781–837) and his pupil and contemporary, Junaid. They attempted to combine asceticism and mysticism with a proper observance of Sharia.[21] This new spiritual path within Islam continued to enlarge through writers such as al-Sarraj, who penned the first surviving Sufi writing in 988.[22] Sufis hold that the path to God is not based on doctrine but on feeling, experience, and introspection.[23] Ruthven comments on this tendency.

> Yet from the first there were Muslims whose psychic or spiritual needs were unsatisfied by mere obedience to the deity and the dutiful observance of his commandments. They sought a closer and more intimate relationship by means of ascetic practices, arduous spiritual exercises and complicated liturgies. They came to be known as *Sufis*, after the woolen garments (*suf*=wool) allegedly

---

[18] Religious officials, "from 'alim or scholar." See Ahmed, *Islam Today*, 9 (see chap. 1, n. 1).

[19] See Ruthven, *Islam in the World*, 225 (see chap. 2, n. 6).

[20] Parshall, *Bridges to Islam*, 12 (see intro., n. 4).

[21] See Ruthven, *Islam in the World*, 227.

[22] See Parshall, *Bridges to Islam,* 15.

[23] See Braswell, *Islam*, 97.

worn by the early exemplars of this movement, as well as by the followers of Jesus whom they particularly admired.[24]

Ernst proposes another origin of the word *Sufi*.

> The term *Sufi* was linked with the Arabic word *suffa* or bench (source of the English word *sofa*), and in this sense it invokes the historical memory of the People of the Bench, a group of poor followers of the Prophet Mohammad who were homeless and slept on a bench in Medina, sharing their meager belongings and supplies.[25]

It fell to Abu Hamid al-Ghazali (1058–1111) to bring respectability to Sufism. A Muslim scholar with theological training, Ghazali experienced a personal religious crisis that drove him to attempt to reconcile mysticism with official Islam.[26] Ghazali believed both in the necessity of the religion's ritual observances and feeling.[27] As a theologian-mystic he held that religious certainty depends upon religious experience.[28] His unique synthesis won him the name of *mujaddid*, or renewer, of Islam.[29] Of the impact of al-Ghazali, Ruthven writes:

> Ghazali's work served to reintegrate the whole legal superstructure with the psychic or spiritual infrastructure, re-injecting into the Quran and the *Sunna*, and into the edifice of law built upon them, the sanctity of the Prophet's mystic consciousness. For this **he has been called the greatest Muslim after Muhammad**.[30]

---

[24] Ruthven, *Islam in the World*, 221–22.

[25] Ernst, *The Shambhala Guide to Sufism*, 22. This is a minority view as to the meaning of Sufi but is a possibility.

[26] See Braswell, *Islam*, 98.

[27] See Ruthven, *Islam in the World*, 233.

[28] See Braswell, *Islam*, 98.

[29] See John L. Esposito, Darrell J. Fasching, and Todd Lewis, *World Religions Today*, 3rd ed. (New York: Oxford University Press, 2009), 252.

[30] Ruthven, *Islam in the World*, 235, bold mine.

As Sufism grew, this expression of Islam became less orthodox in both faith and practice.[31] For this reason, Sufism can be viewed as one of the major streams of folk Islam.[32]

Sufi Influences on Folk Islam

Some orthodox Muslims relegate all Sufism to the sphere of folk Islam[33] while others reject only its excessive elements.[34] It is difficult either to define Sufism or explain exactly what Sufis believe.[35] Muslim writer Khalifa Hakim concurs, writing, "Islam itself has never classed *Sufism* under any one heading and that explains the fact why *Sufism* is not regarded as a doctrine with any definite boundaries to mark it off either from orthodox Islam or from any system of metaphysics."[36] As Chittick writes, "Rather than trying to domesticate *Sufism* by giving it a more familiar label, we should recognize at the outset that there is something in the *Sufi* tradition that abhors domestication and definition."[37] This difficulty is evident in these Sufi sayings collected by Al-Qushayri:

> *Sufism* is entry into exemplary behavior and departure from unworthy behavior. *Sufism* means that God makes you die to yourself and makes you live in him. The *Sufi* is single in essence; nothing changes him, nor does he change anything. The sign of the sincere *Sufi* is that he feels poor when he has wealth, is humble when he has power, and is hidden when he has fame. *Sufism* means that you own nothing and are owned by nothing. *Sufism* means entrusting the soul to God most high for whatever he wishes.[38]

---

[31] See Braswell, *Islam*, 97.
[32] See Parshall, *Bridges to Islam*, 4.
[33] See Ernst, *The Shambhala Guide to Sufism*, xii.
[34] See Ahmed, *Islam Today*, 49–50.
[35] See Ernst, *The Shambhala Guide to Sufism*, 18.
[36] Khalifa Abdul Hakim, *The Metaphysics of Rumi: A Critical and Historical Sketch* (1933, repr., New Delhi: Adam Publishers, 2006), 145.
[37] Chittick, *Sufism*, 2.
[38] Al-Qushayri in Ernst, *The Shambhala Guide to Sufism*, 23.

Sufi doctrine can best be gleaned from poring over aphorisms such as these and unraveling the riddle of their meanings. Sufi writers enjoy couching instruction within paradoxical proverbs and witticisms.[39] Sufi (and many Shia) writers practice an allegorical hermeneutic called *tawil*,[40] which is rejected by Sunnis.[41] This special art of Quranic interpretation deciphers the hidden, esoteric, multilayered connotations within Sufi mysticism. The Sufi mining for deeper significance beneath the surface of Islam is ripe for folk religious speculation that borders on Islamic heresy. Chittick presents this accusation thus:

> Constant focus on God leads eventually, God willing, to the **goal of the *Sufi* path, which is union with God,** or the full realization of human perfection, or actualization of the divine image in which human beings were created. . . . Having traversed the path, *Sufis* can say with Hallaj (d. 922), "I am the Real," that is "**I am God.**"[42]

Chittick points out that there are three major Quranic themes in ancient Islamic teaching: (1) submission (*Islam,* السلم), (2) faith (*Iman,* يمَان), and (3) doing the beautiful (*Ibsan,* ابصان).[43] The first two are well-known, representing the Five Pillars and the Six Principles of Islam. Sufism sees the latter, doing the beautiful, as its "special domain."[44] Ibn Khaldun writes the following about the Sufis:

> The *Sufi* approach is based upon constant application to divine worship, complete devotion to God, aversion to the false splendor of the world, abstinence from the pleasure, property and position

---

[39] See Abu 'L-Qasim Al-Qushayri, *Sufi Book of Spiritual Ascent,* trans. Rabia Harris, ed. Laleh Bakhtiar (Chicago: KAZI Publications, 1997), 284.

[40] *Tawil* is the common Arabic word for "long, large, big, tall, high" in Hans Wehr, *Arabic-English Dictionary,* 576. *Sufis* use the word in the sense of the larger, greater, and deeper meaning within Islam.

[41] See Ruthven, *Islam in the World,* 232.

[42] Chittick, *Sufism,* 16–17.

[43] Chittick, 4.

[44] Chittick, 5.

to which the great mass aspire, and retirement from the world into solitude for divine worship.[45]

Sufis worship God in many ways, but the essence of Sufism is a form of meditation called *al-dhikr* (remembrance).[46] *Dhikr* ritual requires the Sufi to pronounce and repeat the ninety-nine names of God in order to unlock the special meaning within each title, producing a spiritual state in the believer.[47] This is normally accomplished by counting a string of thirty-three beads (*subha* or *misbaha*) three times in succession, allowing the Sufi to accurately count the ninety-nine names of Allah. Besides helping express the believer's faith, the Sufi believes this device symbolically links this world with the next. Malek Chabel says, "The symbolism connected to the prayer beads is that of the 'chain of worlds.' A discreet reference to sacred numerology is also contained therein, as the symbolism of numbers permeates the activity of the mediator."[48] The *dhikr*-Allah (counting the ninety-nine names of Allah) appears in the Quran twenty-six times. Sufis believe *dhikr* molds the character of the worshipper, bringing out his spiritual potential.[49] This activity is accompanied by ritual dancing. Ruthven describes the connection between dancing and spirituality thus:

> Controlled ecstasy may also be induced by certain physical movements. Among orders these range from the gentle turning from right to left with which the *Qadiris* accompany the *tahlil* formula, a technique attributed to Abd al-Qadir al-Jilani himself, to the spinning of the *Mawlawiya* or "Whirling Dervishes," who have performed their famous dance in several European cities.[50]

---

[45] Ibn Khaldun in Ernst, *The Shambhala Guide to Sufism*, 17.

[46] See Nasr, *Islam*, 81 (see chap. 1, n. 32).

[47] See Ahmed, *Islam Today*, 50.

[48] Malek Chebel, *Symbols of Islam* (Paris: Ausoline, 2001), 102.

[49] See Chittick, *Sufism*, 58.

[50] The *tahlil* formula is as follows: "*la ilaha il-la allah*: 'There is no deity but God.'" Ruthven, *Islam in the World*, 255.

The recitation of the ninety-nine names in this fashion as an integral part of worship sets the Sufis apart. Chittick writes, "The *Sufis* are distinguished from other Muslims partly because they consider the remembrance of God, in the form of mentioning His names as instructed by their *shaykhs*, as incumbent, not merely recommended."[51]

There are other important emphases within Sufism. Sufis are known for their pursuit of esoteric, mystical knowledge called *'arif* or *Gnostic*.[52] Carl Ernst writes, "When mystical knowledge was emphasized over traditional learning, the preferred term was *ma'rifa* or *'irfan*,[53] meaning a special knowledge or *gnosis* that transcended ordinary reality."[54] Sufi author Al-Qushayri says, in his chapter on *gnosis*, that "*ma'rifa* is the trait of someone who knows the Truth in His names and attributes and then bears witness to the divine in all his actions."[55] In other words, Sufis receive direct knowledge (gnosis) from God.[56] This is unacceptable in orthodoxy.

Sufism began, according to adherents, when Muhammad started receiving the first of 114 *suras* on the "Night of Power" in the year 610.[57] The "Night of Power" during Ramadan is very important to Muslims today. Folk Muslims believe that through prayers and devotion they have the opportunity to alter what is "written" in predestination.[58] According to Ruthven, Ghazali and other Sufis believe[d] in "modes of cognition lying beyond the realm of the intellect."[59]

Sufis also place great importance on the love of God. Although Sufism began in asceticism, it gave way to devotion and love.[60] In fact, Omar

---

[51] Chittick, *Sufism*, 57.

[52] *'Arif* is derived from the Arabic word *arafa*, "to know." The term also means "expert, master, or connoisseur." Wehr, *Arabic-English Dictionary*, 607.

[53] Both *ma'rifa* (knowledge) and *'irfan* (gnosis) are also derivatives of *'arafa*, the Arabic word "to know." Wehr, *Arabic-English Dictionary*, 605–6.

[54] Ernst, *The Shambhala Guide to Sufism*, 28.

[55] Al-Qushayri, *Sufi Book of Spiritual Ascent*, 293.

[56] Al-Qushayri, 294.

[57] The chapter divisions in the Quran are called *suras*.

[58] See Musk, "Popular Islam," 123 (see intro., n. 5).

[59] Ruthven, *Islam in the World*, 233.

[60] See Chittick, *Sufism*, 61.

Khayyam says, "Sufism's motive force is love. This love cannot be quite equated with *agape*. Nor is it simply *eros* . . . What the Persians call *'Ishq*, the passion of love, was directed in *Sufism* solely toward God the Creator."[61] This is seen in the poetic verse of Rumi, Junaid, and ibn Arabi. Among their themes are the concepts of affection, beauty, and truth. Their love poetry is striking, as illustrated by the following example:

> If you become a lion, love is a great lion-catcher.
> Become an elephant—love is a mighty rhinoceros!
> If you flee to the depth of a well,
>   love's rope will bind your neck like a bucket.
> Become a hair—love is a great hair-splitter.
> Become a kabob—love is a spit.
> Love is a sanctuary, the source of all justice,
>   even if it waylays the intellects of man and woman.
> Silence! For speech's homeland is Damascus, the heart—
>   with such a homeland, don't call it a stranger.[62]

An emphasis upon a strong master-disciple relationship also characterizes the Sufi orders.[63] Practicing Sufis belong to various orders or brotherhoods called *tariqas. Tariq,* or *tarik,* is the Arabic word for "way, road, highway, trail, track, or path." *Tariqa,* or *tarika*, is a derivative of *tariq* and means "manner, mode, means, way, method, procedure, system, creed, faith, religion, religious brotherhood, or dervish order."[64]

Al-Sanusi compiled a list of the forty traditional Sufi orders.[65] The forty Sacred [Sufi] Traditions of the nineteenth century are still preeminent.[66]

---

[61] Omar Khayyam, *The Ruba'iyat of Omar Khayyam*, trans. Peter Avery and John Heath-Stubbs (London: Penguin Books, 1981), 14.

[62] Rumi in Chittick, *Sufism*, 72.

[63] See Ernst, *The Shambhala Guide to Sufism*, 29–30.

[64] Wehr, *Arabic-English Dictionary*, 559.

[65] See Al-Sanusi in Ernst, *The Shambhala Guide to Sufism*, 112–13.

[66] See Laleh Bakhtiar, *Sufi: Expressions of the Mystic Quest* (New York: Avon Books, 1976), 7.

New Sufi brotherhoods, however, continue to be founded as individuals receive new visions, revelations, and commissions from the Prophet to start new tariqas.[67] Each Sufi order is led by a sheikh, or shaykh. "He who has no *Shaykh*, his *Shaykh* is Satan" is a commonly quoted Sufi aphorism.[68] New initiates enter their Sufi orders individually, taking an oath of fealty to God, Islam, and their sheikh. Often the new disciple receives a "cloak of blessing" to wear as a symbol of their submission.[69]

There are various opinions about the source of the garment given to new Sufi disciples. Some Sufis believe the origin lies in Joseph's coat of many colors in the book of Genesis. Others assert that Abraham received such a coat from the angel Gabriel. Some Sufi orders hold that Gabriel gave Muhammad a special tunic when he made his "night journey" to Jerusalem from Arabia, and the custom was passed down through the generations. Often the cloak is blue, but a patched version was also popular in the past.[70]

The followers of the Sudanese Mahdi wore patched tunics. These are currently on display at the Sudanese Khalifa's house, now a museum, across the street from the Mahdi's tomb in Omdurman, Sudan. The Mahdist Sufi followers of the Sudanese Caliph Abdullah mistakenly believed their patched tunics would repel the bullets of the British during the Battle of Omdurman in 1898.[71]

Orthodox Islam resists the claims of the Sufi masters, as Sunnis believe divine revelation has ceased.[72] Islamic scholar and writer Reza Aslan says, "Sufis consider all orthodoxy, all traditional teachings, the law, theology, and the Five Pillars inadequate for attaining true knowledge of God. Even the Quran, which Sufis respect as the direct speech of God, lacks the capacity to

---

[67] See Giorgio Ausenda, "Leisurely Nomads: The Hadendowa (Beja) of the Gash Delta and Their Transition to Sedentary Village Life" (PhD diss., Columbia University, 1987), 444.

[68] See Abu Yazid al-Bitami in Karrar, *The Sufi Brotherhoods in the Sudan*, 2.

[69] See Ernst, *The Shambhala Guide to Sufism*, 144.

[70] Ernst, 144.

[71] I was told this during a visit to the caliph's house in Khartoum on June 26, 2017.

[72] See Ruthven, *Islam in the World*, 247.

shed light upon God's essence."[73] Additionally, Ruthven says, "Most of the leading [Sufi] *Shaikhs* claim to receive their vocations, or confirmations of them, directly from God or the Prophet in dreams and visions."[74] Christians may see certain parallels here. Catholics believe in apostolic succession where power and authority are passed from priest to priest from the days of the apostle Peter. Many evangelical Christians believe revelation has ceased, while some charismatic Christians believe God still speaks today in dreams and visions through continuing revelation.

While some Sufis are self-possessed "travelers" along a Sufi path, or tariqa, others view themselves as intoxicated "fools of God" who sometimes appear crazy.[75] Like Shiites, Sufis believe in the concept of sainthood (*wilaya*) achieved by especially righteous Muslims.[76] Devotion to their shrines and belief in the saints' spiritual assistance in this life lead to many excesses that can only be called folk Islam. The power of these holy men is known as *baraka*.[77]

Baraka is a very important concept in Sufism. When used religiously, *baraka* is usually translated as either spiritual "power" or "blessing." The reason for the two meanings may be due to the similarities of the Arabic words. The Arabic word *baraka* means "blessing, invoke a blessing, or kneel down (as a camel kneels down in the lush grass of the oasis)."[78] Interestingly, the similar-sounding term *baraqa* conveys "to shine, glitter, sparkle, flash (as in lightning)."[79] I believe there is an intended connection between the

---

[73] Aslan, *No god but God*, 201.

[74] Ruthven, *Islam in the World*, 248.

[75] See Ernst, *The Shambhala Guide to Sufism*, 29.

[76] Ernst, 30.

[77] See Hiebert, Shaw, and Tienou, *Understanding Folk Religion*, 136 (see intro., n. 6).

[78] Wehr, *Arabic-English Dictionary*, 54.

[79] Wehr, 53. The words *baraka* and *baraqa* are not the same words, but they sound similar.

two words (*baraka* and *baraqa*) when the terms are used in a religious sense. *Baraka* also means "blessing" in Swahili.[80]

The spiritual baraka, or power, transmitted from master to disciple in both Sufi and Shia Islam creates a spiritual hierarchy absent in Sunni Islam. Ernst observes, "The basic esotericism of Sufism rested on the principle that only certain qualified people would be able to understand and experience the highest spiritual truths."[81] This places Sufism within the category of folk Islam and separates it from Sunnism.

The practices described below illustrate the extent to which folk religion permeates the dervish orders. Poetry is important to Sufis and considered one of their greatest contributions to Islam.[82] Even Sunnis appreciate the Sufis in this regard,[83] as praising God is incumbent upon all Muslims. Many Sunnis, however, draw the line at the Sufi practice of sama' (listening to chanted or recited poetry),[84] which involves musical instruments and dancing. This practice is designed to produce a state of ecstasy.[85] For Sufis this sama' means "listening with the heart." The Egyptian Sufi Dhu al-Nun said, "Sama' is the rapture of God that incites hearts towards God."[86] Some Sufis even recite poetry as a method of divination. Ernst highlights this fact, writing, "To this day, there are many people who perform elaborate rituals to select at random a lyric from Hafiz, which is then interpreted (as with

---

[80] Frederick Johnson, *A Standard English-Swahili Dictionary* (Nairobi: Oxford University Press, 1982), 1:29.

[81] Ernst, *The Shambhala Guide to Sufism*, 118.

[82] See Ernst, 147.

[83] According to Ruthven, Hassan al-Banna, founder of the Sunni (Egyptian) Muslim Brotherhood (d. 1949), read from the work of the great Sufi al-Ghazali at bedtime, even though he was a fanatical, extremist, orthodox Muslim. *Islam in the World*, 234.

[84] Sama' is the common Arabic word for "listen, hear, pay attention to." Wehr, *Arabic-English Dictionary*, 430.

[85] Wehr, 180, 182.

[86] Dhu al-Nun in Ernst, *The Shambhala Guide to Sufism*, 185.

I Ching)[87] to guide everyday choices in matters as mundane as real estate transactions."[88]

Adherents also believe the power of baraka assists Sufi saints in the performance of miracles (*karamat*). Such attitudes provide a fertile field for cultivating folk Islamic beliefs. Ernst says, "This power can include such unusual abilities as thought-reading, healing the sick, reviving the dead, controlling the elements and animals, flying, walking on water, shape-shifting, and bilocation."[89] These unusual folk practices of Sufis and Shiites continue to divide Muslims.

In his book explaining the Sunni creed, At-Tahawiyy says, "Since Allah is unimaginable, one must not try to imagine the reality of Allah, because this will lead to blasphemies."[90] This is exactly what Sufis do. In addition, the proliferation of intermediaries between God and the ordinary Muslim persists as the major difference between Sunnis and the other two divisions of Islam. Karrar presents the contrast, writing, "A *tariqa shaykh* [sheikh, or leader of a Sufi order] had absolute authority and expected the total submission of his followers. He was believed to be divinely inspired and incapable of sin."[91] Ruthven states the crux of the matter: "Both movements [Shiites and Sufis] centered on the cult of personality rather than on the proclamation of Scripture."[92] This cult of personality remains as the principal issue dividing the Sunnis from the other two segments of Islam (Shiites and Sufis).

---

[87] *I Ching* (or *Yi Jing*) is the divination system of ancient Chinese traditional religion. Both Confucianism and Taoism utilize *I Ching* practices. Diane Morgan, *The Best Guide to Eastern Philosophy and Religion* (New York: Renaissance Books, 2001), 183.

[88] Ernst, *The Shambhala Guide to Sufism*, 170.

[89] Ernst, 68.

[90] Abu Ja'far al-Warraq At-Tahawiyy, *The Creed of At-Tahawiyy: A Brief Explanation of the Sunniy Creed* (Philadelphia: Association of Islamic Charitable Projects, n.d.), 40.

[91] Karrar, *The Sufi Brotherhoods in the Sudan*, 2.

[92] Ruthven, *Islam in the World*, 257.

Conclusion

Many outside Islam believe Sufis are a Muslim sect in the same sense as Sunnis and Shiites. This is not the case. Sufism is a template upon Islam. In other words, there are Shia Sufis and Sunni Sufis but no Sufi Sufis. Aslan writes, "Sufism represents a rare anti-intellectual strain within Islam devoted solely to esotericism and devotionalism."[93] This sketch of the sects of Islam presents the major tenets of Islam in order to later demonstrate popular Islam's divergence from orthodoxy. Having established this framework, a more detailed study of folk religion and popular Islam begins now.

---

[93] Aslan, *No god but God*, 200.

The Origins *OF* Folk Islam: Traditional Religion

When the Hadaway family arrived as missionaries to Tanzania in 1984, our children were small. Our house in the city of Mwanza was located at the bottom of a hill. Behind our house we often heard the nocturnal screech of leopards, mongooses, and monkeys. Perched on top of the hill was an owl's nest. One day, my four-year-old son and seven-year-old daughter brought an adolescent owl with a broken wing back to our home. My children pleaded that we nurse it back to health. I dutifully carried the owl to a veterinarian, who formed a cast for the wing. For several weeks we fed the owl its daily allotment of meat. One day some believers approached me and tactfully said it was not considered appropriate for a missionary to keep an owl as a pet. They explained that traditional Sukuma tribesmen believed sorcerers and witches summon owls to their coven meetings.[1] Some wondered if their missionary was a witch doctor posing as a man of God. These kinds of presuppositions have mixed with both Christianity and Islam in places all over the world where traditional religious customs linger.

---

[1] Piet Van Pelt, *Bantu Customs in Mainland Tanzania*, rev. ed. (Tabora, TZ: T.M.P. Book Dept., 1984), 74.

Popular Islam includes two main aspects: (1) traditional religious practices within African Traditional Religion (ATR), Arabian traditional religion, or Asian traditional religion; and (2) Islamic influences, especially Sufism. Chapter 3 addressed the latter while this chapter and the next examine the former. John Mbiti observes the following about people who have converted to Islam but retain many of their former practices: "This survival of African Religion in predominantly Muslim areas is in the form of beliefs, rituals, magic and medicine. African traditional ideas and practices have been mixed with those of Islam to suit the requirements of the people concerned, so that they get the best out of both religions."[2] Folk Islam blends the Muslim faith with the culture of Africa. This chapter analyzes these ATR roots.

Traditional Religion Defined

There has been much discussion over the years about an accurate and proper definition of traditional religion.[3] John Mbiti calls ancestor worship, superstition, animism, paganism, magic, and fetishism derogatory descriptions.[4] Byang Kato adds idolatry, heathenism, witchcraft, juju, and primitive religion to the list.[5] Animism was the most frequently used term of yesteryear.[6] Concerning it, Mbiti writes, "Animism is not an adequate

---

[2] John S. Mbiti, *Introduction to African Religion*, 2nd ed. (Oxford: Heinemann Educational Foundation, 1991), 188–89.

[3] O. Oladimeji notes that for him traditional religion means "native, that which is aboriginal or foundational; handed down from generation to generation; that which continues to be practiced by living men and women of today as the religion of their forebears, a heritage from the past which people of today have made theirs by living on it and practicing it as that which for them connects the past with the present and upon which we base the connection between now and eternity with all that spiritual hope and fear." *African Traditional Religion* (Imo, NG: Ilesanmi & Sons,1980), 4.

[4] Mbiti, *Introduction to African Religion*, 18–19.

[5] Byang H. Kato, *Theological Pitfalls in Africa* (Kisumu, KE: Evangel, 1975), 18–24.

[6] According to Gailyn Van Rheenen, the term *animism* was originated by Edward B. Taylor in 1873. Van Rheenen, *Communicating Christ in Animistic Contexts* (Pasadena,

description of these religions, and it is better for that term to be abandoned once for all. It needs to be emphasized, that African religions are historically older than both Christianity and Islam."[7] On the other hand, Kuel Jok argues that animism differs from magic and can be used to describe a religion that brings harmony and health to its practitioners. Jok says, "The primary aim of magical performance is to cause its target harm. Believers of Animism among the Nilotics perform 'worship' to God and 'respect' to totem(s) without intent to harm others."[8]

Hiebert and Hesselgrave prefer the word *tribal* when describing indigenous faiths.[9] While many belong to a tribe, a number do not. Kato says that African Traditional Religions[10] (ATR) is the most comprehensive title for the religions of Africa.[11] Traditional religion (TR) best describes indigenous faiths found the world over. Ambrose Moyo offers an excellent model for examining traditional religion.

The following religious phenomena seem to be basic and common to most of them [traditional religions]: **(a)** belief in a supreme

---

CA: William Carey Library, 1991), 19. Taylor called it the most primitive stage in the evolution of religion. Hiebert, Shaw, and Tienou, *Understanding Folk Religion*, 17 (see intro. n. 6). The word is rejected by most current missiologists as either inaccurate or derogatory, as Mbiti and Kato mention above. Nevertheless, older writers, such as Samuel M. Zwemer (*The Influence of Animism on Islam*) employed the term (see chap. 1, n. 5). Contemporary writers who have used the word include Van Rheenen, 20; Bill Musk; "Popular Islam," 238 (see intro., n. 5); and Phil Parshall, *Bridges to Islam*, 62 (see intro., n. 4). I prefer the terms "traditional religion" or "indigenous religion" to describe the phenomenon of localized faiths. When the word *animism* appears in this book, it will only be when quoting other sources.

[7] Mbiti, *Introduction to African Religion*, 8.

[8] Kuel Maluil Jok, *Animism of the Nilotics and Discourses of Islamic Fundamentalism in Sudan* (Leiden: Sidestone, 2010), 31.

[9] See Hiebert, *Transforming Worldviews*, 106–7 (see intro., n. 22) and Hesselgrave, *Communicating Christ Cross-Culturally*, 221–22 (see intro., n. 7).

[10] Kato quotes John Mbiti concerning the plural form of ATR in *Theological Pitfalls in Africa*: "We speak of African Traditional Religions in the plural because there are about one thousand African people (tribes) and each has its own religious system."

[11] Kato, *Theological Pitfalls in Africa*, 24.

being, **(b)** belief in spirits/divinities, **(c)** belief in life after death, **(d)** religious personnel and sacred places, and **(e)** witchcraft and magic practices.[12]

Traditional Religion of the Sukuma of Tanzania

The Sukuma people of northwestern Tanzania compose the largest ethnic group in Tanzania and represent the second-largest tribe in all of East Africa.[13] Numbering approximately six million persons,[14] the Sukuma make up about 16 percent of Tanzania's total population.[15] Nestled along the southern shore of Lake Victoria, the city of Mwanza[16] forms the geographical and cultural

---

[12] Ambrose Moyo, "Religion in Africa," in *Understanding Contemporary Africa*, 3rd ed., April A. Gordon and Donald L. Gordon, eds. (Boulder, CO: Lynn Reiner, 2001), 301.

[13] See April A. Gordon and Donald L. Gordon, eds., *Understanding Contemporary Africa*, 3rd ed. (Boulder, CO: Lynn Reinner, 2001), 81.

[14] See Frans Wijsen and Ralph Tanner, *I Am Just a Sukuma: Globalization and Identity Construction in Northwest Tanzania* (Amsterdam: Rodopi, 2002), v.

[15] The population of the Sukuma has steadily increased over the years. Hans Cory in *The Indigenous Political System of the Sukuma and Proposals for Political Reform* (Nairobi: Eagle, 1954), 1, estimated they approached one million persons in 1954. A 1967 census placed the Sukuma at one and a half million, according to Per Brandström, "The Agro-Pastoral Dilemma: The Underutilization and Overexploitation of Land among the Sukuma of Tanzania" (Uppsala University, Sweden, 1985), 4. A few years later Evie Adams Welch, in "Life and Literature of the Sukuma in Tanzania, East Africa" (PhD diss., Howard University, 1974), 1, numbered the tribe at 2 million out of a total Tanzanian population of 12 million (17 percent of the whole). By 1991 the Sukuma were estimated at between 3 million and 5 million inhabitants (Van Rheenen, *Communicating Christ in Animistic Contexts*, 218). The UN estimated the inhabitants of Tanzania in 2003 at just below 37 million. Since the Sukuma have consistently maintained their population ratio of 16 percent of total Tanzania residents, the Wijsen and Tanner figure of 6 million Sukuma seems to be the most accurate (*I Am Just a Sukuma*, v).

[16] Mwanza boasts a populace of almost a half million people, making the city the second-largest metropolitan area in the country. Welch ("Life and Literature of the Sukuma," 186), said that one-half of the residents were Muslims, one-third Catholics, and 15 percent Protestants. In 1957 this city numbered only 19,877 inhabitants according to R. G. Abrahams in *The Peoples of Greater Unyamwezi, Tanzania* (London: International African Institute, 1967), 22. In those days, the Sukuma composed only 30 percent of

center of Sukumaland. The tribe's homeland is about the size of Switzerland (see appendix 3).[17] The Sukuma rely on farming for sustenance and their livestock, especially cattle, for calculating wealth and social standing.[18]

Sukuma History

Due to the lack of written records, unraveling Sukuma history becomes challenging. Their language, *Kisukuma*,[19] forms part of the Niger-Congo linguistic family known as Bantu.[20] From their origins in Nigeria and Cameroon,[21] the Bantu spread over three-fourths of sub-Saharan Africa, absorbing the original inhabitants along the way.[22] These journeys occurred over thousands of years.[23] The Bantu speakers created fresh cultures as they settled in new territories (see appendix 2).[24]

The emergence of the Sukuma as a distinct people dates from about AD 1500.[25] The Sukuma tribe emerged from a mixture of the original

---

the total population of the city. Pakistanis, Indians, and Arabs comprised 21 percent of Mwanza, accounting for many of the Muslims. Europeans and other non-Africans were 3 percent of the population. Other tribes made up the remaining 46 percent.

[17] See Welch, "Life and Literature of the Sukuma," 60.

[18] See Brandström, "The Agro-Pastoral Dilemma," 3.

[19] *Kisukuma* is the tribal language, the people are called the *Wasukuma*, and the homeland is known as *Usukuma*. Currently most speakers omit the prefixes, using the term *Sukuma* in place of all three terms.

[20] According to Welch in "Life and Literature of the Sukuma," 83, the expression *Bantu* was first used in 1856 in the *Library of Sir George Grey*, 1:40. Welch (90) says the pure Bantu speakers lived in central and southern Africa. Robert O. Collins and James M. Burns in *A History of Sub-Saharan Africa* (Cambridge: Cambridge University Press, 2007) note that ethnic groups speaking Bantu languages number more than 400 (44, 47, 50). They are united by their usage of the root *ntu* for the word *man*, and its plural *batu*. (Individual Bantu languages have variations on this, as Swahili employs *mtu* and *watu* for man and men respectively.) Bantu is a linguistic definition for a family of languages and not a tribal designation.

[21] See appendix 2 for maps explaining the origins of the Bantu people and their migration in Africa.

[22] See Van Pelt, *Bantu Customs in Mainland Tanzania*, 26–27.

[23] See Welch, "Life and Literature of the Sukuma," 84.

[24] See Collins and Burns, *A History of Sub-Saharan Africa*, 47.

[25] See Wijsen and Tanner, *I Am Just a Sukuma*, 37.

inhabitants of the region and successive waves of Bantu immigrants, followed by the entry of a *Hamitic* ruling class.[26] By the time of the arrival of the Europeans in the middle of the nineteenth century, the Sukuma were ruled by approximately fifty chiefdoms among five major clans.[27]

Germany colonized Tanganyika in 1890 but lost the territory to Great Britain in 1919 after the First World War.[28] Britain administered Tanganyika as a protectorate until its independence in 1961. Both Germany and Great Britain governed *Sukumaland* through the traditional chieftainship[29] system.[30] For thirty years the country experimented with socialism but abandoned it, fully transitioning to a free market economy by the end of the twentieth century.[31]

Sukuma Society

Summary justice sometimes surfaces as a means for punishing delinquency and criminality. The *Sungusungu*[32] function as an informal vigilante group to maintain law and order in the community when the national and local governments neglect the responsibility.[33] In 1984 I was driving with my family along the outskirts of Mwanza, Tanzania, on the road toward the Kenyan border, when I encountered a group of twenty *Sungusungu*. Despite

---

[26] See Berta Millroth, *Lyuba: Traditional Religion of the Sukuma* (Uppsala, SWE: Studia Ethnographia Upsaliensia, 1965), 13–14.

[27] See Welch, "Life and Literature of the Sukuma," 87.

[28] See Abrahams, *The Peoples of Greater Unyamwezi, Tanzania*, 26–27.

[29] Both German and British colonialists employed "indirect rule" over Tanganyika (Abrahams, 26–27). The Sukuma idea of chieftainship of their *batemi* (chiefs) differed from the expectations of their colonizers. The traditional Sukuma ruler conducted religious rituals to insure punctual rains and arbitrated disputes among his subjects. Thus, sometimes the British selected their own chiefs from those qualified by lineage and sacked those who proved to be poor at the additional colonial administrative duties. Wijsen and Tanner, *I Am Just a Sukuma*, 75–77.

[30] Wijsen and Tanner, 75.

[31] See Aimee Bessire and Mark Bessire, *Sukuma* (New York: Rosen, 1997), 20.

[32] The *Sungusungu* are not a Sukuma secret society, but an independent (normally nonreligious), informal association of vigilantes.

[33] See Wijsen and Tanner, *I Am Just a Sukuma*, 4.

the early hour of the morning, they were lying in the road, stopping traffic in both directions. When motorists approached their blockade, they charged each vehicle, raising their spears, causing everyone to retreat in the opposite direction. I was able to run the roadblock by hiding my vehicle directly behind a passing bus. As the Sungusungu parted for the motor coach, I slipped by them, hidden by the exhaust fumes of the bus. The Sungusungu rarely bother non-Sukuma, but in this case, I was the exception to the rule. The large number of witches and wizards annually killed in northwestern Tanzania testifies to the Sukuma propensity for taking matters into their own hands.

Of the 4,519 witches and wizards known by the government to have been killed in Tanzania between 1970 and 1988, 49 percent of them perished in Sukumaland. Much of the responsibility for this was blamed on the vigilante group, the Sungusungu.[34] Despite these modernizing tendencies, Wijsen and Tanner state that the leader of the modern Sukuma vigilante group is often called *ntemi*, a traditional framework within a modern structure. The following explains how ATR penetrates contemporary life:[35]

> The "*Sungusungu*" are also based in the spiritual religious outlook of magic and counter-magic. They identify thieves and the routes they have taken after the theft by divination; before they set off on the task of tracking stolen cattle they consult the diviner (*mfumu*). And they smear their bodies with "traditional" protection (*lukago*) and they use medicine (*dawa*) to guard themselves against the dangers that they might encounter on the way. However, the "*Sungusungu*" groups were not just a revival of the past. Their rituals and symbols were partly old and partly new. They did borrow some "traditional" symbols and rituals, but they also added new features.[36]

---

[34] See Wijsen and Tanner, 135.
[35] Wijsen and Tanner, 147.
[36] Wijsen and Tanner, 150–51.

Sukuma Culture

The Sukuma have successfully resisted many of the cultural changes attempted by Muslim and Christian missionaries, two European colonial governments, and most recently, the modern Tanzanian state. Wijsen and Tanner say this about the legendary Sukuma resistance to change: "The Sukuma have managed to keep their culture substantially intact. . . . Significantly, only some 12% have become Christians[37] and a much smaller percentage have become Moslems [*sic*] despite a century of evangelization by missionaries and the even longer presence of Moslems."[38]

Secret societies command great importance in Sukuma culture. Associations practice open membership, but special knowledge and secret powers await the initiate. Two principal types of societies exist: the *mbina* (dance) and the *ngoma* (drum). Subgroups of these associations include *manga* (spirit possession societies), *Bafumu* (associations of diviners), *Buyeye* (snake charmers), *Bunguli* (porcupine hunters), game hunters, and parents of twins.[39] The snake-charming society began as a group of diviners and medicine men treating snakebites. A subgroup, however, evolved, called the *Bagoyangi*: a miming, drumming society of acrobats who actually play with and toss live snakes to one another during their routines.[40] The porcupine society members actively dance and pantomime. Their rigorous initiation ceremony involves throwing and catching live porcupines.

---

[37] Discerning the percentage of adherents to various religious persuasions in the Sukuma area presents major problems, as approximations differ widely. Welch estimates that 50 percent of the Sukuma in the rural areas follow ATR, one-third embrace Catholicism, with less than 10 percent following Protestant denominations. Nonetheless, Welch offers a disclaimer, saying, "The situation thus is complicated, for many times the traditional beliefs and customs still persist under Islamic and Christian practices. "Life and Literature of the Sukuma," 186–87.

[38] Wijsen and Tanner, *I Am Just a Sukuma*, 35.

[39] Parents of twins and parents of children born in the breech position have their own secret societies. A twin birth is a spiritual event with the parents of the phenomenon warranting their own secret society. Welch, "Life and Literature of the Sukuma," 370.

[40] See Millroth, *Lyuba*, 149.

With great understatement, Millroth remarks that membership in this society is understandably small.[41] Most members choose the secret associations to which they will belong based on the advice of a diviner. Many maintain memberships in several different dancing and drum societies, while others belong to none at all.[42] These associations serve both leisure and religious functions.

Sukuma Traditional Religion

Sukuma traditional religion consists more of a loose set of private practices than a faith. Wijsen and Tanner say, "The success of the Sukuma religious system is that, in practice as well as in theory, it is no system at all, except in very general terms."[43]

The Sukuma believe in a Supreme Being. Forty different words describe God in the Sukuma language, with *Liwelelo* being the most prominent.[44] *Liwelelo* describes more of a universal controlling force than a personal God. Ancestors dwell within the deity's life energy. Generally regarded as a benevolent great shepherd, the high god of the Sukuma also judges and punishes wrongs.[45] Sukuma believe Liwelelo created the world and reigns omnipresent and eternal.[46]

Sukuma beliefs in spirits and divinities. The Sukuma venerate many lesser deities in addition to the one high God. These divinities include *Ngasa Ilembe*, the god of the south, who brings the rain; and *Sita*, the god of the wilderness (the spirit of the bush). Sukuma also beseech the

---

[41] Millroth, 149.

[42] See Abrahams, *The Peoples of Greater Unyamwezi, Tanzania*, 64–65.

[43] Wijsen and Tanner, *I Am Just a Sukuma*, 57.

[44] Sometimes the diminutive *Welelo* is used for brevity. Christians in Sukumaland employ Liwelelo as the name for their God, and it is the word translated "God" in the Sukuma Bible. See Welch, "Life and Literature of the Sukuma," 171, 175.

[45] See Millroth, *Lyuba*, 104.

[46] See Welch, "Life and Literature of the Sukuma," 175–76.

ancestral spirits when Sukumaland lacks rain.[47] The tribe also venerates *Kongwa* or *Ndimi*, the lord of the animals.

Traditional Sukuma also fear a water monster called *Ngassa*.[48] This is a deity who appears in the form of a great fish, crocodile, or hippopotamus, living in Lake Victoria.[49] Another deity, *Katabi,* demands reverence as an evil divinity associated with a spirit-possession society.[50] Other minor malevolent ghosts cause storms, floods, and droughts. Such calamities stem from improperly venerating ancestors, but Sukuma believe it is Liwelelo who sends the evil spirits that bring the misfortune.[51]

Sukuma belief in life after death. Life after death for the Sukuma means to dwell in the next world as an ancestor. They believe each person has a soul, and one's shadow represents part of this essence. Many Sukuma hold that the shadow is synonymous with life and believe dead men do not cast shadows. Sorcerers are feared due to their perceived ability to kill someone by stealing part of their shadow.[52] Traditional Sukuma remain uncertain about what transpires after death, except for the belief that the deceased join their ancestors. The dead live among the tribe but only the *mfumu* (medicine men) can see them due to their invisibility.[53]

Concerning ancestors (*masamva*), Oladimeji observes, "It is not easy to draw a line between worship and veneration."[54] Ancestors receive honor, not worship, so veneration more precisely describes the practice.[55] It is inaccurate to characterize ATR as ancestor worship. Rather, ethnic groups like

---

[47] Sukuma do not consider ancestors to be deities nor do they worship them. See Millroth, *Lyuba*, 111; and Welch, 170.

[48] Also called *Mugassa*. Sukuma and even some of the Arabs offer a sacrifice to the lake deity to ensure safe passage. See Millroth, 110.

[49] See Millroth, 107; and Welch, "Life and Literature of the Sukuma," 183.

[50] See Abrahams, *The Peoples of Greater Unyamwezi, Tanzania*, 78.

[51] See Welch, "Life and Literature of the Sukuma," 177.

[52] See Millroth, *Lyuba*, 115.

[53] See Millroth, 115.

[54] Oladimeji, *African Traditional Religion*, 19.

[55] See Van Pelt, *Bantu Customs in Mainland Tanzania*, 54.

the Sukuma generally worship one supreme being, but they pray to ancestral spirits, who mediate between humans and deities.[56]

Ancestors exhibit both good and bad characteristics because the departed can either hurt or help the living.[57] Small huts called *numba ja masamva* (house of the ancestors) dot the compounds of the Sukuma.[58] In this way, the forebears of each clan remain in contact with their descendants. Ancestors communicate with their relatives from the grave through a diviner (*mfumu*) or medium (*manga*). Ancestors cause calamities, while the magicians relay instructions to the living for corrective action. Welch explains the relationship of the living to the deceased as follows:

> Living *Sukuma* will pray to the deceased *Wasukuma* to control the negative forces on earth that cause his life to be unhappy. Aside, it is fitting to explain that the omnipotent spirit of the deceased will exist as long as he is remembered in the minds of his offspring and as long as his spirit is invoked in their prayers. Hence, this is one of the reasons the *Wasukuma* want to have many children. They are not interested so much in continuing a family's name or to have heirs to claim his wealth. Through his children, the traditional *Sukuma* believes he can achieve immortality.[59]

Traditional Sukuma venerate ancestors beginning with their deceased grandparents and going back as many as eight generations,[60] with five of the generations remembered fairly well. After the fifth generation, forebears

---

[56] See Oladimeji, *African Traditional Religion*, 20.

[57] Welch, "Life and Literature of the Sukuma," 176.

[58] Scattered around most Sukuma compounds (usually three to four thatched homes) are small "spirit houses" about the size of a filing cabinet, but round in shape like a soccer ball. Also called *magabilo*, these ancestor dwellings are miniature, thatched, loosely constructed, open-air houses bound with vines. They most closely resemble a large, transparent soccer ball constructed of thatch and vines. See Millroth, *Lyuba*, 160.

[59] Welch, "Life and Literature of the Sukuma," 176.

[60] Living grandparents are not venerated. Other people's ancestors are neither feared nor honored. See Millroth, *Lyuba*, 122.

are invoked only in a general way. Most Sukuma would not kill a snake, thinking perhaps the serpent was an ancestor. Leopards, lions, and porcupines are not killed for the same reason.[61]

Sukuma religious personnel and sacred places. Any discussion of the religious personnel of the Sukuma begins with the *ntemi*,[62] or chief. The Sukuma view their chiefs more religiously than administratively.[63] Hans Cory says, "Every chief was considered to be the earthly representative of the most powerful spirit of the founder. . . . The chief became the bringer of rain and so came to be responsible for the fertility of corn, cattle, and mankind."[64] Paradoxically, Cory continues, despite having to conduct magical ceremonies for ensuring rain, "the chief himself was not a diviner (*mfumu*) and his people never considered him a magician."[65] Instead, each *ntemi* retains an associate called the *ngemi wa mbula*,[66] or rainmaker, who actually causes the rain to fall.[67] Nevertheless, if the rainmaker fails, the chief is held responsible and may be deposed.[68]

The *mfumu* (plural, *bafumu*) ranks as the second most important religious official. This person functions as a traditional medicine practitioner. When a problem surfaces, the sufferer hires a diviner (*mfumu*) or medium (*manga*) that determines which ancestor has been offended and what must

---

[61] See Millroth, 116–20.

[62] The plural of *ntemi* (chief) is *batemi*.

[63] See Wijsen and Tanner, *I Am Just a Sukuma*, 89.

[64] Cory, *The Indigenous Political System of the Sukuma*, 5–6.

[65] With the advent of the Tanzanian state and universal education, Cory also says this about the modern *ntemi*: "Many of the younger chiefs have themselves probably become skeptical of their own powers and perform ceremonies not because they consider them effective, but in order to please the conservative elements among their subjects." Cory, 6–7.

[66] The similarity between the Bantu languages of *Kisukuma* and *Kiswahili* is evident in the third word of this phrase. *Mbula* means "rain" in Sukuma, while *mvula* is the term in Swahili.

[67] See Millroth, *Lyuba*, 134.

[68] See Welch, "Life and Literature of the Sukuma," 164.

be done to satisfy the spirit. Often, the diviners prescribe ritual sacrifices.[69] Most of the *bafumu* also serve as leaders in the Sukuma dance and drum societies. Besides their spiritual activities, the *bafumu* treat illnesses by their knowledge of pharmacology, anatomy, and homeopathy.[70]

The spirit-possessed medium, or *manga*, constitutes another type of diviner. Manga serve as merely channels to the spirit world and interact more passively with the supernatural than the *mfumu*. Some of these mediums display glossolalia (ecstatic utterances) as they interact with the unseen forces.[71] People consult the *manga* when disease, barrenness, accident, or death strikes.[72] Wijsen and Tanner describe how these *manga* work: "Possession is fundamental to the conducting of successful séances, for, without the presence of his ancestors, the *manga* cannot attempt to get any correct solution. During the séance the *manga* works himself into a state of hysteria."[73]

The *nogi* (evil witch or sorcerer) represents the most powerful and feared religious figure within Sukuma ATR. Although some researchers distinguish between witchcraft and sorcery, the Sukuma language uses the terms interchangeably, calling both *bulogi*.[74] Some believe one cannot become a *nogi* except by birth,[75] while others hold that an *mfumu* (diviner) can become a *nogi* (pl., *balogi*) by excelling in evil. Fearing reprisals, *balogi* keep their identities secret. Special powers of invisibility assist in maintaining their anonymity in the community, as Millroth explains: "The word *nogi* is used more generally to acknowledge that someone has a secret, extraordinary

---

[69] See Welch, 179.

[70] See Millroth, *Lyuba*, 143.

[71] See Wijsen and Tanner, *I Am Just a Sukuma*, 42.

[72] See Millroth, *Lyuba*, 141.

[73] Wijsen and Tanner, *I Am Just a Sukuma*, 141.

[74] These terms can be confusing. *Bulogi* means witchcraft, sorcery, and evil magic. *Balogi* describe the sorcerers, witches, and magicians themselves. *Nogi* is the singular of *balogi* and can be of either sex. Sometimes married couples form husband-and-wife sorcery teams.

[75] See Welch, "Life and Literature of the Sukuma," 200.

power to cast an evil spell, which will bring sickness or death. This power can be exercised by personal contact or from a great distance."[76]

Much of Sukuma folk religion consists of preventive medicine and cures for suspected *balogi* spells and curses. The Sukuma fear the charges of witchcraft and sorcery because of the indefensibility of such allegations. Any person indicted must move away, be killed, or die.[77] The charges are impossible to refute due to the following Sukuma rationale: "A *nogi* goes to *kulogwa* (cast his spells) by night in his own body, which he makes invisible, while at the same time he is quietly sleeping at home. Some say that the body asleep at home is not real but an optical illusion."[78] Therefore, one may be visibly asleep at home and still be accused of causing harm.

Sukuma witchcraft and magic practices. Each segment of Sukuma ATR relates to another portion of the religion that, in turn, affects a different part. Nowhere can this be seen more clearly than in the concept of magic (*bufumu*) and diviner (*mfumu*).[79] As Millroth notes, "A secret religious society is called *bufumu*, but this is also an abstract word denoting either the magic bond which links a person with his ancestors or the knowledge of any procedure which contains or is based on a magic element."[80] Therefore, all traditional Sukuma believe they share this supernatural magical bond (*bufumu*) as part of their existence. Their diviners simply possess a greater amount of these special powers than the average member of the tribe. The dance and drum societies to which most Sukuma belong serve as cultural vehicles to cement this bond.

---

[76] Millroth, *Lyuba*, 144–45.

[77] See Welch, "Life and Literature of the Sukuma," 188, 212.

[78] Millroth, *Lyuba*, 144.

[79] *Bufumu* may be loosely translated "magic" but in the sense of "good magic." The practitioners of *Bufumu* are the *Bafumu* (singular, *mfumu*). The terms can be confusing, as *bufumu* is also the word for a secret religious society active among the dance and drum associations.

[80] Millroth, *Lyuba*, 137.

The concept of causation underlies the idea of witchcraft. Unexpected deaths of people under the age of fifty do not just happen, and they must be explained. Sukuma usually attribute life's problems and calamities to offended ancestors, evil spirits, or witchcraft.[81] When misfortune occurs, the sufferer hires a diviner (*mfumu*) to determine the ancestor, spirit, or witch (*nogi*) causing the disaster. If the divination reveals sorcery as the problem, the *nogi* may only receive a beating and be driven out of the village. On the other hand, a death attributed to witchcraft, or a second witchcraft offense, often results in an execution.[82] Tanzania outlawed witchcraft accusations years ago, but those who kill witches are rarely prosecuted.[83] Many traditional Sukuma believe owls summon sorcerers and witches to their coven meetings, riding to their gatherings on the backs of hyenas.[84]

Sukuma practice curative and preventive magic, often wearing beaded necklaces in honor of their protecting ancestors.[85] On a return trip to Mwanza, Tanzania, in January 2006, I visited a Sukuma village with a pastor friend. Pastor Philemoni noticed a young woman carrying a baby wearing such a necklace. Upon questioning the lady and discovering she was a Christian, he asked why her child was wearing a magic charm. Receiving no satisfactory answer, and with the woman's permission, Philemoni burned the *lupingu*. Belief in magic so pervades Sukuma thinking that practitioners often blend traditional and modern medicine to achieve the best results.[86] Sukuma ATR possesses its own version of the "evil eye," known as *wisu*, or jealousy. Envious Sukuma sometimes cry out, *"Bulogi!"* (witchcraft, sorcery)

---

[81] See Welch, "Life and Literature of the Sukuma," 200.

[82] See Millroth, *Lyuba*, 144–45.

[83] Welch, "Life and Literature of the Sukuma," 210.

[84] See Van Pelt, *Bantu Customs in Mainland Tanzania*, 72; Welch, "Life and Literature of the Sukuma," 304.

[85] See Bessire and Bessire, *Sukuma*, 32.

[86] See Millroth, *Lyuba*, 143.

against their richer neighbors.[87] Chiefs can confiscate the property of a convicted *nogi*.[88]

The diviners and mediums recommend to their clients the appropriate sacrifice for each problem or request brought by the inquirer. The simplest offering consists of spitting a mouthful of grain on the grave of an ancestor. Particularly displeased ancestors require the blood sacrifice of an animal. Before cultivation the chief offers different sacrifices to ensure a bountiful harvest.[89] Beja Muslim farmers have a similar practice of sacrificing an animal before planting.

Sukuma believe sorcerers, evil spirits, and displeased ancestors cause all misfortunes.[90] The origin for each must be determined by consulting diviners and remedied through rituals. Much of Sukuma life centers upon resolving these supernatural dilemmas successfully.

African Traditional Religion and Folk Islam

In an interesting and surprising twist, Welch says, "The Islamic religion has made an impact on the traditional religion [of the Sukuma]."[91] This can be seen by the increasing belief by Sukuma in the existence of Muslim spirits called *majini* (Swahili for *jinn*). Special ATR Sukuma rituals supposedly chase them away.[92] Wijsen and Tanner suggest, "It seems probable that their [Sukuma] idea of spirits such as '*mashetani*' [Satan or devil], '*majini*' and '*mapepo*' [evil spirit] entered Sukuma understanding through contacts with Arabs."[93] They use these Muslim spirits to explain misfortune that cannot be attributed to either witchcraft or ancestors.

---

[87] See Welch, "Life and Literature of the Sukuma," 198.
[88] See Cory, *The Indigenous Political System of the Sukuma*, 13.
[89] See Millroth, *Lyuba*, 156–57, 172–73.
[90] See Wijsen and Tanner, *I Am Just a Sukuma*, 63.
[91] Welch, "Life and Literature of the Sukuma," 186.
[92] See Wijsen and Tanner, *I Am Just a Sukuma*, 55.
[93] Wijsen and Tanner, 61.

Conclusion

Traditional Religion (TR) profoundly influences the practice of Islam. Ambrose Moyo says, "For the masses of Muslim Africans, African traditional beliefs and practices have continued, although with some adaptations to conform to similar practices in Islam."[94] In the next chapter, we will explore ATR's influence over folk Islam.

---

[94] Moyo, "Religion in Africa," 323.

6

Traditional Religion's Influence
on Popular Islam

A hundred years ago, Samuel Zwemer wrote, "Islam and Animism live, in very neighborly fashion, on the same street and in the same mind."[1] He quotes Muslim writer Abu'l Fida, who comments on some pagan beliefs entering Islam from Arabian traditional religion:

> "The Arabs of the times of ignorance," he says, "used to do things which the religious law of Islam has adopted. . . . They used, moreover, to make the pilgrimage (Hajj) to the House" (the Ka'aba), "and visit the consecrated places, and wear the Ihram" (the single garment worn to the present day by a pilgrim when running round the Ka'bah), "and perform the *Tawwaf*, and run" (between the hills As Safa and Al Marwa) "and make their stand at all the Stations and cast the stones" (at the devil).[2]

---

[1] Zwemer, *The Influence of Animism on Islam*, 207 (see chap. 1, n. 5).
[2] Abu'l Fida in Zwemer, 4.

Introduction

One of the most difficult aspects of studying folk Islam involves its origins. Questions emerge about the relative percentage of Islam or traditional religion. Bill Musk sees two primary sources: (1) traditional Arabian religious practices dating back to when Muhammad founded the faith, and (2) observances and beliefs that gradually entered Islam as the religion spread.[3] This blending of traditional religion and Islam produces a myriad of traditions across the world known as folk or popular Islam. Traditional religion profoundly influences the practice of Islam. Moyo says, "For the masses of Muslim Africans, African traditional beliefs and practices have continued, although with some adaptations to conform to similar practices in Islam."[4] Ruthven describes how easily Islam absorbed the faith of traditional religion: "The supreme deities which exist in many pagan traditions could be assimilated to Allah. Lesser local deities could be Islamicized or explained away as vernacular terms for God's attributes, or as the *jinn's* or spirits of Quranic folklore."[5]

Traditional Religion and Folk Islam

Islam came to Africa early during the second wave of the Muslim conquests. Umar, the second caliph, extended the western borders of Islam by taking Egypt in the year 640. After his successful conquest of Jerusalem, Caliph Umar did not favor a conquest of Egypt due to the strength of the Roman garrisons at Farama, Fusat, and Alexandria. Yet, he was persuaded by 'Amr b. al-'As, one of his generals, to make the attempt.[6]

The armies of Islam under the third caliph, Uthman, brought Tunisia under their control by 647.[7] By 698 the ninth caliph, Abd al-Malik, had triumphed over the North African coastal strip and placed it under the

---

[3] Musk, "Popular Islam," 238 (see intro., n. 5).
[4] Moyo, "Religion in Africa," 323 (see chap. 5, n. 12).
[5] Ruthven, *Islam in the World*, 259 (see chap. 2, n. 6).
[6] See Shibli Numani, *Umar* (London: I. B. Tauris, 2004), 257–58.
[7] See Braswell, *Islam*, 23 (see intro., n. 28).

banner of the crescent. The Islamization south of the Mediterranean coastal area happened more gradually.

Islam spread into the East African interior through commercial traders and Sufi orders.[8] Along the Red Sea and Indian Ocean coasts, Persian and Arab merchants established a string of settlements. After generations of intermarriage, a new Swahili-speaking African-Arab Islamic culture emerged.[9] Some of these towns were initially founded by the Portuguese but were always primarily composed of Arabized coastal African people. In East Africa, Islam did not spread far beyond the coastal strips of the Red Sea and Indian Ocean, except in the case of a few Arab slave-trading centers, such as Mpatwa, Tabora, and Ujiji (modern-day Tanzania), the route taken by David Livingston, and later by his "rescuer," Henry Morton Stanley.[10]

In West Africa, traders and *marabouts*[11] traveled south of the Sahara into present-day Mauritania, Mali, Nigeria, Burkina Faso, and Senegal, spreading Islam among kings who influenced their subjects to embrace Islam.[12] J. A. Naude says:

> Mediterranean Africa was Islamized at an early date and an integrated Islamic culture with Arabic as a language was formed, so much so that it is at least as much part of the Arab world as it is of Africa. In fact, eight of the twenty-one members of the Arab League are part of the African continent and numerically they represent more than sixty percent of all Arabs. North Africa, therefore, is fully within the Islamic world.[13]

When Muslim culture encounters traditional African civilizations, conflict sometimes ensues. Voll designates the region where Islam meets other

---

[8] See Nasr, *Islam*, 21 (see chap. 1, n. 32).

[9] See Moyo, "Religion in Africa," 321.

[10] See John Bierman, *Dark Safari: The Life Behind the Legend of Henry Morton Stanley* (New York: Alfred A. Knopf, 1990), 100.

[11] *Marabout* is the name for a Muslim holy man in West Africa, similar to a *sheikh*.

[12] See Ruthven, *Islam in the World*, 258.

[13] J. A. Naude, *Islam in Africa* (Braamfontein, ZA: Jan Smuts House, 1978), 4.

societies on the continent, principally indigenous religions and Christianity, the "fault line of Africa."[14] The Beja people of North Africa live along this fault line. While living in their country, I observed a number of practices that resembled the traditional religious customs of the Sukuma tribe of Tanzania covered in the previous chapter. The religious practices of the Sukuma typify the ATR of sub-Saharan Africa and illustrate the religious similarities between traditional religion and folk Islam.

The Folk Islam of the Beja of Sudan, Egypt, and Eritrea

A look at the Beja of North Africa demonstrates how profoundly their popular religion still influences them. The tribe lives along the "fault line" between the Muslim northern region of Africa and the Christian-ATR southern portion of the continent.[15]

Early Egyptian Influences

The earliest ATR influence upon Beja folk religion comes from the faith of the pharaohs. They have lived side by side with the Egyptians for the past 4,000 years, although mostly as enemies. Despite a history of conflict and antagonism, eventually the Hillmen adopted many of the Egyptian gods as their own.[16] In fact, two of the major Egyptian gods, Re and Ammon-Re[17]

---

[14] John Voll, "The Effects of Islamic Structures on Modern Islamic Expansion in the Eastern Sudan," *International Journal of African Historical Studies* 7, no. 1 (1974): 85.

[15] See appendix 1 for a map of the Beja area in Sudan, Egypt and Eritrea.

[16] The Egyptians gave the Beja the nickname *Hillman* in the third century AD, calling them *Beja,* the Anti, or Hillmen. See E. A. Wallis Budge, *The Egyptian Sudan: Its History and Monuments* (London: Kegan Paul, Trench, Trübner, 1907), 174.

[17] Re was the sun god during the Old (Egyptian) Kingdom but later was considered the god of the underworld. Ammon-Re was the principal god of the New Kingdom and closely associated with Re. Budge, 18–19.

(Lords of the thrones of the two lands)[18] were considered Cushitic deities.[19] The pharaohs of Cush ruled most of Egypt during the third Intermediate Period and Late Period (1065–525 BC) of Egyptian history.[20] During the first five centuries AD, the Beja filled the roles of both ally and enemy to the rulers of Upper Egypt.[21] The people and kings of Upper Egypt were Cushitic and ethnically related to the Beja. Candace, queen of the Ethiopians (Acts 8:27), was a Nubian Cushite and ruled ancient Napata and Meroe, now within the borders of modern-day Sudan.[22] The Beja raided both the Nubians and the Romans in antiquity.[23]

According to Beja oral history, two notable practices survive from ancient Egyptian times. Beja men wear their hair in a uniquely long style. Rudyard Kipling called them the "Fuzzy Wuzzy."[24] Besides impressing the opposite sex, the Beja claim that the male Beja hairstyle (*tiffa*) "preserves the eyesight and teeth of the wearer and protects him from the summer's sun and winter's cold, and is good for the brain as well."[25] The other custom dat-

---

[18] Ancient Egypt consisted of a lower (northern) kingdom from the Mediterranean to Luxor (central Egypt along the Nile) and an upper (southern) kingdom from Luxor to Aswan (at the first cataract) to Meroe (at the sixth cataract), north of present-day Khartoum, Sudan.

[19] See B. G. Haycock, "Towards a Better Understanding of the Kingdom of Cush," *SNR* 49 (1968): 10.

[20] See Arthur Goldschmidt Jr., *A Brief History of Egypt* (New York: Checkmark Books, 2008), 28–29.

[21] See L. P. Kirwan, "A Contemporary Account of the Conversion of the Sudan to Christianity," *SNR* 20, no. 2 (1937): 289–95.

[22] See Budge, *The Egyptian Sudan*, 169.

[23] See Budge, 174, 177, 179.

[24] Rudyard Kipling, "Fuzzy Wuzzy" in *A Victorian Anthology: 1837–1895*, ed. Edward Clarence Stedman (Boston: Houghton-Mifflin, 1895), 595.

[25] Only the men of the Beja tribe wear their hair in this unique manner among the Sudanese. The hair, groomed in ringlets, hangs down their backs and in front of the ears. Goat and camel fat (*darisa*) causes the hair to stand up so when the young man dances, the hair shakes upon his jumping. Men sleep on carved wooden headrests (*matras*) so their hair will not be disturbed at night. B. A. Lewis, "Deim el Arab and the Beja Stevedores of Port Sudan," *SNR* 43 (1962): 35–36.

ing from ancient times involves the circumcision of females in infancy and males during boyhood.[26]

In the sixth century AD, the Roman emperor Justinian transformed the temple of Isis at Philae temple[27] near Aswan, Egypt, into a church,[28] depriving the Beja of the center of their religion. A few years later, Jacobite Monophysite missionaries began the conversion of the Nubian kingdoms along the upper Nile between modern-day Aswan and Khartoum.[29] Some of the Beja dwelling near the Nubians adopted Christianity, while others retained their traditional religion or mixed it with the new faith.[30]

During the 500 years of the so-called Beja Christian era, the faith of the Hillmen consisted of the syncretism of sun-and-stone worship, Isis and Osiris Egyptian mythology, and Monophysite Christianity.[31] One custom survives from their Christian past: the cross represents a sign of mercy and redemption to the Beja.[32] Sometimes a Beja shaman marks the sign of the cross on the forehead of a sufferer for healing.

Beja Traditional Religion and Folk Islam

Although separated by distance, comparisons with the popular religion of the Sukuma serve as a frame of reference for observing the lingering influences of traditional religion on the Beja who have abandoned it for Islam. Drawing a line separating the Islamic elements of Beja popular Islam from

---

[26] See Lewis, 34.

[27] Philae temple rests on the Nile River near Aswan, Egypt. This is one of the Nubian monuments rescued and moved to higher ground by UNESCO when the construction of the Aswan High Dam threatened to submerge it. A nightly sound and light show reenacts the worship of the cult of Isis for tourists. The *Ababda Beja* tribal region still includes the area near the temple site.

[28] See Budge, *The Egyptian Sudan*, 297.

[29] "The Jacobites were Monophysites who believed in one nature of God. They were so called from the monk Jagoub el Baradai, who framed the canon of their belief." A. Paul, *A History of the Beja Tribes of the Sudan* (London: Frank Cass, 1954), 62.

[30] See Paul, 62.

[31] See Paul, 62.

[32] See Ausenda, "Leisurely Nomads," 418 (see chap. 4, n. 67).

the influences of African Traditional Religion is difficult. Many Beja practice a version of ATR covered by a veneer of Islam, while others reflect a strict Muslim orthodoxy. Kapteijns describes the Beja as "'mixers' who retain many non-Islamic practices."[33]

Beja belief in a supreme being. The ATR concept of a high God matches well with Islam. When the Beja accepted Islam[34] as their religion, the Allah of the Quran gradually superseded and replaced their earlier concepts of God. Lewis says, "Islam insists on the uniqueness of God as a single omnipotent creator deity. . . . But once this is said, . . . the Quran itself provides scriptural warrant for the existence of a host of subsidiary powers and spirits."[35]

Notwithstanding the adoption by the Beja of the Muslim concept of one high God, a few dissenters remain. I received quite a surprise while driving near a *Hedareb Hadendowa Beja* village in 1992 near Kassala, Sudan. A Beja Christian told me, "In that town my people worship the devil and not God. They do not worship God, only the devil."[36] Although a startling practice for Muslims, it coincides with this account of a *Hedareb* (Beja) ritual:

> They adore the devil, and follow the example of their priests: every
> clan has its priest, who pitches a tent made of feathers, in the shape
> of a dome, wherein he practices his adorations; when they consult
> him about their affairs, he strips naked, and enters the tent stepping
> backwards; he afterwards issues the appearance of a mad and deliri-
> ous person, and exclaims, "The devil salutes you."[37]

---

[33] Lidwien Kapteijns, "The Historiography of the Northern Sudan from 1500 to the Establishment of British Colonial Rule: A Critical Overview," *International Journal of African Historical Studies* 22, no. 2 (1989): 254.

[34] This was a gradual process. The Beja fought against the Muslims during the ninth and tenth centuries. With the defeat of the Christian Nubian kingdoms in 1275 and their steady conversion to Islam (complete by 1400), Bejaland increasingly became Muslim as well. See Budge, *The Egyptian Sudan*, 189, 193, 199.

[35] Lewis, "Deim el Arab and the Beja Stevedores of Port Sudan," 60.

[36] Faisal Farouk, interview with the author, Khartoum, Sudan, January 18, 2005.

[37] Budge, *The Egyptian Sudan*, 182–83.

Beja belief in spirits and divinities. In addition to the jinns and devils so prominent in the Quran, Beja folk Islam adds other spiritual beings to their faith framework. These deities answer to the name of "spirit humans" and may benefit or harm members of the tribe. I asked an English-speaking Beja leader residing in the United States about these spirit humans. Ibrahim said they are not jinns but "helpers of the jinns."[38] These spirits could be classified as "familiar spirits." Beja believe spirit animals and spirit insects accompany spirit humans.[39] These beings populate a pantheon of lesser deities both feared and venerated by the Beja. Jacobsen says, "The cultural world of the Beja is a world inhabited by a host of spirits. Although there are Muslim and good intentioned spirits, most *Hadandowa* Beja are mainly concerned with the malevolent ones as well as the capricious ones, which occasionally create problems."[40]

Werehyenas, who transform themselves back and forth between animals and humans, frighten many Beja. Folklore claims they steal babies and drink their blood.[41] Such lycanthropic superstitions persist among many folk religions worldwide.[42] They also believe in numerous ghosts.[43] In the Beja worldview, diseases consist of spirits who possess both personality and purpose.[44] The diviner or healer, often the same person, discovers the source and prescribes the cure for spiritual and physical maladies caused by evil spirits.[45] As a result, divination rituals command great respect among the Hillmen, who see no conflict between such practices and Islamic rituals. I. M. Lewis states, "Islam does not ask their adherents to abandon their

---

[38] T. A. Ibrahim, interview with the author, Pittsburg, Pennsylvania, May 1, 2010.

[39] See Frode F. Jacobsen, *Theories of Sickness and Misfortune amongst the Hadandowa Beja: Narratives as Points of Entry into Beja Cultural Knowledge* (London: Kegan Paul, 1998), 58.

[40] Jacobsen, 34.

[41] See Ausenda, "Leisurely Nomads," 429; and Jacobsen, *Theories of Sickness and Misfortune*, 36.

[42] See Hiebert, Shaw, and Tienou, *Understanding Folk Religion*, 86 (see intro., n. 6).

[43] See Jacobsen, *Theories of Sickness and Misfortune*, 254.

[44] See Jacobsen, 89, 106.

[45] See Jacobsen, 152–54

accustomed confidence in their mystical forces. Far from it. In the volumi-
nous Quranic storehouse of angels, *jinns* and devils, whose number is legion,
many of these traditional powers find a hospitable home; and passages from
the Quran are cited to justify their existence as real phenomena."[46]

The Zar possession cult comprises the most important and unusual
non-Muslim spiritual phenomenon in the Beja region.[47] Possessing men,
women, and children, zar spirits are agents believed to cause sicknesses,
paralysis, bleeding, swelling, irritability, and even marriage problems.[48]
Satisfying zar spirits often requires a gold payment and the offering of blood
sacrifices,[49] which is a direct violation of Islamic law. Yusuf Al-Qaradawi
states that "the drinking of blood is repugnant to human decency and it
may be likewise injurious to health."[50] Besides the ceremonial consumption
of blood, the Beja sometimes eat blood boiled with milk,[51] like the ATR
Maasai tribe of Tanzania and Kenya.

In cases of severe possession, three-day parties honoring the entity are
often held. Celebrants perform a mock marriage whereby the spirit weds
an individual, attaching the zar to their host for a lifetime.[52] Zar sacrifices
involve a great economic hardship on the Beja. One zar doctor's diagnosis
required seven sheep,[53] while another zar party necessitated the expendi-
ture of the equivalent of half the cost of a Mercedes-Benz automobile.[54] At
these festivals, both the patient and those attending the ritual often fall into

---

[46] I. M. Lewis, ed., *Islam in Tropical Africa*, 2nd ed. (London: Hutchinson University Library for Africa, 1980), 60.

[47] Jacobsen, in *Theories of Sickness and Misfortune*, 62, says Zar possession is more common among the Beja than other Muslim groups in Sudan.

[48] See Jacobsen, 62, 155.

[49] See Ausenda, "Leisurely Nomads," 433; and Jacobsen, *Theories of Sickness and Misfortune*, 219, 231, 235.

[50] Yusuf Al-Qaradawi, *The Lawful and the Prohibited in Islam (Al-Halal Wal-Haram Fil Islam)*, trans. K. El-Helbawy, M. M. Siddiqui, and S. Shukry (Indianapolis: American Trust Publications, 1960), 44.

[51] See Paul, *A History of the Beja Tribes of the Sudan*, 35.

[52] See Jacobsen, *Theories of Sickness and Misfortune*, 156.

[53] See Jacobsen, 211.

[54] See Jacobsen, 238.

trances where they are beaten with whips by zar doctors without feeling any pain.[55] Zar possession ceremonies feature the striking of sacred drums and violent, trancelike dancing, not unlike the drum and dance (*ngoma*) ATR rituals of the Sukuma tribe mentioned in the previous chapter.[56]

The most common kinds of zar spirits include an Ethiopian prostitute, a British colonial military officer, and a western Sudanese woman.[57] Any of these three may possess either sex. Although occurring in other Muslim societies in central and South Asia and the Middle East, Jacobsen says, "*Zar* as a phenomenon has a wide acceptance among the *Beja* in the Sinkat district [E. Sudan],[58] and most of them recognize the necessity of performing *Zar* rituals."[59]

The Beja differentiate between ordinary madness, or insanity, and zar spirit possession.[60] They also distinguish between Muslim spirits, such as *jinns,* and the non-Muslim zar spirits. Understanding that zar spirits are not part of Muslim orthodoxy does not diminish belief in them, as one Beja man stated, "Well, Zar ceremonies are not Islamic but zar spirits are present among us, so what can we do?"[61] Beja exhibit a certain pragmatism in regard to the supernatural and advise negotiating with the evil spirits when necessary.[62]

Beja belief in a life after death. Ali Karrar, leaning on the work of J. S. Trimingham, says Sufism was the most fundamental characteristic of

---

[55] See Jacobsen, 243.

[56] Drums are also beaten after the death of a Beja man at his funeral according to W. T. Clark in "Manners, Customs and Beliefs of the Northern Bega," *SNR* 21, no. 1 (1938): 13.

[57] See Jacobsen, *Theories of Sickness and Misfortune*, 236.

[58] Sinkat sits on the highway between Khartoum and Port Sudan in the Red Sea hills about an hour and a half drive from the coast. Located in the heart of Beja culture, Sinkat provides a cool respite for coastal residents during the summer when the heat becomes oppressive.

[59] Jacobsen, *Theories of Sickness and Misfortune*, 238.

[60] See Jacobsen, 244.

[61] Quoted in Jacobsen, 71.

[62] See Jacobsen, 262.

Islam in Sudan.[63] Sufis emphasize the recitation of the names of God[64] as the key to entering heaven.[65] One of the Beja ATR alterations to Islam involves Sufism and the spiritual activity of their departed Sufi saints. Many Hillmen believe the souls of deceased holy men remain in their tombs and are available to greet and assist supplicants during pilgrimages to their shrines, especially on the saint's birthday.[66] Some researchers view Beja Sufism as "quite close to an ancestor cult."[67] Beja accept the Islamic concept of life after death as a paradise with sensual delights. Popular Islam convinces the Hillmen that the spirits of the departed remain to either help or hinder the living.

Beja religious personnel and sacred places. Beja sacred places consist of the shrines of their Sufi saints and, of course, their mosques. The Hillmen outwardly revere Islam's holy sites but rarely choose to travel the short distance across the Red Sea to participate in the pilgrimage to Mecca.[68]

The Beja recognize quite an array of religious personnel. The *basir* (plural, *busara*) is a diviner who possesses the ability to see the unseen world both physically and spiritually. Combining knowledge of anatomy, herbs, and folk techniques, *busara* discern illnesses and treat patients accordingly, primarily through homeopathic medicine. This specialist also counts bleeding, cutting, and branding as techniques at his or her disposal. The spiritual quality of *Heequal*[69]—blessedness, holiness, or luckiness—

---

[63] Karrar, *The Sufi Brotherhoods in the Sudan*, 1 (see chap. 4, n. 2).

[64] The Hadith, in Braswell, *Islam: Its Prophet, Peoples, Politics and Power*, 47, quotes Muhammad as saying, "There are ninety-nine names of Allah; he who memorizes them and repeats them will get into paradise."

[65] See Ernst, *The Shambhalah Guide to Sufism*, 85 (see chap. 4, n. 4).

[66] See Ausenda, "Leisurely Nomads," 437.

[67] Ausenda, 448.

[68] See F. C. Gamst, "Beja" in *Muslim Peoples: A World Ethnographic Survey*, vol. 1., ed. Richard V. Weekes (Westport, CT: Greenwood, 1984), 130–36.

[69] The Beja believe certain people possess the spiritual essence of a luck-bringing ability that is very prized among healers and diviners of all kinds. Jacobsen, *Theories of Sickness and Misfortune*, 90.

endows some of the *busara* with special powers. Most, however, follow a homeopathic approach.[70]

The female cowry-shell reader serves as the primary fortune-telling caste among the Beja. She predicts the future or diagnoses a disease by casting seven cowry shells on the ground and reading a story by their random placement. The fortune-teller may prescribe a cure, but a faki or zar doctor usually administers the treatment.[71]

The faki is akin to a shaman or witch doctor, while the zar doctor is a medium. The faki sometimes employs herbal remedies, but usually treats patients through the agency of the Quran. Treatments include reading, wearing, eating, or drinking Quranic verses as magical charms or potions. A common cure consists of whispering Quranic verses over the affected parts of the body.[72]

Most fugara (singular, *faki*) utilize spirit helpers (familiar spirits) in their duties.[73] Serving their communities often in a dual role as Sufi sheikhs, fugara easily blend the medicinal and spiritual aspects of their healing arts.[74] Traditional Beja folk Muslims believe the fugara possess a hereditary power (baraka)[75] passed down from sheikh to sheikh.[76] Many Beja hold that baraka can be essentially "stored up" from generation to generation and passed through the holy lineage of Sufi sheikhs.[77]

Fugara discern the cause and prescribe treatment for most of the physical, emotional, and spiritual problems of the Beja. Alternatively, possession by an unpredictable and troublesome zar spirit requires a specialist. Should a faki fail to effect a cure, the patient often resorts to visiting a zar doctor.

---

[70] See Jacobsen, 63–64.

[71] See Ausenda, "Leisurely Nomads," 419.

[72] See Jacobsen, *Theories of Sickness and Misfortune*, 105, 154.

[73] See Jacobsen, 67–68

[74] See Ausenda, "Leisurely Nomads," 425.

[75] Spiritual power and blessing. Anders Hjort af Ornäs and Gudrun Dahl define *baraka* also as "divine grace." Hjort and Dahl, *Responsible Man: The Atmaan Beja of North-eastern Sudan* (Uppsala: Stockholm Studies in Social Anthropology, 1991), 84.

[76] See Idris Salim el Hassan, "On Ideology: The Case of Religion in Northern Sudan" (PhD diss., University of Connecticut, 1980), 102.

[77] See Jacobsen, *Theories of Sickness and Misfortune*, 158.

Not categorized as a Muslim healer, the zar doctor is a medium possessed by a powerful spirit who successfully negotiates with the zar spirit dwelling inside his patient.[78] Blood sacrifices form the foundation for curing zar maladies.[79] Zar doctors often intertwine herbal, homeopathic, medical, and supernatural elements in treating zar spirit possession.[80]

Beja witchcraft and magic practices. An interdependent relationship exists between the personal beliefs and practices of traditional religion. Some additional Beja witchcraft and magic practices not covered previously will be addressed here.

The Beja observe a number of cultural taboos. They possess a fear of person and foodstuffs originating outside of their tribal lands.[81] Although Beja territory borders the Red Sea, the tribe has a taboo against eating fish.[82] Unlike the Arab and African tribes in other parts of Sudan, the Beja enforce a ban prohibiting females from milking livestock;[83] only men are permitted to do so.[84] Camel milk products protect consumers from illness, according to Beja theory, but pregnant women should avoid crossing the trail of a camel so as not to incur the risk of a miscarriage.[85] Mother-in-law avoidance constitutes another taboo that endures as a strong cultural observance.[86]

The Beja believe certain magical practices bring good fortune and protect from evil influences. After speaking about an illness, many Beja spit on the ground, asking for God's protection from the evil forces.[87] Traditional Beja families hang a decorated straw mat or an embroidered blanket on the

---

[78] See Jacobsen, 156.
[79] See Jacobsen, 231.
[80] See Jacobsen, 85.
[81] See Jacobsen, 261.
[82] See Ausenda, "Leisurely Nomads," 340.
[83] See Hjort and Dahl, *Responsible Man*, 99.
[84] See Ausenda, "Leisurely Nomads," 92.
[85] See Jacobsen, *Theories of Sickness and Misfortune*, 26, 257.
[86] See Paul, *A History of the Beja Tribes of the Sudan*, 239.
[87] See Jacobsen, *Theories of Sickness and Misfortune*, 109.

walls of their homes to repel the *jinns* from their dwellings at night.[88] Some Beja burn medicine pills like incense, inhaling the smoke instead of ingesting the medicine.[89] Magical ornaments adorn marriage houses to convey luck and fertility to newlyweds.[90] Most Beja children wear amulets to protect from attack by spirits; additionally, parents place hyena's teeth necklaces around their children's necks for safety.[91] Furthermore, the northern Beja believe the last Thursday of the month and all Fridays to be unlucky to begin a journey. The *Arteiga* and *Hadendoa* (Hadendowa) believe Wednesday is the unlucky day to start a trip.[92]

Beja popular religion places a high value on sacrifice. At the one-year anniversary of the death of a prominent Sufi sheikh, Hadendowa Beja offer special sacrifices at his tomb. The new sheikh's followers pledge their loyalty to the successor by ceremonially placing tree branches upon his head. The people also sacrifice a calf or sheep, allowing the blood to ritually fall upon the new sheikh's feet. The new leader receives the best of the meat and distributes the remainder to the people.[93] Many Beja sacrifice animals to spiritually prepare the soil before cultivation and planting.[94]

Beja fear the "evil eye," which represents the most prominent practice of witchcraft observed by the Hillmen. The Beja believe that a person can contract an evil-eye sickness, called *siir*, from an envious person.[95] The Hillmen also suppose witches and sorcerers move around in the evenings eating the souls of their enemies.[96] The Beja practice the projection of evil thought and

---

[88] See Ausenda, "Leisurely Nomads," 414–15.

[89] See Jacobsen, *Theories of Sickness and Misfortune*, 82.

[90] See W. T. Clark, "Manners, Customs and Beliefs of the Northern Bega," *SNR* 21, no. 1 (1938): 11.

[91] See Jacobsen, *Theories of Sickness and Misfortune*, 150–51, 174, 193.

[92] See Clark, "Manners, Customs and Beliefs of the Northern Bega," 19.

[93] See Ausenda, "Leisurely Nomads," 455.

[94] Hjort and Dahl report that this practice was still followed as late as 1980. *Responsible Man*, 119.

[95] See Jacobsen, *Theories of Sickness and Misfortune*, 169–70, 264.

[96] See S. F. Nadel, "Notes on Beni-Amer Society," *SNR* 26, no. 1 (1945): 84.

contagious magic[97] to improve the power of their swords.[98] According to W. T. Clark, the following are two spells exercised by the Beja:

> **Sorcery to cause dissension between a man and his wife:** A man named Mohammed must catch a chameleon and a man named Ali cut off its head. This is dried and powdered, and mixed with donkey dung. The mixture is then deposited underneath the bed or sprinkled near the house of the couple whose future happiness is to be jeopardized.

> **A spell to kill one's enemy:** A dung beetle is wrapped in a piece of cloth cut from the clothing of the person against whom the spell is directed and his name written thereon. It is then buried or burned and as it decays or is consumed the bewitched person falls ill and dies.[99]

Conclusion

"You have to seek good things, but bad things come out of their own accord," observes a Beja proverb.[100] The Hillmen view life as capricious, unpredictable, and inhabited by whimsical and sometimes malicious spirits.[101] Most of the nominally Muslim Beja approach the supernatural through their unique blend of Islam and traditional religion. Folk Islam includes two divisions: (1) traditional religious practices (including ATR) and (2) Islamic influences (especially Sufism).

While working with the Beja people of Sudan, I noticed their religion had much in common with the ATR practices that I had also observed

---

[97] With contagious magic, the object of the magic comes in contact with the agent of the magician to effect the cure or curse. Claude Levi-Strauss, "The Sorcerer and His Magic" in *Magic, Witchcraft, and Religion: An Anthropological Study of the Supernatural,* 2nd ed., ed. Arthur C. Lehmann and James E. Myers (Mountain View, CA: Mayfield, 1985), 194–95.

[98] See Gamst, "Beja," 135.

[99] Clark, "Manners, Customs and Beliefs of the Northern Bega," 17.

[100] Jacobsen, *Theories of Sickness and Misfortune,* 35.

[101] See Jacobsen, 34.

among the Sukuma tribe of Tanzania. For this reason, I present the Sukuma ethnic group as a baseline and model for observing the residual traditional religion of another people group (the Beja) who follow folk Islam.

The question arises whether or not traditional religious practices remain among the Beja and other folk Islamic ethnic groups. Concerning the contemporary nature of traditional Beja practices, Jacobsen writes, "When I once went through old literature describing native medical practice among Hadendowa [Beja], I was struck by the similarities between practices I myself encountered and the ones described up to 200 years ago."[102]

A word of caution is in order. Rare is the folk Muslim who follows popular practices exclusively. There is a sliding scale, so to speak. Some folk Muslims, especially Sufis, observe popular Islam often. On the other end of the spectrum are those who turn to traditional practices only when in a crisis. For example, a married couple who worked for me in North Africa befriended a Jordanian family while in language school. These friends had been married for more than five years but were childless. Both were educated professionals, living in an upscale apartment complex in Amman. First, they went to a medical specialist, who prescribed fertility drugs. This course of treatment was not successful. Finally, they consulted a shaman, who directed them to sacrifice a sheep and spread the blood on the roof above their apartment. After obeying this folk Islamic injunction, the wife conceived, and a child was born some months later.

Since such customs continue all over the Muslim world, methods for reaching those practicing folk Islam must be calibrated for an encounter with Muslims that differs greatly from Quranic orthodoxy.

---

[102] Jacobsen, 256.

7

The History *OF* Evangelizing Muslims

E very Sunday afternoon for more than ten years, an American missionary mounted a portable stepladder on Speaker's Corner in Hyde Park
in London, England. Jay Smith, and several assistants, openly confronted
Muslims about the errors of Islam and attempted to win them to faith in
Christ.[1] Although the debate was spirited, no violence took place.

This chapter reviews the history of evangelizing Muslims and examines
the important contextualization concepts underlying efforts to witness to
them. Although there were many attempts at apologetics from AD 700 until
1800, Peter Pikkert identifies four historical transitions of Protestant missionary interaction with Muslims,[2] which will be explored in this chapter.

---

[1] Jay Smith, a third-generation Christian worker, serves with the Brethren in Christ
in London. Smith responds to Muslims by calling into question portions of the Quran
and the Prophet Muhammad. Smith is a friend of the author.

[2] See Peter Pikkert, *Protestant Missionaries to the Middle East: Ambassadors of Christ
or Culture?* (Ancaster, ON: Alev Books, 2008), 26–27. The subheadings in the historical
section are taken from Pikkert's book.

History of Contextualization

Era of the Late Ottoman (Turkish) Empire (1800–1918)

During this era, Protestants of the Enlightenment Age working in Muslim majority countries were often accompanied by occupying colonial European powers.[3] Christian workers in this day viewed Islam as one faith and generally failed to take it seriously.[4] Polemics dominated the landscape of Christian interaction with Muslims during this period. Although some Christian workers possessed great knowledge of Islam, many identified Muhammad as the Antichrist of the Bible[5] and termed the Quran a false book advocating all manner of fleshly passions.[6] Of course, many of their points were true, but the arguments widened the gap between the two faiths.

The first great Christian apologist to oppose Islam, Karl Pfander of Germany, penned *The Balance of Truth* in 1829 at the age of twenty-six. Although courteous in tone, Pfander called for Muslims to choose between Muhammad and Christ while quoting liberally from the Quran, the Hadith, and biographies of the Prophet.[7] A lack of contextualization, either theologically or culturally, characterized this first era of missions.

The lack of response to these direct and confrontational evangelism methods as well as government restrictions caused the denominations working in Muslim countries during the nineteenth century to turn to evangelizing members of the existing Eastern Orthodox and Roman Catholic churches. The "Great Experiment," as it was called, advocated reaching Muslims through "reforming and reviving the Eastern church."[8] Although

---

[3] The Enlightenment, also known as the Age of Reason, began in Europe in the seventeenth century and extended through the nineteenth century. William Lane Craig, *Reasonable Faith: Christian Truth and Apologetics*, 3rd ed. (Wheaton, IL: Crossway Books, 2008), 248.

[4] See Craig, 70.

[5] See 1 John 2:18, 22.

[6] See Pikkert, *Protestant Missionaries to the Middle East*, 30.

[7] See Pikkert, 50.

[8] Pikkert, 41.

the Great Experiment failed to reach Muslims with the gospel in the nineteenth century,[9] the descendants of the converts from Orthodoxy are leading the way in missions to Muslims in the twenty-first century.[10]

Era of Colonialism and Nationalism (1919–1946)

After the end of the First World War, missiologists began questioning the polemical method of evangelism. Out of the Enlightenment Age, new social science disciplines emerged, emphasizing the study of society, culture, and comparative religions.

This reevaluation resulted in new strategies for the Muslim world. Pikkert notes that Samuel Zwemer and Temple Gairdner insisted on the necessity of proper views of the atonement and Jesus's incarnation,[11] but argued for "a sympathetic understanding of Islam and of Christianity's reaction to it without compromising their own mission and message."[12] This irenic approach sought to reach Muslims with minimal offense while appreciating their culture.[13]

During this era, the first extensive attempts at contextualization with Muslims emerged. Gairdner urged not just an adaptation in surface matters, such as dress and demeanor, but also in regard to devotional life, worship forms, and music.[14] This new thinking in missions promoted the first extensive use of Islamic Arabic vocabulary in missionary publications and emphasized the power of prayer to overcome demonic forces.[15] Despite these innovations, many missionaries during this period disliked the "soft"

---

[9] See Pikkert, 60.

[10] The Evangelical church in Sudan consists of the descendants of the first converts out of the Sudanese Coptic Church (related to the Egyptian Coptic Church). This is also true in Egypt and other parts of the Middle East.

[11] Pikkert, *Protestant Missionaries to the Middle East*, 82.

[12] Pikkert, 93.

[13] See Pikkert, 94.

[14] See Pikkert, 98–100.

[15] See Pikkert, 103–4.

approach toward Islam and continued the polemic methods of the nine-teenth century.[16]

Era of the Rise of the Arab World (1947–1978)

Protestant evangelism to Muslims stalled during this period as significant events rocked the Muslim world. Israel received independence in 1948, causing the displacement of a significant number of Palestinian refugees. Western support of the new nation enraged Muslims all over the world, ush-ering in an era of Islamic fundamentalism.[17] The post–World War II retreat from colonialism, and the perceived humbling of Palestinian Muslims, awakened a resurgent pan-Arab nationalism.[18] Even non-Arab Muslims sympathized with the Palestinian cause. The newfound oil wealth of many Muslim countries buoyed Islam's belief in their favored destiny.[19] This new consciousness sowed the seeds for the Islamic revival that would begin in the closing decades of the twentieth century.

During this era, missionaries continued with methods such as medi-cal ministry, education, literature, social centers, and humanitarian relief.[20] These ministries succeeded in gaining access to ordinary Muslims.

Apologists retained the debate method of Christian witness. For exam-ple, Josh McDowell famously debated the late Ahmed Deedat in 1981.[21] Others, such as Jay Smith, continue the method today. Schlorff calls the debate or polemic method the "direct approach."[22] The latter technique differs little from the former, except the direct approach uses polemic

---

[16] See Pikkert, 100.

[17] See Ahmed, *Islam Today*, 134 (see chap. 1, n. 1).

[18] See Kenneth Cragg, *The Call of the Minaret* (Ibadan, NG: Daystar, 1985), 24; Ahmed, *Islam Today*, 137; and Pikkert, *Protestant Missionaries to the Middle East*, 119.

[19] See Pikkert, *Protestant Missionaries to the Middle East*, 124.

[20] See Pikkert, 128–30.

[21] See Pikkert, 134.

[22] Samuel P. Schlorff, *Missiological Models in Ministry to Muslims* (Upper Darby, PA: Middle East Resources, 2006), 13.

arguments only as a last resort.[23] The direct approach favors not "beating around the bush."

A new approach developed alongside the direct approach during this period was called "dialogue."[24] The dialogue method, as popularized by Bishop Kenneth Cragg, advocates the diametrically opposite approach from the direct approach. It calls for Muslim and Christian unity in Christ. The dialogue technique sees Christianity not displacing Islam but rather fulfilling "what is there."[25] Dialogue epitomizes the most indirect of methods and has become linked to the World Council of Churches and its condemnation of evangelism.[26] The acknowledgment of truth in the Quran has led to relativism and a resultant weak witness to Muslims. Despite their good intentions, neither the dialogue nor the debate method ultimately wins many Muslims to Christ. Pikkert writes, "Instead of dialogue and debate leading to mutual understanding, discord between Christians and Muslims has been growing."[27]

Era of Islamic Fundamentalism (1979–Present)

During the last thirty-five years, regimes indebted to resurgent Islam replaced secular governments in many Muslim majority countries.[28] Since the Iranian revolution of 1979, Iran, Palestine, Turkey, Indonesia, and Pakistan all feature administrations drawing their support from the Islamic revival.[29] Religious fundamentalism increasingly influences nations such as Iraq, Afghanistan, Algeria, Egypt, Sudan, and Saudi Arabia.[30] Two wars in

---

[23] J. Christy Wilson Sr., writing in the middle of the twentieth century, said, "Today he who would present Christ to the Moslem heart should be an expert in avoiding argument." Quoted in Schlorff, 13.

[24] See Pikkert, *Protestant Missionaries to the Middle East*, 131.

[25] Schlorff, *Missiological Models*, 20.

[26] See Schlorff, 22.

[27] Pikkert, *Protestant Missionaries to the Middle East*, 187.

[28] See Esposito and Mogahed, *Who Speaks for Islam?*, 42, 44 (see chap. 2, n. 4).

[29] See Wheatcroft, *Infidels*, 301 (see chap. 2, n. 40).

[30] See Sookhdeo, *Global Jihad*, 299 (see chap. 2, n. 2).

Iraq and Afghanistan,[31] and the ongoing Palestinian conflict with Israel, cause many Muslims to view Western nations with suspicion and harden resistance to Christianity.[32]

Despite these formidable hurdles to evangelism, the number of Christian workers to Muslim countries has increased. Representatives from both the baby boomer generation and Generation X replaced the cohort of veterans on the field.[33] Recent emphasis on the so-called 10/40 Window increased interest in missions to the Islamic world.[34] With most of the world's Muslims living within the 10/40 Window, and the call for personnel publicized, many new workers have responded.[35] As a younger and more diverse force arrives in Muslim countries,[36] they demonstrate more of a willingness to test new techniques in evangelism.

Older approaches, such as debate, dialogue, social centers, literature, and relief work, continue. However, newer methods, such as "tentmaking,"[37] and technologies such as radio, satellite television, and the Internet have gained ground in the effort to spread the gospel.[38] Modern travel and the relative financial prosperity of Western church members allow short-term and nonresidential missionaries easier access to formerly inaccessible

---

[31] Esposito and Mogahed, *Who Speaks for Islam?*, 92. While most Americans view the wars in Iraq and Afghanistan as political conflicts, many Muslims view these wars as invasions of Muslim nations by Christian countries.

[32] See Pikkert, *Protestant Missionaries to the Middle East*, 154–55.

[33] Those born between 1946 and 1964 comprise the baby boomer generation. Generation X consists of those born between 1965 and 1981.

[34] Gailyn Van Rheenen writes, "At the 1989 Lausanne II Conference in Manila, Luis Bush proposed that if the goal of missions is to reach the unreached, mission finances and personnel must focus on what he called the '10/40 Window.' This 'window' extends from ten degrees north of the equator and stretches from North Africa through the Middle East to China and Japan." *Missions: Biblical Foundations and Contemporary Strategies* (Grand Rapids: Zondervan, 1996), 209.

[35] See Pikkert, *Protestant Missionaries to the Middle East*, 152.

[36] See Pikkert, 152–53. Pikkert notes that an increasing number of missionaries to Muslim countries come from South America and Asia.

[37] "Tentmakers" use a secular skill for the purpose of Christian witness in order to enter closed countries. See Acts 18:1–3.

[38] See Pikkert, *Protestant Missionaries to the Middle East*, 168, 171.

countries.[39] Some of the older methods, like relief work, do not always yield the expected results. Colin Adams of the Fellowship for African Relief (FAR) told me about overhearing two old men comment on his organization's food distribution program in North Africa. "Allah has tricked the infidel into feeding us," they said.

Advances in the social sciences in the early part of the twentieth century also led Christian workers to experiment with new methods[40] and contextualized approaches to Muslims.[41] After a renewed emphasis on learning the local languages and identifying with culture, the new contextualized missionaries set their sights on Islamic forms. Instead of using the Quran solely as a foil for refuting Islam, they began searching for linguistic and cultural "bridges" within the book.[42] The "Dynamic Equivalence" model adopts the following premise:[43]

> On the assumption that Islamic culture is a neutral vehicle, Islam is considered a legitimate starting point for contextualization. This means that, in theology, Quranic passages may be used as a theological starting point or source of truth for the gospel (e.g., trying to prove the crucifixion on the basis of certain Quranic passages). As concerns the church, it means importing Muslim ritual forms, such as the ritual prayer, into the convert church and attempting to fill them with Christian meanings.[44]

Such modern methods are quite controversial and will be analyzed next.

---

[39] See Pikkert, 173.
[40] See Pikkert, 175, 187.
[41] See Schlorff, *Missiological Models*, 25.
[42] See Schlorff, 25–26.
[43] This model is also known as the "Translational" model.
[44] Schlorff, 26.

Contextualizing *TO* Orthodox *AND* Folk Islam

A number of years ago, a band of clandestine Christian missionaries settled in a North African city to begin their work. The female missionaries wore veils and Islamic garb. Their husbands grew closely cropped beards and appeared as Muslim as possible. Although Christians, they claimed to be "Muslims submitted to *Isa* [Quranic Arabic for Jesus], the Messiah" and were Messianic Muslims. Although they were from the United States, they attempted to contextualize with Islamic culture. One night, the security police knocked on the door of one of the apartments and interrogated the missionaries all night long. The next day the missionaries were expelled from the country.

Most evangelism techniques, like these missionaries tried, confront either theological issues or experiment with contextualized Islamic forms. Although attempted in good faith and with the best intentions, their motives were misunderstood. Nonetheless, such strategies are still used by nationals and a few missionaries in Muslim lands. This chapter analyzes such methods.

Introduction to Contextualization Issues

I. C. Brown states, "No custom is 'odd' to the people who practice it."[1] As evangelists encounter different cultures, they consider how to best communicate the gospel message. *Contextualization* is the term that commonly describes the process of translating the unchanging gospel into a form understandable to a current culture. Byang Kato says of contextualization, "We understand the term to mean making concepts or ideals relevant in a given situation."[2] Hesselgrave says, "There is not yet a commonly accepted definition of the word *contextualization*, but only a series of proposals, all of them vying for acceptance."[3] Despite a lack of agreement on an exact definition of *contextualization*, missiologists favor using the concept as best they can when supported by biblical truth.[4]

Contextualized Approaches with Muslims

As the current generation of missionaries to Muslims experiment with new methods, these issues take on special relevancy. Contextualization approaches abound in Christian ministry, especially to Muslims.

Debate/Polemic (Non-Contextualized) Method

As mentioned in the last chapter, older apologists used a negative proof-text technique in the nineteenth century. The debate/polemic approach, later called the "direct method," returned toward the end of the twentieth

---

[1] I. C. Brown in Van Pelt, *Bantu Customs in Mainland Tanzania*, 17 (see chap. 5, n. 1).

[2] Kato in David J. Hesselgrave and Edward Rommen, *Contextualization: Meanings, Methods, and Models* (Pasadena, CA: William Carey Library, 2000), 33.

[3] Hesselgrave and Rommen, 35.

[4] Gailyn Van Rheenen says, "According to David Hesselgrave, 'Acceptable Contextualization is a direct result of ascertaining the meaning of the biblical text, consciously submitting to its authority, and applying or appropriating that meaning to a given situation.'" *Communicating Christ in Animistic Contexts*, 4 (see chap. 5, n. 6).

century as Muslims living in Western countries challenged Christians to debates. Although boosting morale on both sides, these contests changed few minds.

Those currently using the direct approach encourage courtesy in their confrontations. "The Quran has huge errors in it, enormous errors," says third-generation missionary Jay Smith, who debates Muslim preachers at Speaker's Corner in London and has trained others to do the same. "My goal is to eradicate the whole edifice of Islam so that [Muslims] can then look for the alternative."[5] This non-contextualized theological model communicates the truth of the gospel without significantly adapting the message to the audience. Although some converts have responded to this method,[6] it has failed to bring significant numbers of Muslims to Christ.

Quranic Contextualization Methods

Many Quranic passages feature phrases and refer to characters that seem biblical at first glance. This common ground often tempts Christians to select proof texts from the Quran to support Christian doctrines. Although the Quran rejects Christ's divinity (*Sura* 5:17, 72, 75; 9:30–1) and denies the Trinity (*Sura* 4:171; 5:73, 116), Christians favoring this approach often bend Quranic teaching to mirror their own presuppositions. Schlorff gives the following examples:

> As we have seen, the Quran calls Christ "the Word of God" and "a Spirit from Him" (4:171; 3:45). It has Him born of a virgin (19:16–35) and calls Him "Illustrious (*wajiih*) in this world and the next, and among those closest to God" (3:45). He is the only prophet who is said to have created, and to have raised the dead

---

[5] Quoted in Stan Guthrie, "Deconstructing Islam: Apologist Jay Smith Takes a Confrontational Approach," *Christianity Today* 46, no. 10 (2002): 37.

[6] See Pikkert, *Protestant Missionaries to the Middle East*, 66 (see chap. 7, n. 2).

(3:49). And of all the prophets, including Mohammad, Christ is never said to have sinned (see 3:36).[7]

The approach of using the Quran as a so-called bridge to the gospel contains at least two pitfalls. First, it is deceptive for Christians to quote the Quran and claim it means something not acceptable to orthodox Islam. For instance, Christians do not appreciate Muslim apologists identifying Muhammad in Quran *Sura* 61:6 as the "other comforter" of John 14:16.[8] In the same way, knowledgeable Muslims bristle when Christians bend Quranic words into odd (to them) Christian interpretations. Second, when a missionary's argument includes references to Christ in portions of the Quran, the Christian unwittingly confers tacit approval upon it.

The "new hermeneutic" of Quran interpretation. Many early-twentieth-century Christian apologists used the Quran as their point of departure with Muslims. They debated Islam by referring to parts of the Quran they thought agreed at least tangentially with biblical ideas. Schlorff calls the tactic of mining Quranic truth in order to unveil its deeper meaning in the Bible a "new hermeneutic" in Quranic interpretation.[9]

Geoffrey Parrinder's *Jesus in the Quran* asserts "the undoubted revelation of God in Muhammad and in the Quran."[10] In *The Event of the Quran* and *The Call of the Minaret*, Kenneth Cragg looks sympathetically at the meaning of the Quran as a whole. Cragg's hermeneutic sees actual revelation in the Quran as Muslims and Christians search together for truth.[11]

The end of the twentieth century witnessed a return to extensive Quranic quoting in Christian outreach.[12] Although few present-day evangelicals ascribe actual revelation to the book,[13] some present-day missionaries

[7] Schlorff, *Missiological Models*, 63–64 (see chap. 7, n. 22).

[8] See Cragg, *The Call of the Minaret*, 257 (see chap. 7, n. 18).

[9] Schlorff, *Missiological Models*, 72.

[10] Geoffrey Parrinder, quoted in Schlorff, *Missiological Models*, 74–75.

[11] See Schlorff's analysis of Cragg in *Missiological Models*, 75.

[12] See Schlorff, 71.

[13] See Schlorff, 77–78.

and missiologists advocate a tolerant view toward the Quran. Ralph Winter suggests the benign approach, stating, "Cannot we think of the Quran as we do the Apocrypha and let it gradually take a back seat to our Bible simply because it is not as edifying intellectually or spiritually?"[14]

Another writer not only views the Quran rather uncritically, but quotes from it extensively. Abdiyah Akbar Abdul-Haqq writes in *Sharing Your Faith with a Muslim*, "The rejection of the idea that Jesus Son of Mary was the Son of God is in line with the Nestorian position."[15] Abdul-Haqq seems to view Muslims more as wayward Nestorian Christians than members of an entirely different religion.[16]

The late Muslim apologist Ahmed Deedat describes true Islamic belief about the Christ as follows:

> "Christ in Islam" is really Christ in the Quran: and the Holy Quran has something definite to say about every aberration of Christianity. The Quran absolves Jesus (pbuh) from all the false charges of his enemies as well as the misplaced infatuation of his followers.[17] His enemies allege that he blasphemed against God by claiming Divinity. His misguided followers claim that he did avow Divinity, but that was not blasphemy (*kufr*) because he was God. What does the Quran say? Addressing both the Jews and the Christians, Allah

---

[14] Ralph D. Winter, "Going Far Enough?" in *Perspectives on the World Christian Movement*, 4th ed., ed. Ralph D. Winter and Steven C. Hawthorne (Pasadena, CA: William Carey Library, 2009), 670–71.

[15] Abdiyah Akbar Abdul-Haqq, *Sharing Your Faith with a Muslim* (Bloomington, MN: Bethany House, 1980), 70–73.

[16] "Nestorians stressed the independence of the divine and human natures of Christ and, in effect, suggested that they were two persons loosely united." Nestorius was an early bishop of Constantinople whose views were condemned at the Council of Ephesus in AD 431 and have been considered heretical ever since. William Chauncy Emhardt and George M. Lamsa, *The Oldest Christian People: A Brief Account of the History and Traditions of the Assyrian People and the Fateful History of the Nestorian Church* (Macmillan, 1926; Eugene, OR: Wipf & Stock, 2012), 50–56. Nestorius himself did not fully subscribe to the views for which he was condemned.

[17] *Pbuh* is the abbreviation for "peace be upon him." Muslims recite this formula after saying or writing the name of any of the prophets.

says: "O People of the Book! Commit no excesses in your religion: Nor say of God aught but the truth. Christ Jesus the son of Mary was (no more than) an apostle of God, and His Word, which He bestowed on Mary, and a spirit proceeding from Him: So believe in God and His messengers" Holy Quran 4:171.[18]

Analytical Quranic contextualization. Propositional techniques featuring step-by-step arguments clash with the literary form of the Quran. Most non-Western cultures communicate truth by poetry, narrative, and song. Many Muslims, such as the late Ahmed Deedat, certainly understand and utilize propositional arguments. Nonetheless, the implanting or mixing of biblical ideas with Quranic concepts offends the informed and attracts only marginal Muslims. Rather than constructing a false Christian template (to Muslims) over the Quran, a better method is to preserve the context of the Quran.[19] An analytical approach respects the intended meanings of both the Christian and Muslim scriptures. Schlorff contends, "The focus is on what Mohammad understood the terms to mean and how his original hearers would have understood him. In practical terms, this means that Quranic language may not be interpreted in terms of what one might think similar biblical language might have meant. It cannot be filled with Christian content."[20]

Quoting a few selected verses of the Quran while respecting the traditional Islamic interpretation focuses the issues without compromising the beliefs of either side. For example, the Christian may say, "The Quran speaks of *'Isa*,[21] whom the Bible calls Jesus Christ. Our holy book says this

---

[18] Ahmed Deedat, *Christ in Islam* (Jaipur, India: Islamic Organization of India, 1983), 31.

[19] See Schlorff, *Missiological Models*, 123.

[20] Schlorff, 133.

[21] Opinions diverge regarding the use of the Quranic word for Jesus, *'Isa* as opposed to *Yasuu'*, a transliteration of the Greek word, *Iesous* (widely used by Christian Arabs). Forty-two New Testament translations employ the latter, while seventeen (including Henry Martyn's renowned 1814 Persian translation) use the former (Schlorff, 36). Some

about Him . . ." One national leader from my work in North Africa advocates quoting two brief Quranic statements, not as bridges, but as quick references. He states:

> We start talking about [Jesus] from [the] Quran because [the] Quran says, "Jesus is the Word of God and the Spirit of God and is the Prophet of God," so we are talking [about that] He is the Word of God. . . . So we go back to [the] Bible in John 1:1: "In the beginning there was the Word and the Word was with God," and also that "Jesus is the Spirit of God." So we start from there [the Quran] and we end up in [the] Bible. Sometimes people, they start in here, in the Quran, and they stay there. When we start here [in the Quran], we just move very fast to come here [to the Bible].[22]

Such a reference does not ascribe authority to the Quran. Instead, a short citation of the Quran serves as a starting point. This approach differs from reading the Quran from the standpoint of a Christian interpretation, which offends many Muslims and indirectly confers truth on the Quran. Again, Schlorff helps here:[23]

---

missiologists prefer *'Isa* since Muslims know the term. Others argue that the Quranic meaning of *'Isa* differs too radically from the biblical understanding of Jesus. John Ankerberg and Emir Caner, *The Truth about Islam & Jesus* (Eugene, OR: Harvest House, 2009). Nevertheless, Schlorff (37) concludes that since both Christians and Christian cults use Jesus with different connotations, evangelicals can safely use *'Isa* when speaking to Muslims about Christ. The same arguments apply in the question concerning the name of God. J. D. Greear, *Breaking the Islam Code* (Eugene, OR: Harvest House, 2010), 160. This case differs slightly, as no good alternative exists for God apart from Allah in Arabic. Every reputable Arabic Bible translation utilizes the term despite the fact that Christian and Muslim concepts of God differ significantly. Christians worship the God of Abraham, Isaac, and Jacob. Muslims revere the Allah of Abraham and Ishmael. In addition, some of the ninety-nine names of God do not reflect a Christian idea of the diety (e.g., *Al-Qahhar*, the All Compelling Subduer; *Al Khafid*, the Abaser; *Al-Mudhill*, the Giver of Dishonor; *Al Mumit*, the Bringer of Death, the Destroyer; *Al-Mu'akhkhir*, the Delayer; *Al-Wali*, the Patron; *Al-Ghani*, the All Rich, the Independent).

[22] Hamid Jonadab, in an interview with the author, Khartoum, Sudan, January 8, 2006.

[23] See Parshall, *Bridges to Islam*, 667 (see intro., n. 4).

It would be improper to begin the contextualization process from within Islam on the assumption that Islam contains "moments" of truth.[24] One cannot use the Quran as a source of truth for proclaiming the gospel or try to fill Muslim forms with Christian meanings. One may sometimes refer to something in the Quran or Islamic culture to get an idea across to Muslims, but that is not the same thing. And one may do so only on certain conditions.[25]

Cultural Contextualization with Muslims

Muslims seamlessly blend cultural and religious elements of their society. This section covers the contextualization issues specifically related to Muslim culture and their associated worship forms. Due to the close relationship between form and meaning in Islam, theological and doctrinal conundrums often surface.

Muslim Customs

The all-pervasive nature of Islamic culture impresses anyone living in a Muslim-majority country. Most men in northern Sudan and the Northern Red Sea region of Eritrea wear the flowing white robes synonymous with Islam. Although most Muslims dress in Western style in the cities of Egypt, Jordan, Turkey, and Syria,[26] their counterparts in the countryside prefer more traditional clothing. As the call to prayer rings out in the air, and Muslims flow in and out of the mosque, Christians wonder how they might engage the people of Islam.

---

[24] Kevin Greeson, in *The Camel*, takes the opposing view, saying, "Remember, there is not enough light in the Quran to bring Muslims to salvation, but there are enough **flickers of truth** to draw out God's person of peace among them. As soon as possible, you want to bridge them out of the Quran and into the Bible where they can see the truth for themselves" (Arkadelphia, AR: WIGTake Resources, 2007), 102 (bold mine).

[25] Schlorff, *Missiological Models*, 149.

[26] See Wheatcroft, *Infidels: A History of the Conflict between Christendom and Islam,* 315 (see chap. 2, n. 40).

Contextualizing culture, custom, and clothing predates modern missions, going back to the nineteenth century.[27] Christian workers today, with some exceptions, appreciate the food, dress, and customs of the people they serve. Although all cultures value outsiders enjoying their societies, investigation should be made and judgment used when adopting certain national clothing styles and eating certain foods. For instance, Muslims wash ceremonially before prayer, but this ritual contains religious significance.[28] I dined at an outdoor restaurant in a Muslim city on my birthday in 1991. When presented with the Arabic menu, one of the Ethiopian Orthodox men accompanying me said, "I do not eat Muslim meat." His religious beliefs required an Eastern Orthodox slaughtering of animals. On another occasion during *Carnival* (Brazilian *Mardi Gras*) ministry in Salvador, Brazil, I noticed a woman selling fish cakes from a sidewalk outdoor griddle. As I approached the vendor to make a purchase, a Christian worker told me the Spiritist priestess had dedicated the fish cakes to a West African deity. I decided to abstain.

Opinions differ about contextualization in dress. In some Muslim countries, such as Pakistan and Egypt, Western women who cover themselves like nationals can successfully avoid male harassment. In other places, for instance in Turkey, Sudan, and Jordan, women feel comfortable in modest Western clothing. Male Christian workers also face dilemmas on the subject of national dress. Since many Western-oriented nationals wear European-style clothing within Muslim majority countries, some nationals wonder about the agenda of a foreigner dressing in an Islamic manner.

Once, a Scandinavian evangelist decided to adopt the Sudanese national dress with rather humorous results. Port Sudan is a city of almost five million people with only about ten permanent European residents. When the six-foot, three-inch, blond-haired, blue-eyed man donned a flowing white robe and walked into the marketplace, virtually the entire crowd followed

---

[27] See J. Herbert Kane, *A Concise History of the Christian World Mission*, rev. ed. (Grand Rapids: Baker 1982), 166, 169.

[28] See Braswell, *Islam: Its Prophet, Peoples, Politics and Power*, 62–63 (see intro., n. 28).

and stared at the strange foreigner. Rather than blending in with the culture, quite the reverse occurred. Contextualization even in surface matters should be approached carefully.

Islamic Forms

Since the 1970s, a movement to contextualize Christianity within Islam has emerged, generating much controversy. Drawing from the field of linguistics, Charles Kraft applied the concept of "dynamic equivalency" to the discipline of missiology.[29] Specifically, a dynamic equivalent version of Islam advocates conversion to Christianity while remaining within the Muslim faith. The Insider Movements cite as its model the recent phenomenon of Hebrew Christians who remain in Judaism,[30] calling themselves Messianic Jews.[31] John Travis writes,[32] "In the past four decades, tens of thousands of Jews have accepted Jesus as their Messiah yet remain socio-religiously Jewish."[33] In the same way, the Insider Movements support Messianic

---

[29] Charles H. Kraft, "Dynamic Equivalent Churches in Muslim Society," in *The Gospel and Islam: A 1978 Compendium*, ed. Don McCurry (Monrovia: Missions Advanced Research and Communication Center—MARC, 1978), 114.

[30] The Insider Movements advocate staying within Islam while accepting *'Isa* as the Messiah. "They want to see movements to Jesus within Islam rather than from Islam. These are called insider movements." Greear, *Breaking the Islam Code*, 153. Rebecca Lewis says, "Insider movements can be defined as movements to obedient faith in Christ that remain integrated with or inside their natural community." Lewis, "Insider Movements: Retaining Identity and Preserving Community" in *Perspectives on the World Christian Movement*, 4th ed., Ralph D. Winter and Steven C. Hawthorne, eds. (Pasadena, CA: William Carey Library, 2009), 673.

[31] See Schlorff, *Missiological Models*, 80–81.

[32] John J. Travis, one of the leading proponents of the Insider Movements, is a pseudonym for a missionary in Asia who has been involved in contextualized Muslim ministry since 1987 (John Travis in *Perspectives on the World Christian Movement*, 664). I know John Travis and his true name. Travis, *Perspectives on the World Christian Movement*, 4th ed., 664.

[33] John Travis, "Response One" in "Four Responses to Timothy C. Tennent's Followers of Jesus (Isa) in Islamic Mosques: A Closer Examination of C-5 'High Spectrum' Contextualization," International Journal of Frontier Missions 23, no. 3 (2006): 125.

Muslims acknowledging *'Isa* the Messiah while retaining their Islamic cultural identity.[34]

The so-called C-Spectrum serves as a framework for discussing issues related to the Insider Movements by both proponents and opponents of varying degrees of Muslim contextualization. To differentiate between the different levels of contextualization with Muslims, Travis developed the following scale:

The C-Spectrum: a practical tool for defining six types of "Christ-centered communities" found in Muslim contexts:

C1—Traditional Church Using a Language Different from the Daily Language of the Surrounding Muslim Community.

C2—Traditional Church Using the Daily Language of the Surrounding Muslim Community. Essentially the same as C1 except for language.

C3—Contextualized Community Using the Daily Language of the Surrounding Muslim Community and Some Non-Muslim Cultural Forms. . . . Islamic elements are "filtered out" so as to use purely "cultural" forms. . . . C3 congregations are comprised of a majority of Muslim background believers. C3 believers call themselves Christians.

C4—Contexualized Community Using the Daily Language and Biblically Acceptable Socio-religious Islamic Forms. Similar to C3, however, *Biblically acceptable Islamic religious forms and practices are also utilized.* . . . C4 believers are seen as a kind of Christian by the Muslim community. C4 believers identify themselves as "followers of Isa the Messiah."

---

[34] See Rick Brown's response to question two in Gary Corwin, "A Humble Appeal to C5/Insider Movement Muslim Ministry Advocates to Consider Ten Questions," *International Journal of Frontier Missiology* 24, no. 1 (2007): 9.

C5—Community of Muslims Who Follow Jesus Yet Remain Culturally and Officially Muslim. C5 believers remain legally and socially within the community of Islam. Somewhat similar to the Messianic Jewish movement . . . C5 believers are viewed as Muslims by the Muslim community and think of themselves as Muslims who follow 'Isa the Messiah.[35]

Whereas Quranic contextualization methods involve theological arguments and hermeneutic interpretation, the Insider Movements focus on bridging the cultural chasm between Christians and Muslims. Easier entry into Christianity represents the goal of advocates such as Rebecca Lewis.[36] John Travis clarifies the goal of C-5 Insider Movements contextualization:

> If perhaps the single greatest hindrance to seeing Muslims come to faith in Christ is not a theological one (i.e. accepting Jesus as Lord) but rather one of culture and religious identity (i.e. having to leave the community of Islam), it seems that for the sake of God's kingdom much of our missiological energy should be devoted to seeking a path whereby Muslims can remain Muslims, yet live as true followers of the Lord Jesus.[37]

Encouraging Christian converts to remain in Islam disturbs many, both Christian workers and nationals. Phil Parshall, a proponent of C-4 contextualization, questions C-5 methodology. He sees problems with Messianic Muslims worshipping in the mosque, except transitionally, and participating in Islamic prayers that affirm Muhammad as a prophet of God.[38] The principal difference between C-4 and C-5 contextualization involves

---

[35] John J. Travis, "The C-Spectrum: A Practical Tool for Defining Six Types of 'Christ Centered Communities' found in Muslim Contexts," in *Perspectives on the World Christian Movement*, 664–65.

[36] See Lewis, "Insider Movements," 674.

[37] John J. Travis, "Must All Muslims Leave 'Islam' to Follow Jesus?" in *Perspectives on the World Christian Movement*, 672.

[38] Phil Parshall, "Going Too Far?" in *Perspectives on the World Christian Movement*, 666.

the *identity* of the believers, both from the point of view of the community and the believers themselves. Timothy Tennent explains:

> The crucial issue at stake is *self*-identify. C-5 believers are fully embedded in the cultural and religious life of Islam. That is why their presence in the Mosque is referred to as an "insider movement," because they really *are* insiders. It is even inaccurate to refer to them (as they often are) as MBBs [Muslim Background Believers], because, for them, Islam is not in their *background*, it remains as their primary *identity*.[39]

Whereas C-4 believers may retain some Muslim cultural forms, both the community and the believers themselves identify C-4 practitioners as Christians. While C-4 contextualization focuses on Muslim culture, many C-5 believers practice some Islamic faith forms, including praying in the mosque. Since C-5 proponents advocate Muslim converts staying within Islam,[40] the controversy has been associated primarily with this form of Muslim contextualization.

Islamic Meaning

Problems surface when outsiders attempt contextualization in unfamiliar territory. C-5 contextualization assumes Muslim forms can be separated from their meanings.[41] This assumption ignores the fact that meanings and forms stem from tacit agreements by insiders among themselves within a

---

[39] Timothy C. Tennent, "Followers of Jesus ('Isa) in Islamic Mosques: A Closer Examination of C-5 'High Spectrum' Contextualization," *The International Journal of Frontier Missions* 23, no. 3 (2006): 104.

[40] John Travis and most other C-5 proponents do not advocate foreign Christian workers becoming Muslims (or saying they are Muslims to reach Muslims). C-5 is for those already within Islam who have converted to Christ. See Travis, "Must All Muslims Leave 'Islam' to Follow Jesus?", 669; and Tennent, "Followers of Jesus ('Isa) in Islamic Mosques," 108.

[41] See Schlorff, *Missiological Models*, 150.

culture.[42] Outsiders reformulate the ethnic and religious paradigms of others at their peril. Hiebert sounds this warning:

> When we try to reinterpret symbols used by the dominant society, however, we are in danger of being misunderstood and ultimately of being captured by its definitions of reality. . . . We are not free to arbitrarily link meanings and forms. To do so is to destroy people's history and culture. . . . The greatest danger in separating meaning from form is the relativism and pragmatism this introduces.[43]

This is especially true in Muslim societies. Christian workers wrongly suppose that they can innocently introduce Christian interpretations into Muslim forms without consequences. This sort of accommodation is often done to make Muslim converts feel more comfortable as they move from Islam into Christianity, thereby reducing the potential for persecution and cultural isolation. Such practices make conversion to Christianity more of a gradual process than a onetime event. Prolonging a Muslim Background Believer's (MBB's) exposure to Muslim practices may result in confusion. Schlorff says, "There are no neutral 'religious structures' (such as ritual prayer) that may be joined to Christian faith-allegiance without creating serious semantic distortion and theological confusion. This is one reason I reject the intuitive approach suggested by some—contextualization by experimentation."[44]

An MBB leader in Sudan advises converts not to worship in the mosque due to the danger of confusion. He says if the MBB attends services in the mosque and the church, they become perplexed. Jonadab comments as follows on MBBs continuing in the mosque:

> That is not also good. That will make them confused again. They will be here and here and also, we saw people like that here in Sudan. They are Muslim converts and they are afraid, especially that first year. He goes to the mosque and then sometimes he goes

---

[42] See Hesselgrave, *Communicating Christ Cross-Culturally*, 67 (see intro., n. 7).
[43] Paul Hiebert in Schlorff, *Missiological Models*, 150.
[44] Schlorff, 151.

to the church, but that also is very confusing. When he has accepted Christ, we ask him to stop going to the mosque and to pray in his house and join us in our house meetings.[45]

Jonadab, the son of strict Muslims, became a Christian at the age of nineteen. He told me that when he and seventeen other young men became believers, they were threatened with death. Inside the prison, they were beaten with whips. Due to this punishment and the threat of execution, thirteen of the eighteen renounced Christianity and returned to Islam. Jonadab and 'Isa (his associate) have started more than 200 Baptist churches and preaching points (smaller house churches) among Muslims in North Africa.[46]

Even some seemingly innocuous cultural practices and clothing styles carry religious significance. The Beja decorate their red prayer mats, blankets, and other artifacts with seashells. The tribe believes the magical power of the shells keeps away *jinns* and can be used to predict the future.[47] According to Sam Schlorff, well-meaning attempts at "cutting-edge" ministry lead to "ill-advised adventurism and the misuse of Muslim forms."[48] Words possess subjective meanings that often transcend translation. The Arabic sense of the word "Muslim" means "one who is submitted to God," according to C-5 proponent John Travis.[49] However, people calling themselves Muslims attach additional significance to the term. J. D. Greear believes Christians should neither acknowledge Muhammad as a prophet[50] nor refer to themselves as "Messianic Muslims."[51] Parshall concurs:

> The mosque is pregnant with Islamic theology. There, Muhammad
> is affirmed as a prophet of God and the divinity of Christ is

---

[45] Jonadab, interview with the author.

[46] Jonadab.

[47] See Jacobsen, *Theories of Sickness and Misfortune*, 65 (see chap. 6, n. 39).

[48] Schlorff, *Missiological Models*, 149.

[49] Travis, "Must all Muslims Leave 'Islam' to Follow Jesus?," 670.

[50] "The best bridge to overcome the barrier to Mohammad is to simply say: 'I agree with what the Quran says about Mohammad.'" Greeson, *The Camel*, 144.

[51] Greear, *Breaking the Islam Code*, 160.

consistently denied. Uniquely Muslim prayers (*salat*) are ritually performed as in no other religion. These prayers are as sacramental to Muslims as partaking of the Lord's Supper is to Christians. How would we feel if a Muslim attended (or even joined) our evangelical church and partook of communion. . . all with a view to becoming an 'insider'?[52]

Reciting the *shahada* potentially confuses the convert and possibly deceives the Muslim community about the faith allegiance of the MBB.[53] Rick Brown, a C-5 advocate, defends against the charge of deception those converts who retain their Islamic practices:

> Some Messianic Muslims say the *shahada*, but not all of them are true believers in it. Nominal Muslims say the *shahada*, but they are not true believers. Some of them [Messianic Muslims] are engaging in dissimulation—masking one's inner thoughts and intentions. That is not the same as deceit, which involves manipulation or exploitation of others rather than mere social conformity or self-protection.
>
> Deceit is wrong, but is dissimulation[54] categorically wrong or can it be used as a last resort?[55]

I am personally sympathetic with MBBs who are persecuted for their faith. Two national leaders associated with my work were arrested, beaten, and tortured for thirty-seven days in 1996. When I offered my sympathy, they said, "We did this for Jesus." Another national Baptist leader (also beaten for his faith) shares a unique viewpoint about the downside of deception:

---

[52] Parshall, "Going Too Far?," 666.

[53] The Islamic *shahada* intones, "There is no god but God and Muhammad is His prophet."

[54] To dissimulate is "to hide one's feelings, motives, etc., by pretense." Guralnik, *Webster's New World Dictionary*, 408 (see chap. 3, n. 33).

[55] Brown in Corwin, "A Humble Appeal," 12.

If you accept Christ and stop going to the mosque, people will feel a difference in you; your speech, your life; it will be different from [them]. And when they see that there is a difference between your life and their life and they start [to] ask, at that time you can witness also for Christ. If they stay in the mosque, then the Muslims say, "Look at him, he has become a good person because of Islam." But if he stays away from [the] mosque and they see his changed life, then they give the glory to Christ.[56]

While affirming C-4 methodology, Greear rejects C-5 methodology.[57] Although expressing doubts about the C-5 approach, Tennent[58] and Parshall[59] allow it briefly for new believers transitioning to open Christianity. I concur with Greear and reject the C-5 contextualization.

Evaluating Contextualization with Muslims

Some evangelists today continue the debate and polemic methods with Muslims that originated in the nineteenth century. Much of current mission activity directed at orthodox Islam employs some type of contextualization by cultural adjustment (C-4), or the retention and augmentation of more substantive Islamic forms (C-5). A few missiologists, however, call into question the effectiveness of much current contextualization. Musk observes, "While such bridging movements may be meaningful to the intellectual Muslim, they fall a long way short of communicating with Muslims committed to a folk-Islamic worldview."[60] Schlorff goes further, claiming that "contextualization is not the key, whatever the model [that] is followed."[61] Pikkert says, "Islam and Christianity are simply too different in

---

[56] Jonadab, in an interview with the author.
[57] See Greear, *Breaking the Islam Code*, 159–60.
[58] See Tennent, "Followers of Jesus ('Isa) in Islamic Mosques," 113.
[59] See Parshall, "Going Too Far?," 666–67.
[60] Musk, "Popular Islam," 285 (see intro., n. 5).
[61] Schlorff, *Missiological Models*, 161.

both doctrine and worship styles to build a contextual bridge from one to the other. . . Hence even the most contextualized of churches will not look like a mosque. It will not have that 'Muslim flavor' which is supposed to ease entry into Christianity."[62]

Simply stated, neither polemics nor most contextualization techniques speak to the average person in Islam. Since folk Islam composes approximately 70 percent of the total religion,[63] most Christians miss this majority population by directing their evangelism toward the Muslim minority who read the Quran and understand Islamic theology. Musk says, "Most folk Muslims value the Quran, not for its intrinsic cognitive content, but for its proven power as a protective talisman or book of fortune."[64]

Conclusion

Since polemics and contextualization methods usually fail with the majority of orthodox Muslims, chances of reaching folk Muslims with the gospel diminishes even further.[65] Folk Muslims fear evil spirits, calamities, and the unknown. They respect the Quran, Muslim theology, and Islamic forms, but choose folk prescriptions over religious rituals to solve everyday problems and ensure a better life. Gospel presentations and contextualized arguments carry little weight and seem irrelevant. Therefore, other avenues merit exploration. Musk says, "The Gospel, in its presentation to ordinary Muslims, must 'fit' the folk-Islamic world in order to do battle with the demonic therein."[66]

---

[62] Pikkert, *Prostestant Missionaries to the Middle East*, 187.
[63] See Parshall, *Bridges to Islam*, 2.
[64] Musk, "Popular Islam," 262–63.
[65] See Musk, 262–63.
[66] Musk, 341.

9

Contextualizing *TO THE* Worldviews *OF* Folk Islam

A t sundown, among the tombs in a cemetery in the capital city of a North African country, the dervishes gathered for their weekly ritual. Each Friday for two hours, more than 100 men assemble in long white robes and rhythmically chant over and over the name Allah. Swaying up and down and back and forth to the beat of a large drum, the Sufis believe their actions keep the evil spirits at bay, and their repetition of God's name concentrates their inner hearts on the divine. As I watched the spectacle in the tombs, I thought to myself, *Is this Islam?*

Introduction

The vast majority of Muslims practice folk Islam rather than orthodoxy.[1] Many evangelicals have attempted to evangelize Muslims through apologetic arguments or contextualized strategies.[2] Apologetic approaches include both confrontational and nonconfrontational methods. Contextualized techniques range from small cultural concessions to the borrowing of Islamic

---

[1] See Parshall, *Bridges to Islam*, 2 (see intro., n. 4).
[2] See Pikkert, *Protestant Missionaries to the Middle East*, 187 (see chap. 7, n. 2).

forms. None of these approaches has resulted in many breakthroughs in Muslim evangelization.[3] Intellectual arguments, cultural contextualization, and experimentation with Islamic forms usually miss the mark with popular Islam because folk religion poses different questions. Orthodoxy answers theological concerns while folk religion deals with the here and now.[4]

Some suggest folk Muslims should be evangelized at their worldview level. Hiebert, Shaw, and Tienou present a threefold model[5] for proclaiming salvation in different kinds of societies. They explain that individualistic cultures like those in the West, based upon the rule of law, operate largely from a guilt/innocence worldview. Many group-conscious societies in Asia, North Africa, and the Middle East follow a shame/honor orientation. The fear/power concept dominates the traditional societies of Africa, Asia, and the Americas.[6] Bill Musk and Roland Muller say the gospel should be contextualized toward a shame/honor axis among Muslims in the Levant.[7]

Arab Muslims live mostly in North Africa and the Middle East. Since orthodoxy springs from the Arabian Peninsula, most apologetic and contextualized approaches for Muslims have been tailored largely toward Arab audiences. Writers such as Musk, Muller, Parshall, and Jabbour have written extensively about reaching Muslims through the shame/honor worldview.[8]

This emphasis sometimes neglects folk Muslims, who possess a worldview resembling more traditional societies. Many African tribes mix African Traditional Religion (ATR) with Islam. Similarly, peoples in Saudi Arabia, Turkey, India, Pakistan, and Indonesia superficially embrace orthodox Islam while clinging to traditional practices. Many of these ethnic groups exhibit

---

[3] See Pikkert, 187.

[4] See Hiebert, *Transforming Worldviews*, 131 (see intro., n. 22).

[5] Nabeel Jabbour adds a fourth paradigm to the list of worldviews. In addition to the guilt/righteousness, shame/honor, and fear/power concepts, Jabbour presents the idea of defilement/clean. Jabbour, *The Crescent through the Eyes of the Cross: Insights from an Arab Christian* (Colorado Springs: NavPress, 2008), 169–72.

[6] Hiebert, Shaw, and Tienou, *Understanding Folk Religion*, 224–26 (see intro., n. 6).

[7] Quoted in Pikkert, *Protestant Missionaries to the Middle East*, 177–78.

[8] See Pikkert, 177–78.

a fear/power worldview. Hiebert, Shaw, and Tienou observe, "Most folk religions seek power as the key to prosperity, health, success, and control over their life."[9]

This chapter presents an approach to evangelizing folk Islam through a fear/power worldview. Among traditional people, the shame/honor and guilt/innocence characteristics also surface as secondary themes. In addition, I introduce a fourth worldview present among folk Muslims like the Sufis, which will be addressed in the next chapter. Folk Islam yearns for a deeper spiritual life, a release from the legalism of formal Islam and the monotony of everyday life. I call this the existential/transcendent worldview.

Worldviews

Numerous proposals for finding common ground when evangelizing non-Christian faiths have been suggested.[10] Parshall observes, "As millions of Muslims move beyond cold, dead orthodoxy, we see them desiring that felt needs be met."[11] Analyzing a culture's felt needs is an important step in determining how to approach a society with the gospel. This "fulfillment approach"[12] seeks to meet humanity's yearning for God, satisfying this and other needs. In addition, people possess unknown and unfelt needs from an eternal perspective. It also stands to reason that people may feel needs that are not appropriate to gratify, such as immorality, anger, jealousy, and slander, to name just a few.

Another method, the "similarity approach,"[13] seeks to discover redemptive analogies and cultural points of contact in order to find common ground with other religions. This method observes the worldview of a society through the prism of understanding. Muller says, "Cross-cultural

---

[9] Hiebert, Shaw, and Tienou, *Understanding Folk Religion*, 373.

[10] See David J. Hesselgrave, *Paradigms in Conflict* (Grand Rapids: Kregel, 2005), 100.

[11] Phil Parshall, *Muslim Evangelism*, 2nd ed. (Waynesboro, GA: Gabriel, 2003), 3.

[12] Hesselgrave, *Paradigms in Conflict*, 100, 102.

[13] This is the classification of Hesselgrave in *Paradigms in Conflict*, 2.

contextualization is simply knowing how to start the Gospel message from a place of common understanding."[14] Hiebert, Shaw, and Tienou emphasize that when approaching different societies with the gospel, the evangelist should emphasize first the Bible passages most understandable to that culture.[15] The effective communicator matches the felt needs of the culture with the biblical needs of the people by crafting a presentation best understood by the society.[16]

This chapter evaluates the components of each of the three major worldviews as to their making sense to folk Muslims. Muller suggests a three-part model:

> Thus, when analyzing a culture, one must look for the primary cultural characteristic, and then the secondary ones. As an example, many North American Native cultures are made up of elements of both **(1) shame-based** and **(2) fear-based cultures**. On the other hand, much of North American culture has been made up almost exclusively of **(3) guilt-based** principles, although this has changed in the last two decades.[17]

Muller says, "All cultures are made up of a mixture of all three [cultural worldviews], and individual families and even individuals in the West identify with different worldviews."[18] Therefore, even though people from fear-based cultures may respond better to an approach that matches their own worldview, they still must be instructed in the biblical concepts in the other paradigms. This chapter identifies the most suitable scriptures to each worldview framework and applies them for use with folk Muslims influenced by traditional religion.

---

[14] Muller, *Honor & Shame*, 105 (see intro., n. 15).

[15] Hiebert, Shaw and Tienou, *Understanding Folk Religion*, 234.

[16] Meeting the felt needs of Muslims is a legitimate way of approaching Muslims. I address meeting the spiritual needs of folk Muslims later in this chapter.

[17] Muller, *Honor & Shame*, 20.

[18] Muller, 70.

Guilt/Innocence Worldview

Westerners understand this worldview because it more closely fits their cultural orientation. A guilt/innocence theme dominates many propositional gospel presentations, such as the "Four Spiritual Laws,"[19] "Steps to Peace with God,"[20] and "The Bridge to Life."[21] Hiebert, Shaw, and Tienou summarize gospel presentations crafted this way:

> In individualistic societies with a strong sense of law, sin is violating rules, and leads to feelings of guilt, fear, and judgment. Salvation is seen as paying the penalty and being declared just before the law. Here the entry point is to preach the good news that through Christ's sacrifice people are forgiven and they are restored to a right standing before God. This has been the dominant motif in Western theology which inherited the Roman forensic system of law, and Hebrew tradition of covenant commandments. There is a danger, however. It is easy to see law as an autonomous, overarching code of moral righteousness, and justification as simply paying the penalties meted out by that law.[22]

This approach has merit, as the Bible contains these ideas. The concept of guilt and innocence before God not only characterizes a legitimate religious-worldview value but represents biblical truths that must be communicated to all cultures when presenting salvation. The apostle Paul speaks of salvation in Rom 2:14–16 from the guilt/innocence perspective:

> So, when Gentiles, who do not by nature have the law, do what the law demands, they are a law to themselves even though they do not have the law. They show that the work of the law is written on their

---

[19] Bill Bright, *Have You Heard of the Four Spiritual Laws?* (Peachtree City, GA: New Life Resources, 2006).

[20] *Steps to Peace with God* (Minneapolis: Billy Graham Association, 2005).

[21] "The Bridge to Life," Navigators (2010), https://www.navigators.org/resource/the-bridge-to-life.

[22] Hiebert, Shaw, and Tienou, *Understanding Folk Religion*, 226.

hearts. Their consciences confirm this. Their competing thoughts either accuse or even excuse them on the day when God judges what people have kept secret, according to my gospel through Christ Jesus.

Although various people groups possess many worldviews, everyone has an internal witness of guilt and innocence.[23] Such an understanding may not be the dominant theme in a culture, but Scripture indicates that all people comprehend some elements of this worldview. Paul continues in Rom 3:21–26 to describe humanity's guilt and God's plan for restoring righteousness through faith in Christ. Evangelizing through these arguments is known as the "Roman Road" witnessing method.[24]

Difficulties exist in trying to reach non-Westerners through the guilt/innocence worldview. While traveling off-road in the Sudanese desert between Tokar and Karora with Abraham, a *Dinka* (Southern Sudanese tribe) Christian, we encountered some *Rashaida* tribesmen on camels. My colleague, trained in propositional witnessing by another Western agency, drew the "Bridge to Life" presentation in the sand with a stick, showing the confused nomad in Arabic how he could cross the "bridge" from his sin and guilt to forgiveness in Christ. The nomad's lack of understanding stemmed partially from the fact that there are no bridges in that part of Sudan, and I doubt he had ever seen one. Despite the flaws within Western propositional presentations, I believe all ethnic groups need to understand a few of the basic guilt/innocence concepts as they come to Christ. Samuel Zwemer said

---

[23] Commenting on this passage, Charles Hodge says, "Men generally, not some men, but all men, show by their acts that they have a knowledge of right and wrong." Hodge, *A Commentary on the Epistle to the Romans* (Edinburgh: Banner of Truth Trust, 1864; repr. 1973), 54–55.

[24] Since the Roman Road is an extrapolation from a number of Scriptures in the apostle Paul's Epistle to the Romans, it is not normally copyrighted. Usually Rom 3:23; 6:23; 5:8; 10:9–10, 13 are the principal verses cited in the Roman Road to Salvation.

that Muslims have to be confronted with the incarnation and atonement and believe they are realities in order to be saved.[25]

Guilt/Innocence in Islam. Orthodox Islam somewhat comprehends the guilt/innocence perspective due to its legalism. A Muslim friend in North Africa shared his faith with me in the following way: "Christianity is too hard. Islam is very easy—you just follow five commandments and straightaway, you are fine." Muslim websites feature propositional illustrations similar in structure to Western evangelical gospel presentations. *Evangelism Explosion*[26] and *FAITH*[27] introduce gospel presentations utilizing the human right hand. Scriptures or ideas signified by the five digits make propositional points. In the *FAITH* presentation, widely used by Southern Baptist churches in the United States, the first finger represents "F" for "Forgiveness" (Rom 3:23); the second signifies "A" for "Available," referring to salvation (John 3:16); the third finger corresponds to "I," symbolizing it is "Impossible" to get to heaven on your own (Eph 2:8–9); the fourth finger denotes "T" for "Turn," as in repentance from sin (Luke 13:3); and the fifth signifies "H" for "Heaven" (John 14:6). Muslims have adopted a similar "hand" illustration.[28] The five fingers represent the sign of *Allahu* (his God). The Sufis also state that in Arabic numerology the two hands together number the ninety-nine names of God.

---

[25] See Pikkert, *Protestant Missionaries to the Middle East*, 82.

[26] Ken Silva, "Share Your Faith," Evangelism Explosion International, accessed February 10, 2021, https://evangelismexplosion.org/ministries/share-your-faith/.

[27] "FAITH: New Revised FAITH Gospel Presentation" (Nashville: Lifeway Christian Resources, 2006), 4–5.

[28] Allah Hand Illustration, accessed November 4, 2020, https://www.bing.com/images/search?q=allah+hand+illustration+for+muslims&qpvt=Allah+hand+illustration+for+Muslims&form=IGRE&first=1&scenario=ImageBasicHover.

Orthodox Islam places an undue emphasis on obeying rules,[29] stressing law over doctrine.[30] Although many Muslims lean more toward a shame/honor or fear/power worldview, their legalistic bent helps them understand guilt/innocence issues. Of course, Muslims do not accept the Christian doctrine of original sin or believe Jesus paid a substitutionary death on the cross.[31] Nevertheless, enough parallels exist between Christianity and Islam that many educated Muslims can be approached through a guilt/innocence worldview. For folk Muslims and the less educated, however, concepts must be explained in other ways.

The idea of sacrifice communicates to the ordinary Muslim. The ritual slaughtering of animals on the tenth day of *Dhu al-Hijjah* (twelfth lunar month) during the Hajj (pilgrimage) mirrors the sacrificial system in the Hebrew Old Testament.[32] Braswell explains, "*Id al-Adha* is the 'feast of the sacrifice' or 'the great feast.' It is obligatory upon all Muslims whether they are in Mecca on the pilgrimage or at home. . . . It also commemorates the sacrificing of an animal in the place of Abraham's son, Ishmael."[33]

The writer of Hebrews uses the Jewish sacrificial system to illustrate Christ's sacrifice upon the cross. This cultural point of contact assists Muslims in understanding the greater sacrifice Christ offered for sins.

By this will, we have been sanctified through the offering of the body of Jesus Christ once for all time.

Every priest stands day after day ministering and offering the same sacrifices time after time, which can never take away sins. But this man, after offering one sacrifice for sins forever, sat down at the right hand of God. (Heb 10:10–12)

---

[29] See Ruthven, *Islam in the World*, 121 (see chap. 2, n. 6).

[30] See Kate Zebiri, *Muslims and Christians Face to Face* (Oxford: Oneworld, 1997), 8.

[31] See Greear, *Breaking the Islam Code*, 62 (see chap 8, n. 21).

[32] The first Muslim convert that I baptized, Muhammad, told me that a Muslim cannot understand the New Testament without the Old Testament.

[33] Braswell, *Islam*, 80 (see intro., n. 28).

Muslims object to both the history of the event and its theological implications (substitutionary atonement). However, they understand the sacrificial reference. When I lived in North Africa, we observed an interesting practice during feast days. On many street corners, vendors kept goats and sheep for sale, penned inside of enclosures. Families stopped to buy an animal on the hoof to take home in obedience to this Islamic injunction. On the opposite street corners of the same intersections, men with axes squatted, waiting for customers to hire them to prepare the animals to eat. These were the butchers. My children, ages four, nine, and twelve, received a lesson in how animals are slaughtered during Muslim holidays according to Islamic law.

Using the customs within a host society to point out scriptural truths represents a "redemptive analogy" or cultural point of contact. Don Richardson coined the term and describes it in the following manner:

> When a missionary enters another culture, he or she is conspicuously foreign. This is to be expected, but often the gospel is labeled as foreign, too. How can it be explained so that it seems culturally right? The New Testament approach is to communicate by way of *redemptive analogy*. Consider these examples: The Jewish people practiced lamb sacrifice. John the Baptist proclaimed Jesus as the perfect, personal fulfillment of that sacrifice by saying, "Behold the lamb of God, who takes away the sin of the world!" This is *redemptive analogy*.[34]

Even though Muslim culture is not generally oriented toward a guilt/ innocence worldview, the sacrificial concept within Islam helps Muslims understand the biblical principles of blood atonement and redemption.

Guilt/Innocence in popular Islam. Despite the Beja tribe's poor practice of Islam,[35] their identification as Muslims and respect for piety offer

---

[34] Don Richardson, "Redemptive Analogy," in *Perspectives on the World Christian Movement*, 430 (see chap. 8, n. 14).

[35] Only 10 percent of rural Beja pray before dawn. See Ausenda, "Leisurely Nomads," 22, 331 (see chap. 4, n. 67); and Jacobsen, *Theories of Sickness and Misfortune*, 21 (see chap. 6, n. 39).

Christians avenues for gospel presentation through the guilt/innocence worldview. As Muslims, the Beja understand blood sacrifices from the Islamic perspective but retain some non-Islamic practices from their popular religion. For instance, when the *Hadendoa* Beja consecrate a new Sufi sheikh, they slaughter a calf so blood spills on his feet.[36] They also believe that "by offering a *karama* [sacrifice to God] involving animal blood, or an apparent equivalent," drought and infertility can be alleviated.[37]

Tribal customary law (*Salif*) trumps Islamic law and governmental statutes.[38] Beja law centers upon the payment of fines for various infractions.[39] Therefore, the Beja understand analogies involving payment for legal and moral infractions mentioned in the Scriptures referenced earlier in this chapter. Nonetheless, such analogies should be used judiciously because the Beja concept of guilt/innocence differs from the biblical idea. Just as the *Sawi* people of *Irian Jaya* described in *Peace Child* consider treachery a virtue,[40] so the Beja view of deceit is not the same as the Western concept.

Visiting the Beja in the early nineteenth century, Swiss traveler and journalist John Lewis Burckhardt observed, "Treachery is not considered here as criminal or disgraceful, and the Hadendoa is not ashamed to boast of his bad faith, whenever it has led to the attainment of his object."[41] No doubt, tribes with unusual (to the Christian worker) value systems should be taught biblical ideals. The communication of these ideals, however, should be through alternative communication methods, such as storytelling.

---

[36] See Ausenda, "Leisurely Nomads," 455.

[37] Jacobsen, *Theories of Sickness and Misfortune*, 259.

[38] See Lewis, "Deim el Arab and the Beja Stevedores of Port Sudan," 37 (see chap. 6, n. 25).

[39] Lewis writes, "The Beja have a complicated scale of customary compensation for wounds ranging from 100 camels or 1,000 *rials* for a death payment, to 20 *piasters* for a day's incapacity resulting from a stick wound. For the loss of an eye, hand, or leg, half payment (£S.30) is paid, for a finger or toe, £S.5. Sword or knife wounds are compensated for a minimum of 50 *piasters*, and if the injury is serious it is assessed" (36).

[40] Don Richardson, *Peace Child*, 4th ed. (Ventura, CA: Regal Books, 2005), 9.

[41] Quoted in D. C. Cummings, "The History of Kassala and the Province of Taka," *SNR* 20, no. 1 (1937): 4.

The ancient Beja practice of sacrificing a sheep, bull, or camel to ensure fertility of the land continues in North Africa.[42] The transfer of livestock constitutes the most common form of payment for both offenses and marriages.[43] Beja fugara[44] (singular, *fagir*) continue to prescribe the slaughtering of animals for offerings designed to satisfy the spirits. A Beja woman reports, "When I went to Saleh [the *fagir*], he said to me that 'the treatment of your son requires a big party [for the *zar*[45] spirit], which needs seven sheep for slaughtering.'"[46]

The biblical concept of guilt may be illustrated for the Beja in two ways. First, the sacrificial offerings graphically depict the crucifixion event. Second, a belief in causality within Beja folk Islam translates into an understanding of mankind's guilt. Beja folk religion acknowledges, but does not readily accept, the claim that Christ's death satisfies God's wrath against mankind's sin. Romans 5:8–10 presents the concept:

> But God proves his own love for us in that while we were still sinners, Christ died for us. How much more then, since we have now been justified by his blood, will we be saved through him from wrath. For if, while we were enemies, we were reconciled to God through the death of his Son, then how much more, having been reconciled, will we be saved by his life.

The Beja also understand the notion of reconciliation because of their cultural mediation practices. They prefer arbitration to fighting,[47] possess a general willingness to compromise,[48] and enjoy councils and lengthy negotiations.[49] A. Paul writes, "This gift for compromise I believe to be one of the

---

[42] See Hjort and Dahl, *Responsible Man*, 119 (see chap. 6, n. 75).

[43] See Ausenda, "Leisurely Nomads," 57.

[44] Traditional healers, plural of *fagir*.

[45] A non-Muslim spirit that possesses individuals.

[46] Qtd. in Jacobsen, *Theories of Sickness and Misfortune*, 211.

[47] See Hjort and Dahl, *Responsible Man*, 82.

[48] See G. E. R. Sandars, "The Amarar," *SNR* 18, no. 2 (1935): 213.

[49] See Ausenda, "Leisurely Nomads," 289.

most deep-seated of all Beja characteristics."[50] Hjort and Dahl state, "One of the most important qualities in a Beja leader is to be a good mediator in the sense of a negotiator and peacemaker."[51] Sandars notices that the Beja refer particularly difficult quarrels to any person of high character inside or outside the tribe, even foreigners.[52] Hjort and Dahl confirm that this practice continues.[53] They call the development of the mediatory role a "striking cultural trait" among the Beja.[54] Parshall claims that the mediatory role of Jesus[55] represents the most important bridge with folk Muslims such as Sufis.[56] The scriptural concept of mediator constitutes a powerful cultural illustration for Muslims and should be utilized. Hebrews 12:22–24 declares:

> Instead, you have come to Mount Zion, to the city of the living God (the heavenly Jerusalem), to myriads of angels, a festive gathering, to the assembly of the firstborn whose names have been written in heaven, to a Judge, who is God of all, to the spirits of righteous people made perfect, and to Jesus, the mediator of a new covenant, and to the sprinkled blood, which says better things than the blood of Abel.

Although the Beja need to understand the gospel in terms of some of the concepts of the guilt/innocence worldview, I do not believe this should be the primary approach with them. Jacobsen says an unwillingness to state matters absolutely represents a central cultural trait among the Beja, which is evidenced by their subjunctive answers to many questions.[57] The general Beja cultural climate flies in the face of rule-keeping, concrete thinking,

---

[50] Paul, *A History of the Beja Tribes of the Sudan*, 4 (see chap. 6, n. 29).

[51] Hjort and Dahl, *Responsible Man*, 84.

[52] G. E. R. Sandars, "The Bisharin," *SNR* 16, no. 2 (1933): 147.

[53] Hjort and Dahl, *Responsible Man*, 85.

[54] Hjort and Dahl, 44.

[55] Muller also sees the mediator concept as important in witnessing to Muslims but places the idea under the category of shame/honor. *Honor & Shame*, 63.

[56] Parshall, *Bridges to Islam*, 121.

[57] "Maybe" (*yumkin*), "possibly" (*mumkin*), "if God wills" (*'in sha'allah*). See Jacobsen, *Theories of Sickness and Misfortune*, 263–64, 267, 309.

and the yes-or-no answers inherent in the Western worldview. Hesselgrave and Rommen describe the contextualization avenues with the most chance of success with folk Islam. They write, "Armed with an understanding of the penchant for concrete relational thinking among Africans, Chinese, and various tribal peoples, the contextualizer will give more attention to the importance of history, myths, stories, parables, analogies, aphorisms, pictures, and symbols in communicating within these contexts."[58] This approach is important in the selection of scriptural passages for use with folk Islam. These are explored more fully in the following worldviews.

Shame/Honor Worldview

Much has been written concerning this worldview. Patai says "One of the importance differences between the Arab and the Western personality is that in Arab culture, shame is more pronounced than guilt."[59] Concerning salvation and shame, Hiebert, Shaw, and Tienou write:

> In strong group-oriented societies, such as Japan and China, people find their identity in belonging to a group. For them, sin is the breaking of relationships and offending community, and leads to feelings of *shame*, embarrassment, unworthiness, and remorse. These feelings are often associated with concepts of sin as defilement or uncleanness. Salvation is seen as reconciliation and restoration of good relationships and cleansing portrayed as washing with water or purging by blood.[60]

The Bible repeatedly presents teachings, stories, and illustrations that draw upon the shame/honor theme. Jesus's parable about the banquet guests in Luke 14:7–11 centers on this idea:

---

[58] Hesselgrave and Rommen, *Contextualization*, 205–6 (see chap. 8, n. 2).

[59] Quoted in Muller, *Honor & Shame*, 113.

[60] Hiebert, Shaw, and Tienou, *Understanding Folk Religion*, 226.

He told a parable to those who were invited, when he noticed how they would choose the best places for themselves: "When you are invited by someone to a wedding banquet, don't sit in the place of honor, because a more distinguished person than you may have been invited by your host. The one who invited both of you may come and say to you, 'Give your place to this man,' and then in **humiliation**, you will proceed to take the lowest place.

"But when you are invited, go and sit in the **lowest** place, so that when the one who invited you comes, he will say to you, 'Friend, move up **higher**.' You will then be **honored** in the presence of all the other guests. For everyone who **exalts** himself will be **humbled**, and the one who **humbles** himself will be **exalted**." [bold mine]

Another biblical example of the shame/honor theme occurs in 1 Cor 1:27: "Instead, God has chosen what is foolish in the world to **shame** the wise, and God has chosen what is weak in the world to **shame** the strong" (bold mine). Another instance surfaces in Luke 9:26 when Jesus says, "For whoever is **ashamed** of me and my words, the Son of Man will be **ashamed** of him when he comes in his glory and that of the Father and the holy angels" (bold mine).

The book of Hebrews contains much shame and honor imagery as well. Hebrews 12:2 describes Jesus as "the pioneer and perfecter of our faith. For the joy that lay before him, he endured the cross, despising the **shame**, and sat down at the right hand of the throne of God" (bold mine). In the paradoxical phrasing Arabs enjoy, the shame of the cross bestows honor upon the sufferer. Hebrews 2:9 announces the following about Jesus: "But we do see Jesus—made lower than the angels for a short time so that by God's grace he might taste death for everyone—crowned with glory and **honor** because he suffered death" (bold mine). Although Muslims reject the historicity of the crucifixion, and the possibility of Jesus dying, they understand the concepts of shame and honor in these passages.

Shame/honor in Muslim societies. Hamady states, "Arab society is a shame-based society. . . . There are three fundamentals of Arab society;

shame, honor and revenge."[61] Of course, not all Muslims are Arabs. Nevertheless, Patai says, "Despite the historical difference between the Arab world and the Muslim world, Arabs often tend to identify Arabism with Islam and Islam with Arabism."[62] Muller observes, "Honor in an Arab society is understood in a complex way, as the absence of shame. Honor and shame are diametrically opposed factors, and the fundamental issue that defines society."[63] Patai notes that "the major features that predominate in the Arab ethics of virtue can be summarized by three syndromes, which are themselves related: (1) the courage-bravery syndrome; (2) the hospitality-generosity syndrome; and (3) the honor-dignity syndrome. These syndromes are found everywhere in the Arab world, and . . . constitute the bulk and body of Arab ethics."[64]

In the Arab world this includes a multitude of different kinds of honor. Shame and honor values are significant to Muslim societies in regard to ethics, especially with respect to the family. A person's relatives either honor or shame them.[65] It is important in Muslim societies for families to extend gracious hospitality to all.[66] Conversely, retaliation and revenge represent the polar opposite of this ideal. The Quran sanctions this in *Sura* 11:73. In fact, one forfeits honor by not taking revenge for an injury suffered.[67] Since the Bible addresses the shame/honor worldview, the Christian must discover the parallels and draw them out. In the following verses Jesus's teaching confronts some of the presuppositions of the Arab world.

In John 8:3–11 a woman caught in adultery receives forgiveness from Jesus rather than the stoning required by Jewish and Islamic law. In Luke 6:27b–29a, Jesus says, "Love your enemies, do what is good to those who hate you, bless those who curse you, pray for those who mistreat you. If

---

[61] Sania Hamady in Muller, *Honor & Shame*, 79.
[62] Raphael Patai, *The Arab Mind*, rev. ed. (New York: Hatherleigh, 1983), 15.
[63] Muller, *Honor & Shame*, 98.
[64] Patai, *The Arab Mind*, 103.
[65] See Muller, *Honor & Shame*, 91.
[66] See Ruthven, *Islam in the World*, 430.
[67] Patai, *The Arab Mind*, 221.

anyone hits you on the cheek, offer the other also."[68] In the parable of the prodigal son, Jesus portrays the father as pardoning the son who has shamed his family.[69] In another parable Jesus appeals to the honor concept implicit in Arab hospitality:

> He also said to them, "Suppose one of you has a friend and goes to him at midnight and says to him, 'Friend, lend me three loaves of bread, because a friend of mine on a journey has come to me, and I don't have anything to offer him.' Then he will answer from inside and say, 'Don't bother me! The door is already locked, and my children and I have gone to bed. I can't get up to give you anything.' I tell you, even though he won't get up and give him anything because he is his friend, yet because of his friend's shameless boldness, he will get up and give him as much as he needs.
>
> "So I say to you, ask, and it will be given to you. Seek, and you will find. Knock, and the door will be opened to you." (Luke 11:5–9)

These parables resonate in a shame/honor culture, while confronting their core presuppositions. The stories may not appear evangelistic, but the ethical contrast between Jesus and Islam is so striking that a number of Muslims come to Christ this way. Pikkert says, "The most common reason why Muslims become Christians is the person of Jesus Christ, sometimes through fascination by the Quran's testimony about Him."[70] One of the national leaders in North Africa told me that he came to faith because Jesus taught forgiveness instead of taking revenge.[71]

---

[68] The apostle Paul writes in Rom 12:19, "Never take your own revenge, beloved, but leave room for the wrath of God, for it is written, 'Vengeance is Mine, I will repay,' says the Lord." (NASB)

[69] See Bill Musk, *Touching the Soul of Islam: Sharing the Gospel in Muslim Cultures* (Oxford: Monarch Books, 2004), 105–6.

[70] Pikkert, *Protestant Missionaries to the Middle East*, 192.

[71] Jonadab, interview with the author (see chap. 8, n. 22).

Shame/honor among the folk Muslim Beja people. In reflecting on the three major worldviews, Muller writes, "It is possible to find all three dynamics in most cultures, but usually one or two are more dominant."[72] Since the Beja claim Islam as their religion, the shame/honor religious idea certainly exists among them. Hjort and Dahl even call the shame/honor model the predominant Beja worldview paradigm: "When we met it, this culture appeared to us to have more in common with Mediterranean honor and shame based cultures than with the Cushitic cultures we knew about."[73] By contrast, two other researchers view Beja society as leaning more toward a fear/power worldview.[74] In addition, the vast literature about the Beja in *Sudan Notes and Records* (*SNR*), and my interaction with them, leads me to conclude that the worldview of the Beja reflects a fear/power orientation. Nonetheless, Hjort and Dahl see shame and honor as a prominent Beja value. They write, "The strong emphasis the Beja place on honor is a key element for understanding not only the Beja historical perspective, but also the current situation. . . . To comply with social norms, the individual Beja man is expected to be 'a Responsible Man.' By achieving this goal, he becomes an honorable person."[75]

Numerous examples abound illustrating the Beja cultural aspect of honor. The blood feuds of the *Beni-Amer* Beja are quite ferocious and persistent.[76] Lewis calls these feuds "a common and accepted custom, and tribal warfare almost a pastime."[77] The missionary can draw out the biblical analogy, because Beja customary law (*Salif*) allows for "the automatic right to

---

[72] Muller, *Honor & Shame*, 69.

[73] Hjort and Dahl, *Responsible Man*, 5. Authors Anders Hjort af Ornäs and Gudrun Dahl each lived for five months in the Red Sea Province in 1980 (viii).

[74] Giorgio Ausenda, author of "Leisurely Nomads: The Hadendowa (Beja) of the Gash Delta and Their Transition to Sedentary Life," spent ten months in the field (Ausenda, iv). Frode F. Jacobsen, the author of *Theories of Sickness and Misfortune amongst the Hadandowa Beja of the Sudan*, lived in the field for twelve months (Jacobsen, 4).

[75] Hjort and Dahl, *Responsible Man*, 9.

[76] See Nadel, "Notes on Beni-Amer Society," 68 (see chap. 6, n. 96).

[77] Lewis, "Deim el Arab and the Beja Stevedores of Port Sudan," 35.

pardon" the offender with an exchange of money or livestock even in the case of a death.[78] Both the pardon and the compensation are face-saving devices in the shame/honor tradition.[79]

Ancient Israel's King David writes in Ps 103:2–3, "My soul, bless the LORD, and do not forget all his benefits. He forgives all your iniquity; he heals all your diseases." As already mentioned, the basis of forgiveness of sins in Christianity consists of the blood payment of Jesus's death upon the cross. No clearer symbol for this exists for shame/honor societies than Christ's institution of the Lord's Supper based on the Jewish Passover meal. As the death angel (Exod 12:23) passed over those who had placed the blood of a sacrificial lamb on their doorposts, so Jesus said in Luke 22:20, "This cup is the new covenant in my blood." John the Baptist cried out, "Look, the Lamb of God, who takes away the sin of the world!" (John 1:29). These images are striking in a shame/honor Muslim setting.

The related ideas of hospitality and sanctuary represent a subtheme typically found in shame-and-honor societies. In this regard there exists some cultural discord among the Beja. The Hillmen are standoffish, reserved, and suspicious of strangers, but they are also extremely hospitable.[80] One Beja said, "As a guest you are allowed to be a king for three days."[81] The following common Beja story is a redemptive analogy from the shame/honor worldview:

> A man fleeing from a murder he had committed took refuge in the house of Gwilai'or [a famous *Amarar* Beja sheikh]. The relatives of the dead man intent on their revenge followed the killer to his sanctuary and demanded that he be surrendered. Gwilai'or tried every means to save the refugee . . . but the avengers were unmoved and insisted that unless their quarry were produced they would drag him by force. . . . At this Gwilai'or consented to parley with

---

[78] Ausenda, "Leisurely Nomads," 282–83.
[79] Ausenda, 283.
[80] See Hjort and Dahl, *Responsible Man*, 44.
[81] Jacobsen, *Theories of Sickness and Misfortune*, 25.

them. . . . He said, "What you propose to do would forever disgrace me and pollute my house, but since you insist on this man's blood I will show you the tree under which he spends the night and thus you can come on him unawares as he sleeps and dispatch him." The pursuers somewhat reluctantly agreed to this plan and having made sure of the exact spot they departed.

All that day Gwilai'or spent in dividing up his wealth in money and animals. . . . For he had decided to lay himself down beneath the fatal tree and so expiate the crime of the man who had taken sanctuary in his house.

But his son, discovering his purpose refused to allow his father to carry it out insisting that he would take his father's place beneath the tree and so uphold their family honor.

That night . . . one of [the avenging party's] number was visited by doubts that Gwilai'or . . . would so sacrifice anyone who had taken refuge in his house. He told his companions . . . to make sure that whoever they found under tree was the man they sought. . . .

And so the son of Gwilai'or was discovered and the murdered man's folk were so impressed with the magnanimity of Gwilai'or that they gave up their plan of vengeance and spared the life of the refugee.[82]

In this story, the beloved son offers to represent his father and lays down his life as the blood payment for a condemned stranger. Writing about such analogies, Hiebert, Shaw, and Tienou contend that "local beliefs associated with sacrifice can be used as redemptive analogies to help people understand Christ's death for sinners."[83] A scriptural parallel to this is Rom 5:6–10:

---

[82] Clark, "Manners, Customs and Beliefs of the Northern Bega," 26–27 (see chap. 6, n. 90).

[83] Hiebert, Shaw, and Tienou, *Understanding Folk Religion*, 223.

For while we were still helpless, at the right time, Christ died for the ungodly. For rarely will someone die for a just person—though for a good person perhaps someone might even dare to die. But God proves his own love for us in that while we were still sinners, Christ died for us. How much more then, since we have now been justified by his blood, will we be saved through him from wrath. For if, while we were enemies, we were reconciled to God through the death of his Son, then how much more, having been reconciled, will we be saved by his life.

Although the Beja possess significant shame/honor themes and values, their society lacks some of the more important and dominant Arab world-view concepts. They, for example, merely levy fines for adultery,[84] and the offending parties are rarely divorced or punished in any other way. Children born out of wedlock receive no social stigma.[85] Historically, the Beja consider adultery a minor matter.

Family life among the Beja differs significantly from the domestic situation usually found among Arabs in the larger Muslim world.[86] For instance, Beja men never beat their wives.[87] In fact, custom constrains them to treat their wives with kindness, never behaving harshly with them.[88] In addition, Beja men do not want their women to work. Unlike many tribes in the ATR world, females do not cultivate land or keep livestock, but only tend the camp and cook meals.[89] Beja women are quite autonomous from their

---

[84] Unusual in the Muslim world, a Beja woman has the right to claim compensation in gold or money from an unfaithful husband. When a man finds his wife unfaithful, compensation in camels is required in equal parts from both the male and female adulterers. See Hjort and Dahl, *Responsible Man*, 103.

[85] See Clark, "Manners, Customs and Beliefs of the Northern Bega," 5–6, 12.

[86] This is in contrast to what Patai describes as "the characteristic Arab male attitude to women: that the destiny of women . . . is to serve men and obey them." *The Arab Mind*, 34.

[87] See Hjort and Dahl, *Responsible Man*, 102.

[88] See Ausenda, "Leisurely Nomads," 226.

[89] See Hjort and Dahl, *Responsible Man*, 99–100.

husbands, who seek their opinion on a number of key issues, such as where to live, when to move, and whom their children should marry.[90]

According to Raphael Patai, Arab men raise their sons in a harsh manner.[91] In contrast, Beja men treat their children with kindness. In fact, a father never disinherits his son.[92] I believe the parable of the prodigal son would resonate with the forgiving Beja heart and could serve as a redemptive analogy to reach them.

Fear/Power Worldview

David Hesselgrave aptly notes, "Primal religionists are 'easily reached' but 'hard to win.' They lack or automatically misconstrue the categories we use—*Creator God, Redeemer, Savior, sin, salvation,* [and] *faith.*"[93] The fear/power concept represents the third worldview religious value paradigm in this study. Concerning cultures that see the world as a battle between supernatural forces, Muller observes, "The paradigm that these people live in is one of fear versus power."[94] Van Rheenen states that the traditional religionist's "relationship with spiritual beings is conceived in terms of power. Spiritual beings are propitiated, coerced, and placated because they have power."[95] In this worldview a close relationship exists between both power over and fear of the supernatural. Hiebert, Shaw, and Tienou summarize the foundation of such cultures thus:

> In many traditional societies, the dominant emotion is *fear*: fear of ancestors, arbitrary spirits, hostile enemies, witchcraft, magic, and invisible forces that plague everyday life. Evil is manifest in demonic oppression and witchcraft, leading to withdrawal, fear of

---

[90] See Ausenda, "Leisurely Nomads," 227.
[91] See Patai, *The Arab Mind,* 36.
[92] See Ausenda, "Leisurely Nomads," 278.
[93] Hesselgrave, *Paradigms in Conflict,* 91.
[94] Muller, *Honor & Shame,* 42.
[95] Van Rheenen, *Communicating Christ in Animistic Contexts,* 21 (see chap. 5, n. 6).

life, self-hatred, and suicidal tendencies (Mark 1:23–26; 5:2–9). Salvation in these societies consists primarily of being saved from the *powers* of evil and the problems, hardships, misfortunes, injustices, sicknesses, and death people experience in this world.[96]

Westerners tend not to take this worldview seriously and some disdain it completely.[97] Despite this disregard, such practices flourish even in Western countries. Cautioning against classifying ATR only in terms of superstition, spirits, and magic, Mbiti says about ATR, "Africans believe that there is a force or power or energy in the universe which can be tapped by those who know how to do so, and then used for good or evil towards other people."[98] According to C. S. Lewis, there are two dangers in approaching the supernatural. One consists of denying its existence while the other is an excessive preoccupation with the demonic.[99]

Denying the supernatural in ATR. Writing about the supernatural power within ATR, John Mbiti vouches for its reality, claiming, "This mystical power is not fiction: whatever it is, it is a reality, and one with which African peoples have to reckon."[100] I agree with Mbiti's declaration. Real power exists in ATR, and people fear it with just cause. Musk asserts, "Magic, sorcery and occult practices are demonstrably real, according to the Bible. The devil is conceived of as a personal being heading a hierarchy of evil spirits."[101] Jesus Christ recognized the reality and power of the devil when He said, "My friends, don't fear those who kill the body, and after that can do nothing more. But I will show you the one to fear: Fear him

---

[96] Hiebert, Shaw, and Tienou, *Understanding Folk Religion*, 224–25.

[97] See Van Pelt, *Bantu Customs in Mainland Tanzania*, 25 (see chap. 5, n. 1); and Hiebert, *Anthropological Insights for Missionaries*, 153 (see intro., n. 25).

[98] Mbiti, *Introduction to African Religion*, 19 (see chap. 5, n. 2).

[99] C. S. Lewis, in Hiebert, Shaw, and Tienou, *Understanding Folk Religion*, 277.

[100] John S. Mbiti, *African Religions and Philosophy*, 2nd ed. (Oxford: Heinemann Educational Publishers, 1989), 193.

[101] Musk, *Touching the Soul of Islam*, 240.

who has authority to throw people into hell after death. Yes, I say to you, this is the one to fear!" (Luke 12:4–5)

The Bible teaches the presence of both good and evil spirits dwelling above humans, but inferior to the Lord.[102] The ministering spirits referenced in Heb 1:14 represent God's angels, who assist the Almighty.[103] These beings should not receive worship or sacrifice. Conversely, the Scriptures identify the evil spirits as demons. Jesus confirms their reality in Luke 13:32, saying, "Look, I'm driving out demons and performing healings today and tomorrow, and on the third day I will complete my work." Cornelius Olowola recognizes that "sacrifice to the spirits is indeed the centre of much African traditional worship,"[104] and these sacrifices are thought to appease the spirits and ward off misfortune in ATR.[105]

According to ATR theory, specialists tap the supernatural power from the unseen realm through magic. Medicine men (and women), diviners, and rainmakers dispense "good magic," while sorcerers, witches, and malevolent magicians practice evil enchantment.[106] Obviously, counterfeit conjuring also infiltrates ATR. Nonetheless, all magic strikes terror in the heart of the traditional religionist. For those within the culture, the real power of darkness and the imagined influence of sympathetic[107] and homeopathic magic frighten with equal force. The question arises, How does the Christian worker approach those within a fear/power worldview? Does one replicate the power of ATR with an equally significant manifestation of Christian power?

---

[102] See Cornelius Olowola, *African Traditional Religion and the Christian Faith* (Ghana: Africa Christian Press, 1993), 31.

[103] "Are they [angels] not all ministering spirits, sent out to render service for the sake of those who will inherit salvation?" (Heb 1:14 NASB).

[104] Olowola, *African Traditional Religion*, 39.

[105] See Oladimeji, *African Traditional Religion*, 44 (see chap. 5, n. 3).

[106] See Mbiti, *African Religions & Philosophy*, 193.

[107] "Items associated with or symbolic of the intended victim are used to identify and carry the spell. Obviously, sympathetic magic contains elements of both imitative and contagious magic." Lehmann and Myers, *Magic, Witchcraft, and Religion*, 257 (see chap. 6, n. 97).

Hiebert, Shaw, and Tienou describe a "split-level" Christianity whereby ethnic groups who come to Christ for eternal salvation retain their traditional religions to solve daily difficulties.[108] Split-level theology persists in Western Christianity.[109] Westerners tend to think dualistically, using logic to analyze phenomena in the natural world.[110] This designation consigns the supernatural aspect of ATR to the realm of folklore.

Western theologians generally push ultimate questions toward a loosely defined afterlife. According to Hiebert, modern Christianity often denies or excludes the so-called middle level between religion (faith, miracles, and otherworldly problems) and science (sight, natural causation, and this-world problems).[111] Hiebert contends, "When tribal people spoke of fear of evil spirits, they [the Christian worker] denied the existence of the spirits rather than claim the power of Christ over them."[112] Adherents to a fear/power worldview reside in this middle level between the transcendent and immanent.

The Christian worker must enter the worldview of the host culture in order to communicate the gospel.[113] Van Pelt says, "One has to take into account distrust and fear of sorcery and spirits on the one hand and the recourse to witchdoctors and spirits on the other hand. There is great confidence in medicine-men and their practices."[114] This is especially true when ministering with ATR and the fear/power presuppositions embedded within.

---

[108] Hiebert, Shaw, and Tienou, *Understanding Folk Religion*, 225, 373.

[109] See Hiebert, *Transforming Worldviews*, 154.

[110] See Hesselgrave, *Paradigms in Conflict*, 194.

[111] Hesselgrave calls Hiebert's "excluded middle" thesis tremendously significant. In this view, "questions having to do with the everyday world of sensory experience have been relegated to science and natural laws. Those having to do with such otherworldly matters such as God, miracles, visions, and inner feelings have been relegated to religion." Thus the "flaw of the excluded middle" unnaturally separates the supernatural from the world of sensory perception. Hesselgrave, 194–95.

[112] Hiebert, "The Flaw of the Excluded Middle" in *Perspectives on the World Christian Movement*, 411–12.

[113] See Sherwood G. Lingenfelter and Marvin K. Mayers, *Ministering Cross-Culturally: An Incarnational Model for Personal Relationships*, 2nd ed. (Grand Rapids: Baker Academic, 2003), 117–18.

[114] Van Pelt, *Bantu Customs in Mainland Tanzania*, 14.

Overemphasis on the demonic. Hiebert says, "The second danger is a return to a Christianized form of animism in which spirits and magic are used to explain everything."[115] More recently this second-mentioned danger has taken center stage in missions circles, for some Christians have developed an "undue fascination with and fear of Satan and his hosts."[116] In response to the resurgence of traditional religions, some missiologists advocate staging "power encounters" in order to engage in spiritual warfare with the forces of darkness. As Hesselgrave states, "Numerous disagreements on spiritual warfare and power encounters have emerged in discussion on missions and ministry practice in recent years."[117] Alan Tippet introduced the term "power encounter" as a result of his ministry in Polynesia working with tribal people.

Although Tippett advanced the concept,[118] Charles Kraft, Peter Wagner, and John Wimber grew the movement into what is called "third wave Pentecostalism."[119] Hesselgrave explains how far this concept has been expanded (bold mine):

> **Third wave–type power encounter** usually goes beyond demonstrating the power of the true God in the context of false gods. To engage in Christian ministry itself is to engage in spiritual warfare, and power encounter is an inherent part of it. Included are such supernatural phenomenon as healing the sick, speaking in tongues,

---

[115] Hiebert, "The Flaw of the Excluded Middle," 413.

[116] Hiebert, 214.

[117] Hesselgrave, *Paradigms in Conflict*, 180.

[118] Originally, proponents defined the term in this way: "A 'power encounter' was a 'visible, practical demonstration that Jesus Christ is more powerful than the false gods or spirits worshipped or feared by a given society or people group.'" Hesselgrave, 176.

[119] According to David A. Bledsoe, this term is synonymous with Neo-Pentecostalism in many parts of the world. He says that third-wave Pentecostalism (i.e., Neo-Pentecostalism) includes groups that in some contexts have clearly gone beyond what most evangelicals would consider orthodox in beliefs as well as practices. Bledsoe, "Brazilian Neo-Pentecostal Movement: Development and Distinctions with a Missiological Case Analysis of the Igreja Universal Do Reino De Deus and Its Impact on Brazilian Society" (PhD diss., University of South Africa, 2010), 14, 25, 43.

interpreting tongues, exorcising demons and territorial spirits, neutralizing poisonous bites, overcoming Satanic attacks of various kinds, and even **raising the dead**. Related practices include concerted prayer and fasting, the laying on of hands, anointing with oil, the use of special handkerchiefs and other objects, **slaying in the spirit, spiritual mapping**, and prayer walking.[120]

Of course, many Scriptures speak to the concept and reality of spiritual warfare. Jesus said in 1 John 3:8, "The Son of God was revealed for this purpose: to destroy the devil's works." The apostle Paul, in Eph 6:10–12, exhorts the believer to do battle with supernatural forces:

> Finally, be strengthened by the Lord and by his vast strength. Put on the full armor of God so that you can stand against the schemes of the devil. For our struggle is not against flesh and blood, but against the rulers, against the authorities, against the cosmic powers of this darkness, against evil, spiritual forces in the heavens.

The question centers on the kind of power to be exercised. If the missionary attempts to match the magician miracle for miracle, then they become another shaman displaying power rather than a messenger bringing the gospel. Even Jesus refused the devil's request that he perform displays of power. In response to Satan's challenge that Jesus throw himself from the pinnacle of the temple, Christ said, "It is said: Do not test the Lord your God."[121]

Hiebert, Shaw, and Tienou stress that pointing to the preeminence of the cross better represents the gospel than manifestations of power showing God's supremacy over other deities.[122] Miraculous displays do not necessarily result in conversions. Even the magicians of Egypt replicated the plagues

---

[120] Hesselgrave, *Paradigms in Conflict*, 177.
[121] Luke 4:12.
[122] Hiebert, Shaw, and Tienou, *Understanding Folk Religion*, 374.

that God produced through Moses,[123] yet Pharaoh was not convinced to let the Israelites leave the country. Hiebert, Shaw, and Tienou advise caution:

> In dealing with folk religions, Christians need a theology of discernment. People seek signs to assure them that God is present, but apart from the fruits of the Spirit, there are no self-authenticating phenomena. Miraculous healings, speaking in tongues, exorcism, prophecies, resurrections, and other extraordinary experiences are reported in all major religions.[124]

Regardless of one's stance on the presence or absence today of the first-century apostolic miraculous gifts, few missionaries regularly attempt such displays of power. Their reticence may stem from either a fear of failure or the recognition that God normally works in quieter ways. Although a lot has been written about power encounters, reports of their occurrence tend to be anecdotal and sporadic. I believe God manifests His power spectacularly, but he utilizes the miraculous as more of an ancillary method rather than a primary strategy.

I have seen God's miraculous power manifested on at least two occasions. First, when working in North Africa, I operated a number of relief projects (water, farming, sanitation, and education) for seven years in partnership with nationals and refugees from two neighboring countries. One of our refugee workers threatened to expose our purpose to the government. Since he knew of our evangelistic efforts in the country, our team began to pray fervently. Within a week, Kidani became so sick that we brought him from the project site to a hospital in a major city. Despite bringing him food and medicine, which is necessary in African hospitals, and paying the extra cost for a good doctor in his treatment, Kidani, who was in his early forties, died within weeks of threatening our work.

---

[123] "But the magicians of Egypt did the same [i.e., turned water into blood] with their secret arts; and Pharaoh's heart was hardened, and he did not listen to them, as the Lord had said," (Exod 7:22, NASB).

[124] Hiebert, Shaw, and Tienou, *Understanding Folk Religion*, 374–75.

Second, a year later, the MBBs associated with my work had started a small church that met in the courtyard of the congregation of another denomination in the same city where Kidani had been hospitalized. Boutros threatened to expose the work to the government. Our small group once again began praying. I had a meeting out of the country, but upon my return the national believers told me what had happened. Within a month of threatening to expose our work, Boutros was traveling along a large river in a four-wheel drive vehicle. His car broke down, but he was able to secure a ride in a passing public cross-country bus. The bus driver became disoriented in the desert and the vehicle became lodged in the sands of the Sahara (the roads are not paved in the desert). Thirty-four passengers, including Boutros, died of thirst along the side of the road. The national believers told me in both cases, "God did that." I did not disagree, for I had learned that the power of God protects His church.

Hesselgrave suggests some alternatives to power encounters. The "truth encounter" depends on the Holy Spirit to communicate the message of the gospel. Speaking about John 16:8–11, Hesselgrave says, "Jesus makes it clear that the Holy Spirit has a vital role in persuading, convincing, and convicting the world of sin, righteousness and judgment—not just in a general sense but in specifics."[125] Contrasting with or at least complementing power encounters, a successful truth encounter involves the sharing of the gospel in the power of the Holy Spirit and results in the miracle of a changed life. Despite the attraction of the power encounter, there is no greater miracle than a Muslim coming to faith by an encounter with the truth.

The "empirical encounter" represents another type. Based on the previously mentioned excluded middle of Paul Hiebert, this approach focuses on the fear/power concerns of folk religion. Hesselgrave shows how the empirical encounter differs from the other encounters:[126]

---

[125] Hesselgrave, *Paradigms in Conflict*, 191–92.

[126] Other writers mention several more types of encounters. Charles Kraft adds "allegiance encounters" to the list, writing, "Implied in the allegiance encounter is the

[1] Truth encounter deals with "the ultimate story of the origin, purpose, and destiny of the self, society, and the universe" [quoting Hiebert]. **[2] Power encounter** has to do with "the uncertainties of the future, the crises of the present, and the unexplainable events of the past." But **[3] empirical encounter** deals with *middle-level* concerns having to do with "the nature and order of humans and their relationships, and of the natural world." At this *middle level* (not the religious or the science level) tribals seek answers to *practical questions*: Which of these seeds will grow? How can we make sure this marriage will last? Why has my brother suddenly become ill?[127]

Fear/Power in Islam. Similar tensions exist among Muslims because orthodox Islam attempts to deny the middle-level apprehensions of the common people.[128] According to Musk, "Ideal Islam has no resources to deal with the everyday concerns and nightly dreads of ordinary Muslims."[129] Many folk Muslims approach the supernatural from an ATR orientation. Opposition between these two groups can be intense. Braswell says, "The leaders of orthodox Islam disparage folk religion and preach against it."[130] Despite this aversion, Ruthven explains, "In the long term official Islam was to benefit from the very practices which orthodoxy

---

cultivation of the fruits of the Holy Spirit, especially love toward God and man. We are to turn from love of (or commitment to) the world that is under the control of the evil one (First John 5:19) to God who loved the world and gave Himself for it." Kraft, "Culture, Worldview and Contextualization" in *Perspectives on the World Christian Movement*, 448. Closely related to the allegiance encounter, the "love encounter" demonstrates the love of God to unbelievers through a servant role. A final kind of encounter is the "prayer encounter." Although sometimes linked to the intercessory, spiritual-warfare prayer that occurs within the power encounter grouping, as Hesselgrave maintains in *Paradigms in Conflict* (196–97), others believe prayer encounters stand alone as a separate category.

[127] Hesselgrave, 195 (bold mine).
[128] See Braswell, *Islam*, 77.
[129] Musk, "Popular Islam," 259 (see intro., n. 5).
[130] Braswell, *Islam*, 77.

condemned."[131] Ruthven makes this assertion because the religion spread to the frontiers of the ancient world by Muslim missionaries from Sufi orders who primarily practiced folk Islam.[132] Accordingly, popular Islam and orthodox Islam have formed an uneasy truce over the years, and each rarely criticizes the other.[133]

The tolerance between popular and orthodox Islam is due to the fact that "the *Sharia* accommodated and legitimized many pre-Islamic Arab customs, which made its observance less burdensome to Arabs and other peoples."[134] Samuel Zwemer mentions many of these customs in *The Influence of Animism on Islam*. L. F. Nalder, reviewing Zwemer's book, writes:

> The tree or bush covered with countless pieces of rag, the cairn of stones by the wayside are familiar to all. These, Dr. Zwemer suggests, are relics of the tree and stone worship prevalent in all primitive Semitic religions. Sacred trees abound throughout Islam, and the Black Stone at Mecca is the best example of the survival of stone worship. Still more curious is his account of snake worship in Islam. The provision of a bowl of milk for the serpent protector "believing that calamity would come upon them if the serpent were neglected. This is undoubtedly a survival of the ancient belief that the serpent was the child of the earth, the oldest inhabitant of the land, and the guardian of the ground."[135]

Saal defines folk Islam and its religious practices as follows:

> Folk Islam is a mixture of pristine [orthodox] Islam with the ancient religious traditions and practices of ordinary people. It exists in a world populated by angels, demons, *jinns*, magicians, fortune-tellers, healers and [Sufi] saints both living and dead. . . .

---

[131] Ruthven, *Islam in the World*, 257.
[132] Ruthven, 256.
[133] See Parshall, *Bridges to Islam*, 37.
[134] Ruthven, *Islam in the World*, 257.
[135] L. F. Nalder, "The Influence of Animism in Islam," *SNR* 9, no. 1 (1926): 86.

Ordinary Muslims regularly turn to the practice of folk religion to meet felt needs while considering themselves to be genuine followers of Islam.[136]

What is the best approach to reach the folk Muslims? Since the faith and practice of folk Muslims resembles ATR, I argue for reaching them primarily through the fear/power worldview. Nabeel Jabbour states, "The fear-power paradigm exists in the minds of folk Muslims all over the Muslim world and in some African countries where some people are occupied with the demonic and magic."[137]

This section identifies a number of encounters advocated by missiologists to reach cultures holding to a fear/power worldview. Some suggest the power-encounter approach for evangelizing Muslims. Sometimes this involves visions and dreams. Rick Brown, for example, reports the following about the conversion of a Sufi master:

> One night while Ibrahim was praying to know the way of salvation, Jesus appeared to him, radiant in white clothing. He told him to travel to a certain town and consult a holy man from such-and-such a village whose father and grandfather were named so-and-so. Jesus showed him in a vision the way to the house. Ibrahim was excited, realizing that this man's grandfather had been his very own *Sufi* master. . . . Brother Jacob [the man in the house] told Ibrahim that the Lord had appeared to him in 1969 and had shown him that He is the way of salvation. He read Jesus' words in the gospel, "I am the Way, the Truth and the Life. No one comes to the Father except through Me."[138]

Such stories are common among advocates of C-5 contextualization. Greeson devotes eight pages of his work, *The Camel* to accounts of

---

[136] Saal, *Reaching Muslims for Christ*, 51 (see intro., n. 3).

[137] Jabbour, *The Crescent through the Eyes of the Cross*, 151.

[138] Rick Brown, "A Movement to Jesus among Muslims" in *Perspectives on the World Christian Movement*, 706–7.

Muslims coming to Christ through an experience of a dream or vision of Jesus.[139] He writes:

> One of the most common themes in the dreams that Muslims are experiencing is "a man in a white robe" whom they come to see as *Isa*. . . . Whether this is a new phenomenon or God has been doing this previously in history, we cannot know. What is clear, though, is that this phenomenon is widespread and common.[140]

Greeson urges the formation of "Muslim dream teams" in churches. He implores believers to "pray that the man in the white robe will appear and speak to them [Muslims]."[141]

Although many conversion testimonies from former Muslims attest to dreams and visions,[142] a word of caution is in order. All spiritual experience should be evaluated by Scripture. First John 4:1 warns, "Dear friends, do not believe every spirit, but test the spirits to see if they are from God, because many false prophets have gone out into the world." Several of the Muslim converts associated with my work attest that dreams piqued their interest in the gospel, causing them to consider Jesus. None, however, reported seeing Him. One of my nationals, 'Isa, dreamed that a giant wooden cross hit him on the forehead and woke him. This happened three times in a row. 'Isa asked a missionary what this meant. He replied, "I think God is trying to get your attention."[143] Soon he became a believer and months later was baptized in the Red Sea.

One must be cautious about identifying every man in white in a vision or dream as Jesus. Muslims, especially Sufis, frequently experience dreams and visions. Ausenda reports that since boyhood, the Prophet Muhammad appeared in the dreams of the Beja Sufi sheikh Ali Betai. Betai proclaimed

---

[139] Kevin Greeson, *The Camel*, 82–89 (see chap. 8, n. 24).

[140] Greeson, 80.

[141] Greeson, 91.

[142] See Pikkert, *Protestant Missionaries to the Middle East*, 195; and Musk, "Popular Islam," 304.

[143] 'Isa Esaam, interview with the author, Khartoum, Sudan, January 8, 2006.

to the Beja the content of his special dreams, writing, "Now that I have returned, I saw him [Muhammad] face to face. The Prophet lit the whole countryside, and I saw with my eyes many people with him; all the good men from early times, now dead. The Prophet said to me: 'Build a mosque here in this place.'"[144]

In my opinion, God brings power encounters at the time and place of his choosing. Christian workers who attempt to orchestrate or encourage others to seek these encounters risk falling prey to the very folk practices they reject. Both truth and empirical encounters, therefore, resonate best with the middle-level concerns of the fear/power worldview within popular Islam.

Fear/power among the folk Muslim Beja tribe. The Beja view the world primarily through a fear/power prism. I believe that approaching popular Islam through this worldview holds the most promise for making sense within the traditional religious framework, which resembles ATR. Jacobsen summarizes the Beja mindset, writing, "The cultural world of the Beja is a world inhabited by a host of spirits. Although there are Muslim and good intentioned spirits, most Hadendowa Beja are mainly concerned with the malevolent ones as well as the capricious ones, which occasionally create problems."[145]

Questions of causality dominate the thought of popular religions. Folk religions peer into the supernatural and seek guidance for the cause and meaning of evil, death, sickness, misfortune, and the unknown.[146] Ausenda says, "The [Beja] Hadendowa's greatest concern is his or her health . . . Hadendowa seemed less concerned about death than disease, since they fear the latter's consequence."[147] Family health and welfare issues consume the mind of the Beja, as Jacobsen illustrates:

---

[144] Ausenda, "Leisurely Nomads," 444.
[145] Jacobsen, *Theories of Sickness and Misfortune*, 34.
[146] See Hiebert, Shaw, and Tienou, *Understanding Folk Religion*, 77–79.
[147] Ausenda, "Leisurely Nomads," 423.

A Beja husband ideally will do everything in his power in order to fulfill the wishes of his wife. Paying for treatment expenses for his sick wife is clearly expected of him. . . . . Beja people are expected to do something about sickness and, in some cases seek any kind of treatment, in order to show their responsibility for their own and other family members' health.[148]

The Beja believe sicknesses possess intentional personalities.[149] Most often, women are the administers of homeopathic cures for minor ailments and reproductive concerns.[150] On one hand, drinking foamed goat's milk and inhaling smoke from burning pages of the Quran treat measles. On the other hand, a cure for mumps requires Quranic readings with the sufferer wearing a thread tied in knots.[151] Another magical cure features a leather amulet[152] stuffed with Quranic texts written by a faki. The Beja believe these protect against thefts, assaults, and accidents.[153] Some faki obtain great reputations for special power in devising cures. Sometimes they write a "prescription" that entails the person repeating the *Fateha*[154] a certain number of times.[155] Such recitations treat *jinn* possession and insanity as well as normal sicknesses.[156] As Clark writes:

---

[148] Jacobsen, *Theories of Sickness and Misfortune*, 228, 232.

[149] See Jacobsen, 106–7.

[150] See Ausenda, "Leisurely Nomads," 419, 423.

[151] See Ahmed Abdel Halim, "Native Medicine and Ways of Treatment in the Northern Sudan," *SNR* 22, no. 1 (1939): 40.

[152] Most rural Beja wear these amulets.

[153] See Ausenda, "Leisurely Nomads," 424.

[154] In a translation by N. J. Dawood, the opening of the Quran reads as follows: "In the name of God the Compassionate, the Merciful. Praise be to God, Lord of the universe, the Compassionate, the Merciful, Sovereign of the Day of Judgment! You alone we worship, and to You alone we turn for help. Guide us to the straight path, the path of those who You have favored, Not of those who have incurred Your wrath, nor of those who have gone astray." Dawood, *The Koran: with Parallel Arabic Text* (London: Penguin Books, 1990), xvii.

[155] See Ausenda, "Leisurely Nomads," 426.

[156] See Ausenda, 427.

Belief in *Jinns* and *shawatin* [devils] is universal and I have spoken to people who are sincerely convinced that they have encountered these spirits. In no case have I heard of a benevolent *Jinn*. Their activities are usually evil and harmful to men and many charms are worn to counteract their influence. Among the Atbai peoples certain tribes are reputed to have *Jinns* in subjugation.[157]

The Beja worldview holds spirits responsible for afflictions such as migraine headaches. The Hillmen consult special faki schooled in exorcism for cures. While headaches require readings from the Quran, traditional healers recommend beating deranged persons with Quranic sticks.[158] Hussey says that the beating "is administered to the *Ginn* [*sic*] that possesses the patient and not to the patient himself who is said not even to feel the blows."[159]

Similarly, Beja attribute epilepsy to spirits.[160] They hold evil powers responsible for a special "fright sickness" (*mirguay*) that causes children to cry for extended periods.[161] In the same way, tribal offspring suffer from a malady known as *mingay*, or "left alone." The Beja blame this ailment on paranormal activity as well. The Hillmen fear leaving children unaccompanied lest evil befall them.[162] Indeed, the Beja fault the supernatural for all misfortunes, miscreants, and maladies. A belief in werehyenas[163] (*karai*) pervades Beja culture.[164] The Hillmen employ housing decorations to repel *jinns*.[165] The Beja keep their number of children and animals secret due to a

---

[157] Clark, "Manners, Customs and Beliefs of the Northern Bega," 14–15.

[158] See Jacobsen, *Theories of Sickness and Misfortune*, 60, 243.

[159] E. R. J. Hussey, "A Fiki's Clinic," *SNR* 6, no. 1 (1923): 37.

[160] Epilepsy is called "falling down" (*toodip* in Beja and *sara'a* in Arabic), according to Jacobsen, *Theories of Sickness and Misfortune*, 59.

[161] See Jacobsen, 172.

[162] See Jacobsen, 59.

[163] Beja believe some humans magically turn into hyenas at night in much the same manner as werewolves of Western folklore.

[164] See Ausenda, 429.

[165] See Ausenda, 416.

fear of the evil eye.[166] Both rural and urban Beja believe in the power of the evil eye, spirit attacks, and possession.[167]

The Beja also believe in Zar "spirit humans" who settle permanently in lifelong marriages with their hosts, as mentioned in a previous chapter. Exhibiting both good and bad character traits, Beja call these spirits naughty and unpredictable.[168] One informant reports that Zar spirits desire the blood of sacrificed animals.[169] Zar doctors (fugara) use assistants called spirit helpers in their efforts. Jacobsen says:

> The majority of the fugara employ "spirit helpers" in their work. Although the help of "spirit helpers" is considered invaluable by the *fagir*, the cooperation is not without dangers as my *fagir* friend Ahmad explains. "Being a *fagir* is harmful to your children. When you are weak or make a mistake, they [the spirits] can harm your children. . . . Also, when you get rid of the spirits from a patient, sometimes these spirits harm you."[170]

A Christian worker told me a story about a Beja woman in North Africa. A female missionary who works for my friend met with this Beja woman every Thursday for coffee, for a year. Each week she would pour an extra cup of coffee and leave it sitting on the table. After a number of weeks observing that the extra coffee was never consumed, the female worker asked about the idea of the spare cup. The woman replied, "Oh, that's [a cup of coffee] for my *Zar*."[171]

Since the Beja dwell in such a frightening spiritual reality, a response must be tailored to suit their worldview. As Musk says, "The gospel, in its presentation to ordinary Muslims, must 'fit' the folk-Islamic world in order to do battle with the demonic therein."[172] The question remains, How best to reach them?

---

[166] See Jacobsen, *Theories of Sickness and Misfortune*, 33, 171.
[167] See Jacobsen, 46.
[168] See Jacobsen, 146.
[169] See Jacobsen, 147.
[170] Jacobsen, 68–69.
[171] H. Richard, interview with the author, Pittsburgh, Pennsylvania, April 30, 2010.
[172] Musk, "Popular Islam," 341.

The redemptive analogy concept holds much promise with folk Islam. The goal of a redemptive analogy "is to make the gospel understandable and to facilitate conversion,"[173] with the cross being the most powerful and central element. Pikkert says, "For Zwemer, 'the cross of Christ is the missing link in the Moslem's creed,' for in it the justice of God, sin and salvation come together, and men find true reconciliation."[174] Native ideas about sacrifice can illustrate Jesus's death on behalf of all.[175]

Zar cult practices among the Beja and other Muslim ethnic groups, have potential for redemptive analogies. Jacobsen describes a custom that contains such material:

> Blood is considered of primary importance in healing *zar* afflictions. As discussed before, a person who is host to a *zar* spirit will never get rid of it. First and foremost the red *zar* spirit wants blood. As we have seen, a *zar* ritual ideally involves even drinking sacrificial blood by the sufferer.[176]

The Beja hold a fear/power worldview and should be reached this way. The Bible addresses the ideas implicit in the Zar spirit concept. Hebrews 2:14–15 reminds us, "Now since the children have flesh and blood in common, Jesus also shared in these, so that through his death he might destroy the one holding the power of death—that is, the devil—and free those who were held in slavery all their lives by the fear of death." This verse fits the worldview of the Beja, as both male and female Beja struggle with Zar possession.[177] The passage communicates freedom from the power of evil through Christ's death.

---

[173] Hesselgrave, *Paradigms in Conflict*, 103.

[174] Pikkert, *Protestant Missionaries to the Middle East*, 96.

[175] See Hiebert, Shaw, and Tienou, *Understanding Folk Religion*, 223.

[176] Jacobsen, *Theories of Sickness and Misfortune*, 231.

[177] Although the Zar spirits possess more Beja women than men, possession is reported among both sexes. Jacobsen says the belief about and treatment of Zar spirits are as common in urban areas as in the rural parts of Bejaland. Jacobsen, *Theories of Sickness and Misfortune*, 72, 156, 212, 238.

Surprisingly, the Beja also possess cultural beliefs about the efficacy of the cross itself, probably due to their pre-Islamic history. For instance, when a *Nabatab* (nobleman) *Beni-Amer* Beja marries, a relative of the bride draws the sign of a cross within a rectangle (*hajrat*) with the blood of a slaughtered bull.[178] Quranic fumigation normally treats all kinds of fever, including malaria.[179] Halim says that serious cases with convulsions require special healing procedures involving a cross:

> Some people [Beja] believe that the fever is due to the entrance into the body of certain souls or demons. . . .
>
> When a child gets this fever and when there are convulsions, the parents are not allowed to handle him (a condition which they call *habobat el soghar* i.e., grandmother of young children). To combat this condition a black cross is drawn on the child's forehead and then a mystic fiki[180] is called to read over the child a special incantation.[181]

Jesus demonstrates his power over evil spirits in Mark 9:20: "When the spirit [in the demon-possessed boy] saw him [Jesus], it immediately threw the boy into convulsions. He fell to the ground and rolled around, foaming at the mouth." Similarly, Beja culture contains embedded references to the power of the cross over evil. Ausenda tells of more Beja customs featuring the cross:

> When a boy is born, women pick up a piece of steel or a pan and hit it with a stone making a bell-like sound. They go on for about

---

[178] A. Paul, "Notes on the Beni-Amer," *SNR* 31, no. 2 (1950): 233.

[179] Quranic fumigation involves the healer burning selected pages of the book. The smoke fumigates the patient and cures the sufferer.

[180] In "A Fiki's Clinic" Hussey says of the fiki or faki, "It is generally rendered in English as *holy-man* or *religious leader* and is used, indifferently to describe the Head of a religious sect big or small, the guardian of a holy tomb, a man of well known piety who has no particular diocese or religious function, a curer and a school master of a *khalwa* or Koran school" (35).

[181] Halim, "Native Medicine and Ways of Treatment," 28.

a quarter of an hour, both at dawn and sunset, for seven days. At sunset they will also light a small fire in front of the mother's tent. On the day of the child's birth, a man will kill a sheep or a goat or a small calf. The women will be given the meat to cook. With its blood, they will trace several crescents and crosses on each side of the first birch mat covering the front of the tent. Seven days later during the naming ceremony, the same procedure is followed.

As soon as the crescent [moon] reappears in the sky at sunset, people turn toward it standing and say: "*Afoy aeb*," meaning: "Pardon my shameful (acts)." The two symbols epitomize the two main traditions that have influenced the Beja. The cross, symbol of the Christian tradition, with which Hadendowa [*Beja* division] may have become acquainted during the thousand-year long period of Nubian Christianity, is a sign of mercy and redemption through expiation and purification. The crescent, symbol of the Muslim tradition, is a sign of restoration of health and wellbeing.[182]

The evangelist must take care when using redemptive analogies with those holding a fear/power worldview. After accepting the gospel, Simon the Magician misinterpreted the apostles' miracles and desired to purchase their power with money (Acts 8:9–24). As Hesselgrave warns, "Points of contact have significance, but they also have limitations."[183] Redemptive analogies should not leave the impression that the Christian condones the folk practices, or the cross may become another charm to them. The same cautions apply to encounters with folk Muslims, whose varied customs contain the basis for many redemptive analogies. A good method is to briefly cite the cultural custom and then quickly move to the Bible and the point the passage makes. The apostle Paul exemplifies this tactic in his evangelistic presentation in Athens:[184]

---

[182] Ausenda, "Leisurely Nomads," 417–18.

[183] Hesselgrave, *Paradigms in Conflict*, 106.

[184] Multiple missiologists reference this passage to prove points on different sides of many issues: Hesselgrave in *Paradigms in Conflict*, 105; Van Rheenen in *Communicating*

Paul stood in the middle of the Areopagus and said,[185] "People of Athens! I see that you are extremely religious in every respect. For as I was passing through and observing the objects of your worship, I even found an altar on which was inscribed, 'To an Unknown God.'[186] Therefore, what you worship in ignorance, this I proclaim to you." (Acts 17:22–23)

Paul began his second missionary journey in Asia Minor by assessing the welfare of his newly planted churches. After receiving the "Macedonian call" to preach the gospel in Europe (Acts 16:9), he traveled to Macedonia and Achaia. A brief interlude found Paul in Athens waiting for Silas and Timothy. As he preached in the marketplace, some Greek philosophers heard a message about "strange deities" and took Paul to another location for him to plead his case.[187] In his opening statement to the Areopagus,[188]

Christ in Animistic Contexts, 246; Greeson in *The Camel*, 17; Musk in *Touching the Soul of Islam*, 19; Schlorff in *Missiological Models in Ministry to Muslims*, 120–21; Saal in *Reaching Muslims for Christ*, 149; and Richardson in *Peace Child*, 9–23, represent but a few.

[185] F. F. Bruce, in *The Acts of the Apostles* (Grand Rapids: Eerdmans, 1952), writes, "[The Areopagus was] the most venerable Athenian court. . . . Its traditional power was curtailed as Athens became more democratic but it retained authority over homicide and moral questions generally. . . . Under the Romans it increased its prestige. It had supreme authority in religious matters and seems also to have had the power at this time to appoint public lecturers and exercise some control of them in the interest of public order" (333).

[186] The early Greek historian Diogenes Laertius stated, "The Athenians during a pestilence sent for Epimenides the Cretan who advised them to sacrifice sheep at various spots, and to commemorate the occasion, altars to unnamed gods were set up." Bruce, *The Acts of the Apostles*, 335–36.

[187] Charles W. Carter and Ralph Earle, in *The Acts of the Apostles* (Grand Rapids: Zondervan, 1959), write, "Certainly if our thesis is correct that Paul's address before the Areopagus was his defense against charges of advocating a new, unauthorized religion, then his choice of the inscription from the altar TO AN UNKNOWN GOD was indeed a master stroke. Their UNKNOWN GOD whose worship was fully authorized and thus made legal in Athens, Paul declared to be the subject of his preaching in Athens. Thus the Athenian charge, 'He seems to be a proclaimer of strange deities,' was abrogated by Paul's declaration" (276).

[188] "Whether Paul appeared before the Court of the *Areopagus* in the *Agora* (market) or was led to the top of Mars Hill is a topic of perennial dispute. Ramsey argues at

the apostle quickly made the connection between an element of ancient Greek cultural worship and the gospel. Paul opened his gospel presentation by referring to a centuries-old altar "[t]o an Unknown God." He used their concept of deity as a point of departure[189] for defining the true nature and identity of God. Gerhard Kittel writes:

> In his preaching at Athens, Paul makes use of the pantheistic sense of God common to the Greeks, and attempts on this basis to open up to them the way to a full belief in God. . . . Hence this statement is to be regarded merely as an acknowledged starting-point for his missionary preaching, not as a full confession of his theological convictions.[190]

Contextualization reinterprets, or replaces, non-Christian religious concepts with Christian truths in order to cross-culturally communicate the gospel of Christ. Paul does not link the "Unknown God" with the Christian God in a one-to-one equivalency. Rather, the apostle fills in their concept of divinity with God's true essence. Hesselgrave observes, "Since the 'unknown god' was unknown, Paul did not obligate himself to empty the Greek concept of false notions. And Paul moved quickly from the general idea offered by the Greek writers to the specifics of special revelation and Christ's incarnation."[191]

High-quality redemptive analogies, points of contact, illustrations, eye-openers, and bridges possess several positive characteristics. (1) They

---

length that Paul spoke in the *Agora*. . . . In the first century, the Court of the Areopagus met in a portico northwest of the Agora . . . [but] Cadbury . . . warns us: 'The possibilities must be left open that the council sometimes met on the hill of the Areopagus and not in the *Agora* even in later times, or that Paul spoke on the hill but not to an official group.'" Carter and Earle, *The Acts of the Apostles*, 257.

[189] Don Richardson calls the apostle Paul's allusion an "eye opener," while others see a redemptive analogy. Richardson, *Eternity in their Hearts*, 3rd ed. (Ventura, CA: Regal Books, 2005), 19.

[190] Gerhard Kittel and Gerhard Friedrich, eds., *Theological Dictionary of the New Testament*, trans. Geoffrey W. Bromiley (Grand Rapids: Eerdmans, 1968) 3:718–19.

[191] Hesselgrave, *Paradigms in Conflict*, 106.

explain biblical truth without distracting from the gospel presentation by becoming mired in the example itself. (2) They move quickly from the illustrative idea to the main message. (3) They refer to one of the key gospel concepts, such as the atonement, the crucifixion, or the resurrection, rather than peripheral matters. No better model of these principles exists than Acts 17:16–34.

A Biblical Approach to the Three Worldviews

Previous sections of this chapter identified guilt/innocence, shame/honor, and fear/power as the three primary worldviews. All cultures possess in varied proportions these three elements.[192] While fear/power concerns prevail among ATR groups, issues from the other worldviews also surface. This section offers a biblical pattern for addressing the concerns of popular religion. Three ways of viewing these issues are evident.

The power encounter tries to match the power of folk religion with the miraculous power of God. Missions scholars define the subject differently. Speaking of the power encounter, Van Rheenen says, "These confrontations with the forces of Satan require visible demonstrations of the power of God in animistic contexts."[193] Despite this pronouncement, all of Van Rheenen's modern examples describe national believers defying ATR taboos and other cultural conventions, not actively performing miracles.[194] Over time the power encounter has come to signify the display of signs and wonders in third wave Pentecostalism.[195] No mission scholar disagrees with believers refusing to participate in ATR rites and would accept a power-encounter idea defined this way. Controversy ensues when some missionaries favor miracles as a mission strategy.

---

[192] See Muller, *Honor & Shame*, 70.
[193] Van Rheenen, *Communicating Christ in Animistic Contexts*, 62.
[194] Van Rheenen, 86–90.
[195] See Hesselgrave, *Paradigms in Conflict*, 176–77.

Second, the scientific (or secular) encounter largely ignores the middle-level issues of ATR. Rather, it favors agricultural, medical, educational, and developmental projects in order to alleviate this-world problems so the missionary can present the promise of the next. Christian workers of the modern persuasion often relegate eternal matters to theory while science rules in everyday life.[196] This method fails to answer the causality questions about the supernatural posed by folk religion.

With the power encounter unpredictable and the scientific encounter inadequate, I propose a third method of addressing the concerns of folk religion. The spirit encounter takes seriously people's mystic beliefs and anxieties about the spirit world. Rather than demanding signs and wonders, the spirit encounter welcomes divine power when God chooses to bring a miracle, but confronts the supernatural world with the true spirit, the Holy Spirit.

One of our nationals, Jonadab, told me that one of his members encountered persecution in her village along a large river in North Africa. Her husband was upset because she had become a Christian. He took her Bible outside the house, placed it on the ground, and poured gasoline over it. The Bible refused to burn.[197]

Years later, I was traveling in an open Land Rover between two desert towns in North Africa with another Christian worker and four Ethiopian nationals. The heat was overwhelming, and it had not rained in many months. The rainy season was months away. Despite the cloudless sky above me, I prayed out loud in the hearing of everyone, "Lord, please send some rain to cool us off." Within five minutes, a cloud appeared overhead, and a significant cloudburst rained directly over our vehicle. We stopped the car and stood out in the rain rejoicing. All were quite impressed. Nonetheless, I have only felt led of the Holy Spirit to pray for rain that one time in April 1991. In addition, Jonadab told me that the incident of the Bible

---

[196] See Hesselgrave, 194–95.
[197] Jonadab, interview with the author.

refusing to burn only happened once as well. I believe God brings about power encounters, but they come only at his choosing and certainly solely at his discretion. Communicating these theological truths to ATR constitutes a daunting challenge.

Many missionaries today understand that biblical truths couched in stories, parables, and illustrations better convey cross-cultural spiritual messages than propositional tracts or sermons.[198] Sometimes, however, the missionary lacks the appropriate framework for communicating the content necessary for discipleship. Stories often seem indirect, while propositional arguments fail to inspire. Somehow the world of the theoretical, the reality of the supernatural, and the practicality of the present must all be addressed by the Holy Spirit. To this end, I have selected scriptures from 1 John that speak to the ATR worldview of the Beja of Sudan (and the Sukuma of Tanzania), confronting the guilt/innocence, shame/honor, and fear/power elements of their worldview.

The Beja believe in the activity of the devil and his evil spirits. First John confronts the issues of the spirit world directly. The apostle John (1 John 2:13) tells believers, "You have conquered the evil one," and, "The Son of God was revealed for this purpose: to destroy the devil's works" (3:8). In his letter, the apostle admonishes Christians to "test the spirits" to determine their origin (4:1). In contrast to the evil forces of traditional religion that require exorcism, John presents the promise of another spirit, the "Spirit of truth," who brings joy and fulfillment (John 14:16–17).[199] The apostle writes, "This is how we know that we remain in him and he in us: He has given us of his Spirit" (1 John 4:13).

---

[198] See Pikkert, *Protestant Missionaries to the Middle East*, 202–3.

[199] "I will ask the Father, and he will give you another Counselor to be with you forever. He is the **Spirit of truth**. The world is unable to receive him because it doesn't see him or know him. But you do know him, because he remains with you and **will be in you**." (John 14:16–17, bold mine)

Additionally, 1 John 4:18 speaks directly to the fear/power paradigm: "There is no fear in love; instead, perfect love drives out fear, because fear involves punishment. So the one who fears is not complete in love." The following verses capture the essence of confronting ATR:

> Everyone who has been born of God conquers the world. This is the victory that has conquered the world: our faith.
>
> Who is the one who conquers the world but the one who believes that Jesus is the Son of God? Jesus Christ—he is the one who came by water and blood, not by water only, but by water and by blood. And the Spirit is the one who testifies, because the Spirit is the truth. For there are three that testify: the Spirit, the water, and the blood—and these three are in agreement. If we accept human testimony, God's testimony is greater, because it is God's testimony that he has given about his Son. . . . And this is the testimony: God has given us eternal life, and this life is in his Son. (1 John 5:4–9, 11)

This passage speaks to all three of the worldviews within folk religion. First, the blood addresses the guilt/innocence worldview by fulfilling the legal demands of a blood sacrifice for sin. Second, the water represents baptism, symbolizing a public identification with Christ and his church and humility before God, which deals with shame/honor concerns. Third, the Spirit of God, who honored Christ at his baptism (John 1:32–33), stands in clear contrast to the spirits of ATR. This threefold testimony (the Spirit, the water, and the blood) conquers the world and the spiritual forces of ATR. Overcoming the world by a spirit encounter addresses the middle-level issues of ATR as well as the religious value ideas rooted in the fear/power, shame/honor, and guilt/innocence worldviews. This passage constitutes a simple scriptural framework for discipling ATR background folk Muslims, helping them conquer their fears of the spirit world. In turn, the might of Christ's resurrection enables them to live victoriously in the Holy Spirit's power in the midst of the middle-level challenges of everyday life.

Conclusion

As Hesselgrave aptly observes, "A mind-boggling variety of approaches to 'discipling the nations' has been advocated during the era of modern missions."[200] A few suggest that folk Muslims should be engaged through their worldview rather than by methods such as polemics, apologetics, dialogue, cultural concessions, or adjusting Quranic and Islamic forms.

This chapter presents a contextualized approach for evangelizing popular Muslims like the Beja tribe of Sudan by addressing their fear/power worldview. In addition, I analyze the worldview themes of shame/honor and guilt/innocence that possess secondary significance for them. I propose a scriptural model from the Epistle of First John that presents a threefold testimony of Christ: the Spirit, the water, and the blood. This example addresses the issues and meets the needs of all three of the major worldviews.

---

[200] Hesselgrave, *Paradigms in Conflict*, 184.

Contextualizing *TO THE* Worldview *OF* Sufi Folk Islam

S ome years ago, I approached an old mosque near the foot of a large mountain in North Africa. At the entrance of the mosque stood a shrine commemorating a departed Sufi sheikh. A tattered white robe, encased in glass to preserve the fabric, helped the Sufi folk Muslims remember the past power of their former leader. As I walked by, several prayed to his robe, asking for protection, power, and good fortune.

Folk religions confront different questions than do formal faiths. Orthodoxy cares about doctrines, rules, regulations, prescriptions, and prohibitions. Popular religion, on the other hand, yearns for experience, feeling, and power. Hiebert, Shaw, and Tienou explain, "Folk religions give people a sense of meaning by answering the existential questions of everyday life, and providing the living a sense of place and worth in their society and world."[1]

The previous chapter showed that folk religions frequently address life through fear/power, shame/honor, and guilt/innocence worldviews in their cultures. Nonetheless, there is also a strain within folk religion that searches for a deeper reality. Nilsson says, "There exists in every man a dormant longing to enter into communion with the divine, to feel himself lifted up

---

[1] Hiebert, Shaw, and Tienou, *Understanding Folk Religion*, 95 (see intro., n. 6).

from the temporal into the spiritual."[2] This felt need for spirituality forms the existential/transcendent worldview. Making the transcendence of God immanent in one's life is the essence of this final worldview. This chapter introduces a fourth worldview as a grid for understanding and evangelizing popular Muslims who yearn for a deeper life. I propose reaching them through their existential/transcendent worldview.

Existential/Transcendent Approaches for Islam

Orthodox Islam emphasizes God's transcendence over his immanence.[3] The religious worldview of popular Islam differs markedly from that of official Islam. Braswell writes:

> Folk Islam appears to address the heartfelt and spiritual needs of a people. It desires a God who is near and not far away. Christianity is challenged to understand the differences between Quranic Islam and folk Islam and to determine if folk Islam for Muslims addresses some of the issues and needs of humanity which may be expressed in Christianity but which may be denied or challenged in Quranic Islam.[4]

Muslim orthodoxy emphasizes the concrete rather than the abstract, the lawful over the devotional. The Quran and the Hadith address questions such as the bodily resurrection and heaven's reward in tangible and specific terms.[5] The Islam of orthodoxy consists of adhering to convention and observing the religion's strict statutes. Ruthven states, "The proper

---

[2] William Nilsson, quoted in Parshall, *Bridges to Islam*, 1 (see intro., n. 4).

[3] See Zebiri, *Muslims and Christians Face to Face*, 9 (see chap. 9, n. 30).

[4] Braswell, *Islam*, 286 (see intro., n. 28).

[5] According to the Hadith, the Prophet Muhammad is reported to have said, "Everything of the human body will decay except the coccyx bone (of the tail) and from that bone Allah will reconstruct the whole body." Braswell, 54. The Quran itself pictures heaven in the vivid imagery of the Middle Eastern harem featuring sensual and sexual experiences. Ruthven, *Islam in the World*, 55 (see chap. 2, n. 6).

approach for a Muslim is to submit to the decrees of God, as represented by the laws of nature and the rules laid down in the Quran and the Prophet's Sunna."[6] The difference between official Islam and folk Islam is straightforward: orthodox Muslims follow a faith that is otherworldly, unknowable,[7] and distant from the problems of everyday people.[8] Folk Muslims desire a religion close to home, so to speak, and accessible to answer their supernatural fears and immediate life questions. While many solve these middle-level problems by ATR-like practices, others address these issues by following the Sufi path.

Parshall calls Sufism "a fairly well-defined influence within folk Islam" and claims that "without understanding Sufism, one cannot understand folk Islam."[9] Whereas non-Sufi, ATR-influenced folk Muslims see life through a fear/power worldview, Sufis come at the supernatural differently.[10] They long for a personal relationship with God.[11] Speaking of the Sufi, Parshall claims, "The Muslim mystic hopes, even in this mortal life, to win a glimpse of immortality."[12] Sufis live in the existential "now," contemplating the uniqueness of each moment.[13] In other words, the Sufi desires the transcendent to invade the immanent (his or her[14] own existential reality), bypassing the middle level altogether. Commenting on the Sufis, Ruthven says:

> The Sufi movement brought an inner spirituality into an Islam which otherwise tended to crystallize into a religion concerned mainly with the outward forms of legal observance and the pursuit

---

[6] Ruthven, 221.

[7] See Saal, *Reaching Muslims for Christ*, 43 (see intro., n. 3).

[8] See Pikkert, *Protestant Missionaries to the Middle East*, 198 (see chap. 7, n. 2).

[9] Parshall, *Bridges to Islam*, 4, 12 (see intro., n. 4).

[10] Parshall notes that early Muslim mysticism was fear-based. By the ninth century, however, concepts of God's love, meditation, and ascetic practices entered Islam (6, 15).

[11] See Orville Boyd Jenkins, *The Path of Love: Jesus in Mystical Islam* (Nairobi: Communication Press, 1984), 7.

[12] Parshall, *Bridges to Islam*, 13.

[13] See Chittick, *Sufism*, 45 (see chap. 4, n. 4).

[14] Sufism permits female disciples. See Ernst, *The Shambhala Guide to Sufism*, 143 (see chap. 4, n. 4).

of political power. The contemplation of the "god within" revitalized Islam, replenishing its psychic reserves and fructifying its structures, both legal and intellectual, with a new injection of energy.[15]

Sufis have been called the mystics of Islam.[16] However, Sufi scholars Ernst and Chittick reject the mystic label as too narrow a description. Since Sufism was covered in an earlier chapter, attention here is devoted to scriptural approaches for reaching Sufis by means of an existential/transcendent worldview. Musk advises that the gospel be expressed in "emotive terms" to reach the heart of the Muslim.[17] This rings true especially in the case of the Sufis, who revel in feeling, emotion, and experience. Sufis certainly fit the category of those more guided by their feelings than by reason. One Sufi, named Uways Qarani, claimed to communicate with the Prophet telepathically. Ibn Al-Rawandi says the *Nasqshbandiyaa Tariqa* (Sufi order) still practices this.[18] It seems Sufis are open to anything. Pikkert says, "A 'substantial number' of Muslims testify their conversion to Christianity is the result of 'a search for truth.'"[19] Their longing for a personal relationship with God trumps orthodox Islam's aspirations. Parshall observes, "The Sufi generally places more emphasis on his relationship to God now than on that which is to come."[20] For these reasons Sufism requires special consideration and a unique slant.

I believe the concept of discipleship holds promise for reaching Sufi folk Muslims. In their eagerness to follow God in a disciplined way, individual Sufis submit to a mentor (*Shaykh*) for guidance.[21] A chain of master/disciple relationships links the teacher to the student from generation to generation.[22]

---

[15] Ruthven, *Islam in the World*, 222.

[16] See Sookhdeo, *Global Jihad*, 167 (see chap. 2, n. 2).

[17] Musk, *Touching the Soul of Islam*, 188 (see chap. 9, n. 69).

[18] Ibn Al-Rawandi, *Islamic Mysticism: A Secular Perspective* (Amherst, NY: Prometheus Books, 2000), 118.

[19] Pikkert, *Protestant Missionaries to the Middle East*, 194.

[20] Parshall, *Bridges to Islam*, 13.

[21] See Karrar, *The Sufi Brotherhoods in the Sudan*, 152 (see chap. 4, n. 2).

[22] See Ausenda, "Leisurely Nomads," 448 (see chap. 4, n. 67).

As the Christian worker challenges the Sufi to follow the "Master Teacher" in discipleship, Jesus speaks to the everyday needs of popular Islam, saying, "Come to me, all of you who are weary and burdened, and I will give you rest. Take up my yoke and learn from me, because I am lowly and humble in heart, and you will find rest for your souls. For my yoke is easy and my burden is light" (Matt 11:28–30). These verses appeal to Sufis because their path of asceticism and denial is difficult, not light.

Sufism also contains a concept similar to the new birth in Christianity. Speaking of Islam as an imbibed cup of love seeking the face of God, Sufi writer Zia Inayat-Khan writes, "Befall what may, do not turn aside, and when ceaseless devotion has transported you from self-possession to oblivion and back again, and your heart has been shattered and made whole again, you will become as new, as one reborn, a child of the moment."[23] When taking on the "way of Sufism" (*tasawwuf*), the new initiate "dies to self" (*fana*, self-extinction) in order to "live to God."[24] This new "life in God" (*baqa*, subsistence) allows the Sufi to be "perfected, transmuted and eternalized through God and in God."[25] The Sufi desire for union with God possesses possibilities for parallels in Christianity.[26] In John 3:3, Jesus said to the Jewish ruler Nicodemus, "Truly I tell you, unless someone is born again, he cannot see the kingdom of God." The necessity of a changed spiritual life, even on the part of a religious leader like Nicodemus, speaks to the Sufi heart. In fact, some Sufis refer to this passage and the "born twice" concept in their quest for spiritual truth.[27]

---

[23] Zia Inayat-Khan, *Saracen Chivalry: Counsels on Valor, Generosity and the Mystical Quest* (New Lebanon, NY: Omega Publications, 2012), 151.

[24] Ruthven, *Islam in the World*, 228.

[25] Arthur J. Arberry, *Sufism: An Account of the Mystics of Islam* (London: Allen and Unwin, 1950), 58.

[26] See Ruthven, *Islam in the World*, 227.

[27] Some Sufis suggest that the born-again concept is similar to the Hadith's "die before you die" prescription. Chittick, *Sufism*, 138.

The Sufi respect for all biblical characters mentioned in the Quran offers potential common ground for discussions with Muslims about scriptural truths. Sufi master Junaid names seven biblical characters in the following lesson:

In Sufism, eight qualities must be exercised. The Sufi has:
Liberality such as that of Abraham;
Acceptance of his lot, as Ismail accepted;
Patience, as possessed by Job;
Capacity to communicate symbolism, as in the case of Zachariah;
Estrangement from his own people, which was the case with John;
Woolen garb like the shepherd's mantle of Moses;
Journeying, like the traveling of Jesus;
Humility, as Muhammad had humility of spirit.[28]

Most Muslims think very highly of Jesus Christ, and many of them who become Christians do so because of the lofty description of him in the Quran.[29] Sufis especially revere Christ. The Sufi poet Al-Hallaj "looked to Jesus as the supreme example of glorified, or perfected humanity, as the actualizer of this Quranic concept of the image of God in man."[30] This awe about the person of Christ can serve as a point of entry with folk Islam.

Several other concepts hold promise as redemptive analogies. The Sufi poet Rumi describes the love of God[31] in the following manner: "What is it to be a lover? To have perfect thirst. So let me explain the water of life."[32] Since Sufis view God's love as the water of life, a biblical parallel is evident. Jesus tells the woman at the well (John 4:10) about the living water that He

---

[28] Quoted in Ahmed, *Islam Today*, 51 (see chap. 1, n. 1).
[29] See Pikkert, *Protestant Missionaries to the Middle East*, 192–93.
[30] Jenkins, *The Path of Love*, 27–28.
[31] As a response to inflexible Muslim theological beliefs, "love became the Sufi byword." Parshall, *Bridges to Islam*, 36.
[32] Quoted in Chittick, *Sufism*, 64.

brings.[33] The analogy follows that only Jesus has the true water of life, which is related to the love the Sufi desires.

In addition, Sufis possess quite a developed theology of spiritual "veils." Concerning the Muslim practice of veiling, Fadwa El Guindi writes, "The link between dress, women and sanctity of space is also reflected in the Islamic rituals of 'dressing' [or veiling] the *Ka'ba*, the center of the holy site of pilgrimage in Makka."[34] This interesting concept also has a potential theological point of contact. Veil theory in Sufism flows from interpretations of fourteen occurrences of the Arabic verb *kashf* (remove) in the Quran. Chittick explains one of these:

> In the most significant of these passages for the *Sufi* use of the term [*kashf* or remove], God addresses the soul that has just died: "You were heedless of this—therefore we have *removed* from you your covering, and your sight today is piercing" (50:22). The "covering" (*ghita*)—a term that is taken as one of several synonyms for "veil" (*hijab*)—will be lifted at death. Then people will see clearly. This verse alone is enough to suggest why the quest for voluntary death is one of the basic themes of *Sufi* literature.[35]

Esoteric, nuanced, and complicated summarizes Sufi teaching about veils. Nonetheless, several important features stand out. Complete unveiling takes place at death. Chittick writes that "when the Sufi who achieves the death and annihilation of the lower self already in this life, they also achieve the vision of God, here and now."[36] True Sufis experience the lifting of the veil in this life described in very paradoxical imagery.[37] Ibn Arabi portrays the entire universe as a veil. He further describes the goal of the Sufi path as an obliteration "through which all awareness of the individual self is

---

[33] "Jesus answered, 'If you knew the gift of God, and who is saying to you, "Give me a drink," you would ask him, and he would give you living water.'"

[34] Fadwa El Guindi, *Veil: Modesty, Privacy and Resistance* (Oxford: Berg, 2003), 95.

[35] Chittick, *Sufism*, 138.

[36] Chittick, 139.

[37] See Chittick, 139–40.

erased by the intensity of the unveiling."[38] Muhammad said in the Hadith, according to Sufi teaching, "God has seventy veils of light and darkness."[39] The Sufi poet Niffari speculates that anything other than God is a veil.[40] Mustamli asserts that a number of veils must be lifted before anyone can be a true follower of Allah and Muhammad:

> The veils are four—this world, the self, people and Satan. This world is the veil of the next world. People are the veil of obedience. Everyone who has busied himself at the feet of people has let go of obedience. Satan is the veil of religion. Everyone who conforms with Satan has let go of religion. The self is the veil of the Real. Everyone who goes along with the self's caprice, He says, has made his own caprice his god. God says, "Have you seen him who has taken his caprice as his god" (45:23). . . . As long as these four veils have not been lifted from the heart, the light of *gnosis* will not find a way into it. . . . The sum of all that has been said about the veil is that everything that busies the servant with other than the Real is a veil, and everything that takes the servant to the Real is not a veil. The light of *gnosis* is the strongest of all lights, and everything that tries to veil the *Gnostics* from the Real will be burned away and pushed aside by the light of *gnosis*.[41]

Of course, official Islam deems Sufi mysticism, rituals, and doctrinal speculation un-Islamic.[42] Arberry writes that some Sufis "introduced the *Logos* doctrine into Islam. . . . If any man aspired to know God, he might seek this end by achieving union with the 'Idea of Muhammad.'"[43] Sufism's serious desire for a personal relationship with God impresses Christians.

---

[38] Ibn Arabi in Chittick, 147, 149.
[39] Quoted in Chittick, 139.
[40] See Chittick, 146.
[41] Mustamli in Chittick, 141.
[42] See Ernst, *The Shambhala Guide to Sufism*, 213.
[43] Arberry, *Sufism*, 93.

Rather than arguing veil theories, the Christian should refer to the Bible passages about veils and apply the analogies in them to speak of salvation in Christ. The apostle Paul writes:

> But whenever a person turns to the Lord, the veil is removed. Now the Lord is the Spirit, and where the Spirit of the Lord is, there is freedom. We all, with unveiled faces, are looking as in a mirror at the glory of the Lord and are being transformed into the same image from glory to glory; this is from the Lord, who is the Spirit. (2 Cor 3:16–18)

Paul's veil passage (2 Cor 3:7–4:4) contains some parallel mystical ideas that should intrigue the Sufi seeker. Paul presents the veil as an illustration of the old covenant, represented by Moses wearing a veil to hide the law's fading glory (3:13) and the veiling of Israel's minds and hearts (3:14). Christian unveiling, unlike Sufi unveiling, occurs when a person turns to the Christ. Paul also contends that the gospel is veiled to unbelievers (4:3) due to Satan's influence (4:4). A parallel exists with Sufi veiling at this juncture because Satan is one of the four veils in Mustamli's system.[44]

The Sufi should be challenged to turn to the Lord through Jesus Christ, remove the veil and behold God's glory, receive the Holy Spirit, and be transformed into conformity with God's magnificent image. The Sufi should also be told that only the believer in Jesus experiences real unveiling and receives the opportunity to view God's true glory. Another verse points to Jesus Christ as the true veil for entry into eternal life. The writer of Hebrews explains, "Therefore, brethren, since we have confidence to enter the holy place by the blood of Jesus, by a new and living way which He inaugurated for us through the **veil**, that is, His flesh . . ." (Heb 10:19–20 NASB, bold mine). In this way a favorite Sufi concept illustrates a biblical truth and invites the folk Muslim to enter salvation through the veil of Jesus.

---

[44] See Chittick, *Sufism*, 141.

Existential/Transcendence Approaches for Beja

As previously mentioned, the Beja hold primarily to a fear/power world-view mixed with some elements of the shame/honor and guilt/innocence motifs. Despite this, another worldview has a strong presence inside the countries where they live. Karrar identifies Sufism as "the most fundamental characteristic of Islam in North Africa."[45] Of the twenty-nine Sufi *tarikas* (orders) operating inside North Africa,[46] seven of these claim numbers of Beja among their adherents.[47] Although the majority are nominally Muslim, those who regularly practice Islam's tenets generally follow the Sufi path.[48] Ausenda describes Beja Sufism in this way:

> *Sufi tarikas*, or "ways," are sects, which profess to achieve closeness to God through the teaching of mystical thought and the perfor-mance of special ecstasy-inducing rituals. Perhaps for this reason, *Sufi* movements have had considerable success among Beja in gen-eral and *Hadendowa* in particular.[49]

While most Beja follow an ATR mindset and fall within a fear/power worldview paradigm, a serious Sufi tradition exists among them as well. When I asked an MBB how the Beja viewed the Sufis, he told me that "the people respect them."[50] The previously mentioned methods and concepts for communicating the gospel with Sufis also apply to their Beja broth-ers and sisters. However, another cultural point of contact stands out as a redemptive analogy for Beja Sufis.

Shaaban claims that a Beja territory always contains one particular mountain to which the *diwab* (clan) believes it possesses a particular ritual relationship.[51] For example, the important Beja Sufi shrine, mentioned at

---

[45] Karrar, *The Sufi Brotherhoods in the Sudan*, 1.
[46] Karrar, 233.
[47] See Ausenda, "Leisurely Nomads," 434.
[48] See Jacobsen, *Theories of Sickness and Misfortune*, 22.
[49] Ausenda, "Leisurely Nomads," 434.
[50] Faisal Faruk, in an interview with the author.
[51] Shaaban in Hjort and Dahl, *Responsible Man*, 61 (see chap. 6, n. 75).

the beginning of this chapter, rests at the foot of *Jebel* (Mount) Kassala. This mountain is believed to contain magical powers and possesses unusual significance in Beja folklore. The concept of a special mountain's significance corresponds well to the cultural situation Jesus encountered with the woman at the well near Mount Gerizim:

> [The Samaritan woman said,] "Our ancestors worshiped on this mountain, but you Jews say that the place to worship is in Jerusalem." Jesus told her, "Believe Me, woman, an hour is coming when you will worship the Father neither on this mountain nor in Jerusualem.[52] You Samaritans worship what you do not know. We worship what we do know, because salvation is from the Jews. But an hour is coming, and is now here, when the true worshipers will worship the Father in Spirit and in truth. Yes, the Father wants such people to worship him. God is spirit, and those who worship him must worship in Spirit and in truth." (John 4:20–24)

Sufis are truth seekers, and they believe that by passing through a series of veils, one can obtain gnosis (*ma'rifa*, mystic knowledge) and approach the throne of God spiritually in this life.[53] In the fourth chapter of John's Gospel, Jesus announces the beginning of a new spiritual era. Spirit and truth within the heart would characterize true worship.[54] God's spiritual presence would dwell within His worshippers, not in temporal locations

---

[52] A dispute existed between the Samaritans and the Jews over which mountain was the mountain of God: Mount Moriah in Jerusalem or Mount Gerizim near Jacob's well. The Samaritan nation was formed when the king of Assyria brought five eastern tribes into Palestine after the northern kingdom of Israel was carried away into captivity (2 Kings 17:24–41). They brought their own gods with them but also adopted some practices from Judaism. The Samaritans held that since the Israelites raised an altar on Mount Gerizim in the time of Joshua, and the Jews' subsequent move of the temple site to Jerusalem is nowhere mentioned in the Pentateuch, the true place of worship had to be Mount Gerizim. See Frederick L. Godet, *Commentary on the Gospel of John*, 3rd ed., trans. Timothy Dwight (Grand Rapids: Zondervan, 1969, repr. of 1893 Funk & Wagnalls ed.), 426–27.

[53] See Chittick, *Sufism*, 141.

[54] See Godet, *Commentary on the Gospel of John*, 430.

such as mountains and temples—and by extension to the present-day, fixed locations, such as mosques, shrines, or churches. Real estate issues so important to the officials of high religions fade into obscurity in comparison to the true spiritual worship of God face-to-face. This analogy would make sense to Beja mystics trying to balance an allegiance to their kinship group's attachment to a special mountain with the constraints of their Sufi ritual observances at the shrine of their order's principal saint.

Conclusion

Since about half of all Islam involves some degree of Sufism, Christians must develop biblical approaches that fit this folk Islamic worldview. Because most methods for engaging Muslims center on orthodoxy, Christianity misses those who follow traditional and Sufi practices. This chapter has advocated for searching for scriptures that challenge and fulfill the existential/transcendent worldview of Sufi folk Islam.

CONCLUSION

This book examines folk Islam and the contextualization approaches for evangelizing adherents from this perspective. Most methods for reaching Muslims have focused on apologetic arguments, cultural adjustments, and Islamic forms. These approaches give little attention to folk Islam, which is the religion practiced by the vast majority of Muslims today. This book, therefore, centers on folk Islam and the practices observed by real people. Since the majority of Muslims live outside the Arab world, this book has potential value for places located on the fringes of Islam's heartland.

I have examined the most effective approaches for communicating the gospel and evangelizing folk Muslims. As a result, I believe concepts contextualized to the fear/power worldview better meet the needs and coincide more closely with the beliefs of popular Islam. I have also noticed that elements of the shame/honor and guilt/innocence worldviews persist, although with lesser intensity. For Sufi folk Muslims, I believe an existential/ transcendent worldview approach, customized to those desiring a personal spiritual relationship with God, is the best approach. This is because apologetic arguments and contextualized Islamic and Quranic frameworks possess limited value in reaching folk Muslim mystics such as the Sufis or even traditional religionists.

Christian missions has responded to the Muslim challenge in diverse ways. Some evangelists over the years have formulated apologetic and polemic arguments to refute Islam and demonstrate the superiority of the Christian faith. Other Christians have fallen prey to accommodating Islam by dialogue methods, which attempt to move Muslims from Islam to Christianity through discussion and mutual understanding. Recently, experimentation with various contextualization methods has emerged as a third broad category.[1] Such techniques attempt to fill Islamic forms with Christian meaning or overlay a biblical hermeneutic upon Quranic passages. Although the apologetic approach has produced limited fruit among the adherents of orthodox Islam, such methods fall far short with folk Muslims, who either fail to grasp the arguments or dismiss their applicability. Musk's observations are very much to the point:

> In the experience of the masses, the official faith by and large fails to meet everyday needs. . . . The God of Islamic theology would appear to be so far removed from humans' lives that substitute focuses of power are sought in and through the practitioners of popular Islam.[2]

Similarly, current trends in contextualizing Muslim forms and Quranic passages to Christianity are troubling. While advances in the social sciences assist Christian workers in gaining more cultural understanding of Islam, they have also spawned an ethos of experimentation. Such a trial-and-error approach of blending Christian and Islamic structures has resulted in some syncretism and much confusion. The debate over the use or non-use of apologetic and contextualized methods is a moot point with regard to folk Islam. The presupposition of apologetics stems primarily from a Western guilt/innocence worldview. In other words, apologetic and most contextualized, techniques set out to prove the falsity of Islam over and against the truth of Christianity from a

---

[1] Schlorff rejects "the intuitive approach suggested by some—contextualization by experimentation." *Missiological Models*, 151 (see chap. 7, n. 22).

[2] Bill Musk, *Holy War: Why Do Some Muslims Become Fundamentalists?* (London: Monarch Books, 2003), 114.

right-or-wrong perspective. I certainly believe Christianity represents the true faith, and the Islamic system is false. Such questions, however, rarely cross the consciousness of folk Islam. Folk Muslims fear the spirit world and seek to gain power over it. Little has changed since Musk wrote the following more than forty years ago:[3]

> Much controversy has raged amongst Christians, both in public debate and via printed page (e.g., Schlorff 1980:144) concerning the philosophical and moral implications of attempts to bridge long-long standing Muslim-Christian differences. Our concern in these paragraphs is not with the rights and wrongs of such a methodology. Rather it is to emphasize that, while such bridging movements may be meaningful for the intellectual Muslim, they fall a long way short of communicating with Muslims committed to a folk-Islamic worldview. To commence with the ordinary Muslim "where he is" demands a reappraisal of such attempts at communication, however attractive they may appear to the Western mind.[4]

This book attempts such a reevaluation for reaching folk Islam. Unfortunately, in the past, many have simply tried to refute popular Islam as if it were a wayward form of orthodoxy rather than engaging the religion through its worldview. Hiebert, Shaw, and Tienou correctly point out the more appropriate response:

> It is important to note that a Christian response to folk religions is not to stamp them out. . . . The Christian answer to folk religions is to bring them under the lordship of Christ so that he can transform people in their everyday lives. Christianity does deal with heaven and eternity, but it also answers the questions folk religions

---

[3] In a trip to Sudan in July 2017, I asked a group of Muslim Background Believers if attempts to gain power over the spirit world were still practiced. The leaders of the Christian conference said yes.

[4] Musk, "Popular Islam," 285 (see intro., n. 5).

raise. Its answers, however, must be rooted in a biblical, not an animistic, worldview.[5]

Since the majority of the adherents of Islam are folk Muslims,[6] I propose approaches contextualized to their unique worldview.

Sometimes studies of ethnic groups describe historical practices as current culture when in fact the traditional customs have largely disappeared. This situation is not true among the Beja. Jacobsen observed local medical procedures described in literature written 200 years before to his own research.[7] Another writer reports that Beja culture had changed little during the last 1,000 years, and their religion had been minimally impacted by Islam over the last 500.[8] Even urban Beja culture appears little altered over time. Jacobsen thus reaches some important conclusions:

> Although living in a town clearly has some impact on rural people moving in, the towns themselves may also be changed in the process. Instead of echoing the usual point of view that the people of the Red Sea Hills are getting increasingly urbanized, one might state that the towns in some senses may be becoming increasingly ruralized. . . . I am inclined to argue, however, that the tribal traditions are not weak in the towns. They may even grow in importance as the towns get increasingly "tribalized."[9]

I believe Jacobsen makes a significant point. I have observed this remarkable trend during my eighteen years of living in Africa and South America—rural people importing their lifestyles, beliefs, and practices from the countryside into the city. Often, we assume that urban life impacts the rural person more than vice versa. Jacobsen argues the opposite, and I tend

---

[5] Hiebert, Shaw, and Tienou, *Understanding Folk Religion*, 91–92 (see intro., n. 6).

[6] See Parshall, *Bridges to Islam*, 2 (see intro., n. 4).

[7] Jacobsen, *Theories of Sickness and Misfortune*, 256 (see chap. 6, n. 39).

[8] Lewis, "Deim el Arab and the Beja Stevedores of Port Sudan," 37 (see chap. 6, n. 25).

[9] Jacobsen, *Theories of Sickness and Misfortune*, 44–45.

to agree with him. Sociologists rarely acknowledge the increasing impact of the rural worldview upon the cities of the two-thirds world.

Another important issue in missiology concerns whether or not adherents of traditional religions remain content in their folk beliefs. Jacobsen describes the Beja as terrified of spirits and uncertain about the future.[10] Hiebert, Shaw, and Tienou identify the issue this way:

> A final worldview theme that runs through nearly all folk religious belief systems is near constant fear and the need for security. In a world full of spirits, witchcraft, sorcery, black magic, curses, bad omens, broken taboos, angry ancestors, human enemies, and false accusations of many kinds, life is rarely carefree and secure. . . . Life for common folk, however, is not all fear. People find security in their kinship groups and joy in their community gatherings. They turn to ancestors and gods for help and to magic and divination to protect them from surrounding dangers.[11]

The Christian worker must not forget that folk Muslims are like unbelievers everywhere: people without Christ, coping with life as best they can within the limitations of their culture. The evangelist must proclaim the gospel of Christ to them, for it alone possesses the power to liberate those held captive by fear. As 1 John 4:18 states, "There is no fear in love; instead, perfect love drives out fear, because fear involves punishment. So the one who fears is not complete in love." The Christian must respectfully and tactfully condemn unbiblical popular religious beliefs and their accompanying practices which inspire this fear.

The goal of the Christian worker is to introduce the folk religionist to the One who can take away the fear of death and uncertainty in life, and love them unconditionally. Popular Islam must be confronted by the claims of Jesus. Since folk Islam dwells outside the boundaries of truth, there can

---

[10] Jacobsen, 150, 264.
[11] Hiebert, Shaw, and Tienou, *Understanding Folk Religion*, 87.

be no compromise or accommodation with it. Instead, the Christian must respectfully challenge it and lead its adherents out of Islam's grasp.

Final Thoughts

The religion of Islam is very much in the news today. A number of years ago, an article appeared in a prominent American newsmagazine, asking the question, "Is America Islamophobic?" The cover story reported that the increase in anti-Islamic sentiment in the United States might be partly traced to the controversy surrounding plans by a Muslim congregation to build an Islamic center near the site of the September 11, 2001, terrorist attacks on the World Trade Center in New York City. The following excerpt from *Time* magazine expresses the attitude toward Islam common today:

> The [anti-Islamic] arguments marshaled by Islam's detractors have become familiar: Since most terrorist attacks are conducted by Muslims and in the name of their faith, Islam must be a violent creed. Passages of the Koran taken out of context are brandished as evidence that Islam requires believers to kill or convert all others. Shari'a laws requiring the stoning of adulterers or other gruesome punishments serve as proof that Muslims are savage and backward. The conclusion of this line of reasoning is that Islam is a death cult, not a real religion. . . .
>
> Those railing against new mosques also use arguments of equivalence: Saudi Arabia doesn't allow churches and synagogues, so why should the U.S. permit the building of Islamic places of worship?[12]

Although many Christians advocate tolerance toward Muslims, this article illustrates that the polemic method of engaging Muslims persists. One Christian pastor, explaining his opposition to the construction of a mosque in another American state, said, "The political objective of Islam

---

[12] Bobby Ghosh, "Is America Islamophobic?" *Time*, August 30, 2010, 24.

is to dominate the world with its teaching . . . and to have domination of all other religions militarily."[13] Even when courteously employing theological apologetic arguments, evangelists run the risk of Muslims perceiving their dialogue as polemic in nature. Rather than engaging Muslims in arguments, a worldview approach supported by cultural understanding holds more promise.

Efforts at contextualizing Islamic forms are also met with suspicion. Muslims living in what they perceive as a siege mentality in the West or a majority situation in the Middle East view contextualizing methods of well-meaning Christians as misguided attempts at co-opting their faith and changing their religion into something it is not. Since polemics, apologetics, and contextualization have borne little fruit, I believe evangelism toward Muslims should be slanted in a different direction. I favor reaching Muslims through the felt and unfelt needs of their worldview. Most Christians have focused on the influential minority elite of Islam: the wealthy, the educated, and the powerful. Since folk Muslims compose the majority of Islam, other believers must develop strategies for reaching the poor, the uneducated, and the powerless.

Evangelicals have been slow to engage folk Islam. Many apologetic-minded missionaries believe that when Muslims see the error of their ways, the entire edifice of Islam will fall, including popular Islam. This has rarely happened.

Additionally, both evangelicals and Islamic orthodoxy itself question the authenticity of folk Islam within the Islamic community. The important fact remains, however, that folk Muslims self-identify as Muslims and must be approached as such.[14] Musk notes, "Sometimes the formal Islamic content of ordinary Muslims' lives is minimal. But there is no question in their minds as to whether they are Muslims or not."[15] This self-identity also holds true for the Beja tribe, as they consider themselves "good Muslims" despite

---

[13] Ghosh, 22 (ellipsis in the original).
[14] See Aslan, *No god but God*, 201 (see chap. 4, n. 3).
[15] Musk, "Popular Islam," 338–39.

their ATR proclivities and practices.[16] Consequently, even though traditional religion-influenced folk Muslims may appear indifferent to orthodox Islam, their self-identification as Muslims often causes them to be as resistant to the Christian message as their orthodox brethren.

Most scholars study the Islam of the Arab Middle East, where the shame/honor worldview predominates, and therefore are seldom exposed to or interested in contextualized worldview approaches that might reach the adherents of popular Islam. Some dismiss Islam outside the religion's heartland as superstitious, syncretistic, and therefore not worthy of serious study. Folk Islam demands earnest examination, because most Muslims live outside the Arab world and practice the popular forms of the religion. Such assessments present problems, because the lines separating the Islamic elements from the traditional influences are difficult to detect. If boundaries exist at all, they constantly shift according to the ethnic group as well as the age, gender, and economic situation of the individual.

Approaches for evangelizing Sufi folk Muslims must receive greater attention. Interestingly, the previously mentioned Islamic center site near the World Trade Center in New York City involves a Sufi congregation. The *Time* magazine article describes Sufis as a non-militant sect, a "mystical form of Islam reviled by extremists like Osama bin Laden."[17] Phil Parshall and Bill Musk represent the foremost advocates for engaging Sufi folk Muslims through their unique worldview. These Muslims who desire a deeper spiritual life deserve more attention by evangelicals. Sufi seekers have some common ground with evangelical Christians, as both groups advocate a personal relationship with God, personal discipleship, and an emphasis on the spiritual over the legalistic aspects of their religions. More methods for reaching Sufis must receive a priority in Christian missions.

Finally, Christians who attempt to engage folk Muslims should concentrate on approaches that aim for the heart and not just for the intellect. Although I believe Christianity possesses self-authenticating truth,

---

[16] See Jacobsen, *Theories of Sickness and Misfortune*, 21.

[17] Ghosh, "Is America Islamophobic?" 25.

becoming a Christian represents an act of faith. This act of faith is a response of the heart based on reason. Many in the West come to Christ after understanding their guilt before God and their need for a Savior. Others within consensus-oriented societies perceive God's requirements from a shame/honor perspective. These people often respond to the gospel by desiring to honor Jesus Christ as their Lord. This book argues that folk Muslims who dread the spirit world and desire release from fear of the unknown hold to a fear/power worldview orientation. As Christian workers concentrate on the everyday needs of folk Muslims, I believe more of them will come to Christ and come to know him personally and biblically. Let us pray to this end.

APPENDIX I

Beja Tribe in Sudan, Egypt and Eritrea.[1]

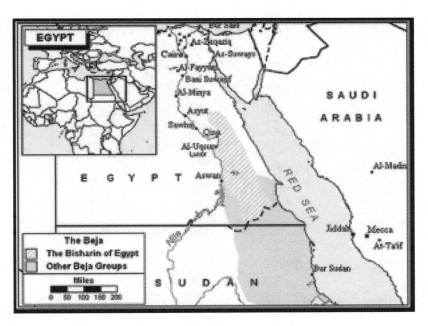

_____

[1] Dianabuja, "Coffee Customs in Eastern Sudan and Egypt: The Beja Tribes and a Recipe," *DIANABUJA'S BLOG: Africa, The Middle East, Agriculture, History and Culture* (blog), May 14, 2014, https://dianabuja.wordpress.com/2011/05/21/coffee -customs-in-eastern-sudan-and-egypt-the-beja-tribes/.

APPENDIX 2

Bantu Migrations in Africa.[1]

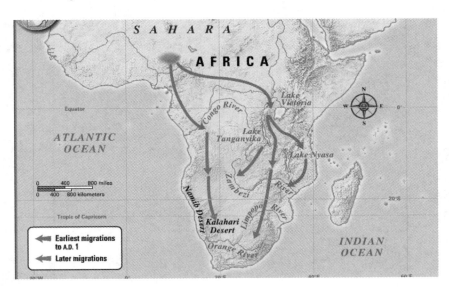

[1] "History of Africa," *Victoria Falls Guide* (blog), https://www.victoriafalls-guide
.net/history-of-africa.html.

APPENDIX 3

Sukuma-Nyamwezi language group area in Tanzania.[1]

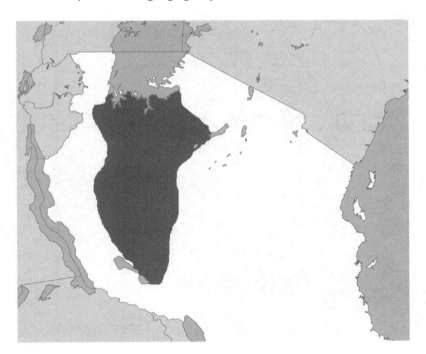

[1] "Sukuma-nyamwezi languages," last modified May 2, 2019, https://commons
.wikimedia.org/wiki/File:Sukuma-nyamwezi_language_in_Tanzania.PNG.

BIBLIOGRAPHY (SOURCES CITED)

Abdalati, Hammudah. *Islam in Focus*, 2nd ed. Indianapolis: American Trust Publications, undated.

Abdi, Vali. "Jacobite Explanation of the Trinity in the Context of Muʿtazilite Theology: Abu Raʾitah al-Takriti. https://www.researchgate.net/publication/340539059_Jacobite_Explanation_of_the_Trinity_in_the_Context_of_Mutazilite_Theology_Abu_Raitah_al-Takriti.

Abdul-Haqq, Abdiyah Akbar. *Sharing Your Faith with a Muslim*. Bloomington, MN: Bethany House, 1980.

Abrahams, R. G. *The Peoples of Greater Unyamwezi, Tanzania (Nyamwezi, Sukuma, Sumbwa, Kimbu, Konongo)*. London: International African Institute, 1967.

Ahmed, Akbar S. *Islam Today: A Short Introduction to the Muslim World*. London: I. B. Tauris, 1999, 2001.

Al Hariri-Wendel, Tanja. *See* Hariri-Wendel, Tanja al.

Allah Hand Illustration. https://www.bing.com/images/search?q=allah+hand+illustration+for+muslims&qpvt=Allah+hand+illustration+for+Muslims&form=IGRE&first=1&scenario=ImageBasicHover.

Al-Qaradawi, Yusuf. *See* Qaradawi, Yusuf al-.

Al-Qushayri, Abu ʾL-Qasim. *See* Qushayri, Abu ʾL-Qasim al-.

Al-Rawandi, Ibn. *See* Rawandi, Ibin al-.

Ankerberg, John, and Emir Caner. *The Truth about Islam & Jesus.* Eugene, OR: Harvest House, 2009.

Arberry, Arthur J. *Sufism: An Account of the Mystics of Islam.* London: Allen and Unwin, 1950.

Aslan, Reza. *No god but God: The Origins, Evolution, and Future of Islam.* New York: Random House, 2006.

At-Tahawiyy, Abu Ja far al-Warraq. *The Creed of At-Tahawiyy: A Brief Explanation of the Sunniy Creed.* Philadelphia: The Association of Islamic Charitable Projects, undated.

Ausenda, Giorgio. "Leisurely Nomads: the Hadendowa (Beja) of the Gash Delta and their Transition to Sedentary Village Life." PhD diss., Columbia University, 1987.

Bakhtiar, Laleh. *Sufi: Expressions of the Mystic Quest.* New York: Avon Books, 1976.

Bessire, Aimee, and Mark Bessire. *Sukuma.* The Heritage Library of African Peoples. New York: Rosen, 1997.

Bierman, John. *Dark Safari: The Life Behind the Legend of Henry Morton Stanley.* New York: Alfred A. Knopf, 1990.

Bledsoe, David Allen. "Brazilian Neo-Pentecostal Movement: Development and Distinctions with a Missiological Case Analysis of the Igreja Universal Do Reino De Deus and Its Impact on Brazilian Society." PhD diss., University of South Africa, 2010.

Brandström, Per. "The Agro-Pastoral Dilemma: The Underutilization and Overexploitation of Land among the Sukuma of Tanzania." Working Paper No. 8, University of Uppsala, Sweden, 1985.

Braswell, George W., Jr. *Islam: Its Prophet, Peoples, Politics and Power.* Nashville: B&H, 1996.

"Bridge to Life." Navigators. https://www.navigators.org/resource/the -bridge-to-life, 2010.

Bright, Bill. "Have You Heard of the Four Spiritual Laws?" Peachtree City, GA: New Life Resources, 2006.

Brown, Rick. "A Movement to Jesus Among Muslims." In *Perspectives on the World Christian Movement*, 4th ed., edited by Ralph D. Winter and Steven C. Hawthorne, 706–7. Pasadena: William Carey Library, 2009.

———. Response to question two in "A Humble Appeal to C5/Insider Movement Muslim Ministry Advocates to Consider Ten Questions." Gary Corwin. *International Journal of Frontier Missiology* 24, no. 1 (2007): 9.

Bruce, F. F. *The Acts of the Apostles*. Grand Rapids: Eerdmans, 1952.

Budge, E. A. Wallis. *The Egyptian Sudan: Its History and Monuments*. London: Kegan Paul, Trench, Trübner, 1907.

Carter, Charles W., and Ralph Earle. *The Acts of the Apostles*. Grand Rapids: Zondervan, 1959.

Chaudhry, Aziz Ahmad. *The Promised Messiah and Mahdi*. Islamabad: Islam International Publications, Ltd., 1996.

Chebel, Malek. *Symbols of Islam*. Paris: Ausoline, 2001.

Chittick, William C. *Sufism: A Short Introduction*. Oxford: Oneworld, 2000.

Churchill, Winston Spencer. *The River War: An Account of the Reconquest of the Sudan*. London: NEL Books, 1899, 1985.

Clark, W. T. "Manners, Customs and Beliefs of the Northern Bega." *Sudan Notes and Records* 21, no. 1 (1938): 1–29.

Collins, Robert O., and James M. Burns. *A History of Sub-Saharan Africa*. Cambridge: Cambridge University Press, 2007.

Corwin, Gary. "A Humble Appeal to C5/Insider Movement Muslim Ministry Advocates to Consider Ten Questions." *International Journal of Frontier Missiology* 24, no. 1 (2007): 5–21.

Cory, Hans. *The Indigenous Political System of the Sukuma and Proposals for Political Reform*. Nairobi: Eagle, 1954.

Cragg, Kenneth. *The Call of the Minaret*. Ibadan, NG: Daystar, 1985.

Craig, William Lane. *Reasonable Faith: Christian Truth and Apologetics*, 3rd ed. Wheaton, IL: Crossway Books, 2008.

Cummings, D. C. "The History of Kassala and the Province of Taka." *Sudan Notes and Records* 20, no. 1 (1937):1–40.

Dabashi, Hamid. *Shi'ism: A Religion of Protest*. Cambridge, MA: Belknap Press of Harvard University Press, 2011.

Daftary, Farhad. "Introduction" in *A Modern History of the Ismailis: Continuity and Change in a Muslim Community*, edited by Farhad Daftary, 1–15. London: I. B. Tauris, 2011.

Dawood, N. J., Trans. *The Koran: with Parallel Arabic Text*. London: Penguin Books, 1990.

Deedat, Ahmed. *Christ in Islam*. Jaipur, India: Islamic Organization of India, 1983.

Dianabuja, "Coffee Customs in Eastern Sudan and Egypt: The Beja Tribes and a Recipe." *DIANABUJA'S BLOG: Africa, The Middle East, Agriculture, History and Culture* (blog), May 14, 2014. https://dianabuja .wordpress.com/2011/05/21/coffee-customs-in-eastern-sudan-and -egypt-the-beja-tribes/.

Donner, Fred M. "Muhammad and the Caliphate." In the *Oxford History of Islam*, edited by John L. Esposito, 6–7. New York: Oxford University Press, 1999.

Donohue, John J. and John L. Esposito, eds. *Islam in Transition: Muslim Perspectives*. New York: Oxford University Press, 2006.

El Guindi, Fadwa. *See* Guindi, Fadwa el.

El Hassan, Idris Salim. *See* Hassan, Idris Salim el-.

Ernst, Carl W. *The Shambhala Guide to Sufism*. Boston: Shambhala Publications, 1997.

Esposito, John L. *Islam: The Straight Path*, 5th ed. New York: Oxford University Press, 2016.

———, ed. *The Oxford History of Islam*. New York: Oxford University Press, 1999.

———, Darrell J. Fasching, and Todd Lewis. *World Religions Today*, 3rd ed. New York: Oxford University Press, 2009.

————, and Dalia Mogahed. *Who Speaks for Islam? What a Billion Muslims Really Think.* New York: Gallup, 2007.

"Extra, Extra, McCain Staffers Knock KC." *Kansas City Star.* April 20, 2008. Section A:2.

"FAITH: New Revised FAITH Gospel Presentation." Nashville: Lifeway Christian Resources, 2006.

Gamst, F. C. "Beja." In *Muslim Peoples: A World Ethnographic Survey*, ed. Richard V. Weekes, 130–136. Vol. 1. Westport, CT: Greenwood, 1984.

Ghosh, Bobby. "Is America Islamophobic?" *Time*, August 30, 2010.

Godet, Frederick L. *Commentary on the Gospel of John*, 3rd ed. Translated by Timothy Dwight. Grand Rapids: Zondervan, 1893, 1969.

Gordon, April A., and Donald L. Gordon, eds. *Understanding Contemporary Africa*, 4th ed. Boulder, CO: Lynne Rienner, 2007.

Greear, J. D. *Breaking the Islam Code*. Eugene, OR: Harvest House, 2010.

Greeson, Kevin. *The Camel*. Arkadelphia, AR: WIGTake Resources, 2007.

Guindi, Fadwa el. *Veil: Modesty, Privacy and Resistance*. Oxford: Berg, 2003.

Guralnik, David B., ed. *Webster's New World Dictionary of the American Language*, 2nd College ed. New York: World, 1970.

Guthrie, Stan. "Deconstructing Islam: Apologist Jay Smith Takes a Confrontational Approach." *Christianity Today* 46, no. 10 (2002): 37.

Hakim, Khalifa Abdul, *The Metaphysics of Rumi: A Critical and Historical Sketch*. New Delhi: Adam, 2006.

Halim, Ahmed Abdel. "Native Medicine and Ways of Treatment in the Northern Sudan." *Sudan Notes and Records* 22, no. 1 (1939): 27–48.

Hamada, Louis B. *Understanding the Arab World*. Nashville: Thomas Nelson, 1990.

Hand, Wayland D. "Folk Medical Magic and Symbolism in the West" in *Magic, Witchcraft, and Religion: An Anthropological Study of the Supernatural*, 2nd ed., Arthur C. Lehmann & James E. Myers, eds. Mountain View, CA: Mayfield, 1989.

Hariri-Wendel, Tanja al. *Symbols of Islam*. New York: Sterling, 2002.

Hassan, Idris Salim el-. "On Ideology: The Case of Religion in Northern Sudan." PhD diss., University of Connecticut, 1980.

Haycock, B. G. "Towards a Better Understanding of the Kingdom of Cush (Napata-Meroe)." *Sudan Notes and Records* 49 (1968): 1–16.

Hesselgrave, David J. *Communicating Christ Cross-Culturally*, 2nd ed. Grand Rapids: Zondervan, 1991.

———, and Edward Rommen. *Contextualization: Meanings, Methods, and Models*. Pasadena, CA: William Carey Library, 2000.

———. *Paradigms in Conflict: 15 Key Questions in Christian Missions Today*, 2nd ed. Grand Rapids: Kregel Publications, 2018.

Hiebert, Paul G. *Anthropological Insights for Missionaries*. Grand Rapids: Baker, 1985.

———. "The Flaw of the Excluded Middle." In *Perspectives on the World Christian Movement*, 4th ed., edited by Ralph D. Winter and Stephen C. Hawthorne, 407–14. Pasadena, CA: William Carey Library, 2009.

———. *Transforming Worldviews: An Anthropological Understanding of How People Change*. Grand Rapids: Baker Academic, 2008.

———, R. Daniel Shaw, and Tite Tienou. *Understanding Folk Religion: A Christian Response to Popular Beliefs and Practices*. Grand Rapids: Baker, 1999.

Higgins, Kevin. "The Biblical Basis for Insider Movements: Asking the Right Question, in the Right Way." In *Muslim Conversions to Christ: A Critique of Insider Movements in Islamic Contexts*, edited by Ayman S. Ibrahim and Ant Greenham, 212. New York: Peter Lang, 2018.

"History of Africa." *Victoria Falls Guide* (blog). https://www.victoriafalls-guide.net/history-of-africa.html.

Hjort af Ornäs, Anders, and Gudrun Dahl. *Responsible Man: The Atmaan Beja of North-eastern Sudan*. Uppsala: Stockholm Studies in Social Anthropology, 1991.

Hodge, Charles. *A Commentary on the Epistle to the Romans*, rev. ed. (reprint edition 1975). Edinburgh: The Banner of Truth Trust, 1864.

Hodgson, Marshall G. S. *The Venture of Islam: Conscience and History in a World Civilization.* Chicago: University of Chicago Press, 1961, 1974.

Houssney, Georges. *Engaging Islam.* Boulder: Treeline, 2010.

Hussey, E. R. J. "A Fiki's Clinic." *Sudan Notes and Records* 6, no. 1 (1923): 35–39.

Ibrahim, Ayman, and Ant Greenham, eds. *Muslim Conversions to Christ: A Critique of Insider Movements in Islamic Contexts.* New York: Peter Lang, 2018.

Inayat-Khan, Zia. *Saracen Chivalry: Counsels on Valor, Generosity and the Mystical Quest.* New Lebanon, NY: Omega Publications, 2012.

Jabbour, Nabeel T. *The Crescent through the Eyes of the Cross: Insights from an Arab Christian.* Colorado Springs: NavPress, 2008.

Jacobsen, Frode F. *Theories of Sickness and Misfortune amongst the Hadandowa Beja: Narratives as Points of Entry into Beja Cultural Knowledge.* London and New York: Kegan Paul International, 1998.

Jenkins, Orville Boyd. *The Path of Love: Jesus in Mystical Islam.* Nairobi: Communication Press, 1984.

Johnson, Frederick. *A Standard English-Swahili Dictionary.* 2 vols. Nairobi: Oxford University Press, 1982.

Jok, Kuel Maluil, *Animism of the Nilotics and Discourses of Islamic Fundamentalism in Sudan.* Leiden: Sidestone, 2010.

Kane, J. Herbert. *A Concise History of the Christian World Mission.* Revised edition. Grand Rapids: Baker, 1982.

Kapteijns, Lidwien. "The Historiography of the Northern Sudan from 1500 to the Establishment of British Colonial Rule: A Critical Overview." *The International Journal of African Historical Studies* 22, no. 2 (1989): 251–66.

Karrar, Ali Salih. *The Sufi Brotherhoods in the Sudan.* London: C. Hurst, 1992.

Kato, Byang H. *Theological Pitfalls in Africa.* Kisumu, Kenya: Evangel, 1975.

Khayyam, Omar. *The Ruba'iyat of Omar Khayyam.* Translated by Peter Avery and John Heath-Stubbs. London: Penguin Books, 1981.

Kipling, Rudyard. "Fuzzy Wuzzy." In *A Victorian Anthology: 1837–1895*, edited by Edward Clarence Stedman, 595. Boston and New York: The Houghton-Mifflin Co., 1895.

Kirwan, L. P. "A Contemporary Account of the Conversion of the Sudan to Christianity." *Sudan Notes and Records* 20, no. 2 (1937): 289–95.

Kittel, Gerhard, and Gerhard Friedrich, eds. *Theological Dictionary of the New Testament*. 10 vols. Translated by Geoffrey W. Bromiley. Grand Rapids: Eerdmans, 1968.

Kraft, Charles H. "Culture, Worldview and Contextualization." In *Perspectives on the World Christian Movement*, 4th ed, edited by Ralph D. Winter and Steven C. Hawthorne, 400–406. Pasadena, CA: William Carey Library, 2009.

—————. "Dynamic Equivalent Churches in Muslim Society." In *The Gospel and Islam: A 1978 Compendium*, edited by Don M. McCurry, 124–28. Monrovia: Missions Advanced Research and Communication Center (MARC), 1978.

Lehmann, Arthur C., and James E. Myers, eds. *Magic, Witchcraft, and Religion: An Anthropological Study of the Supernatural*, 2nd ed. Mountain View, CA: Mayfield, 1989.

Levi-Strauss, Claude. "The Sorcerer and His Magic." In *Magic, Witchcraft, and Religion: An Anthropological Study of the Supernatural*, 2nd ed., edited by Arthur C. Lehmann and James E. Myers, 192–202. Mountain View, CA: Mayfield, 1985.

Lewis, B. A. "Deim el Arab and the Beja Stevedores of Port Sudan," *Sudan Notes and Records* 43 (1962): 16–49.

Lewis, I. M. *Islam in Tropical Africa*, 2nd ed. London: Hutchinson University Library for Africa, 1980.

Lewis, Rebecca. "Insider Movements: Retaining Identity and Preserving Community." In *Perspectives on the World Christian Movement*, 4th ed., edited by Ralph D. Winter and Steven C. Hawthorne, 673–75. Pasadena, CA: William Carey Library, 2009.

Lingenfelter, Sherwood G., and Marvin K. Mayers. *Ministering Cross-Culturally: An Incarnational Model for Personal Relationships*, 2nd ed. Grand Rapids: Baker Academic, 2003.

Marshall, Paul, Roberta Green, and Lela Gilbert. *Islam at the Crossroads: Understanding Its Beliefs, History, and Conflicts*. Grand Rapids: Baker, 2002.

Massey, Joshua. "His Ways Are Not Our Ways." *Evangelical Missions Quarterly* 35, no. 2 (1999): 194–98. https://missionexus.org/his-ways-are-not-our-ways/.

Mbiti, John S. *African Religions and Philosophy*, 2nd ed. Oxford: Heinemann Educational Publishers, 1989.

———. *Introduction to African Religion*, 2nd ed. Oxford: Heinemann Educational Publishers, 1991.

McCurry, Don M., ed. *The Gospel and Islam: A 1978 Compendium*. Monrovia: Missions Advanced Research and Communications Center (MARC), 1979.

Millroth, Berta. *Lyuba: Traditional Religion of the Sukuma*. Uppsala, Sweden: Studia Ethnographica Upsaliensia, 1965.

Morgan, Diane. *The Best Guide to Eastern Philosophy and Religion*. New York: Renaissance Books, 2001.

Moyo, Ambrose. "Religion in Africa." In *Understanding Contemporary Africa*, 3rd ed., edited by April Gordon and Donald L. Gordon, 299–329. Boulder, CO: Lynne Rienner, 2001.

Muller, Roland. *Honor & Shame: Unlocking the Door*. Bloomington, IN: Xlibris Corp., 2000.

Musk, Bill A. *Holy War: Why Do Some Muslims Become Fundamentalists?* London: Monarch Books, 2003.

———. "Popular Islam: An Investigation into the Phenomenology and Ethnotheological Bases of Popular Islamic Belief and Practice." PhD diss., University of South Africa, 1984.

———. *Touching the Soul of Islam: Sharing the Gospel in Muslim Cultures*. Oxford: Monarch Books, 2004.

————. *The Unseen Face of Islam: Sharing the Gospel with Ordinary Muslims at Street Level*. Revised edition. London: Monarch Books, 2003.

Nadel, S. F. "Notes on Beni-Amer Society." *Sudan Notes and Records* 26, no. 1 (1945): 53–94.

Nalder, L. F. "The Influence of Animism in Islam." *Sudan Notes and Records* 9, no. 1 (1926): 75–86.

Nasr, Seyyed Hossein. *Islam: Religion, History, and Civilization*. New York: HarperCollins, 2003.

————. *Sufi Essays*, 3rd ed. Chicago: ABC International Group, 1999.

Nasr, Vali. *The Shia Revival: How Conflicts within Islam Will Shape the Future*. New York: W. W. Norton, 2006.

Naude, J. A. "Islam in Africa." Occasional paper in *The Bulletin of The South African Institute of International Affairs*. Braamfontein: Jan Smuts House, 1978.

Numani, Shibli. *Umar*. London: I.B. Tauris, 2004.

Oladimeji, O. *African Traditional Religion*. Imo, NG: Ilesanmi & Sons, 1980.

Olowola, Cornelius. *African Traditional Religion and the Christian Faith*. Ghana: Africa Christian Press, 1993.

Ornäs, Anders Hjort af, and Gudrun Dahl. *See* Hjort af Ornäs.

Paul, A. *A History of the Beja Tribes of the Sudan*. London: Frank Cass, 1954.

————. "Notes on the Beni-Amer." *Sudan Notes and Records* 31, no. 2 (1950): 223–45.

Payne, Robert. *The History of Islam*. New York: Dorset, 1959, 1987.

Parshall, Phil. *Bridges to Islam: A Christian Perspective on Folk Islam*. Downers Grove, IL: InterVarsity Press, 2006.

————. "Going Too Far?" In *Perspectives on the World Christian Movement*, 4th ed., edited by Ralph D. Winter and Steven C. Hawthorne, 666. Pasadena: William Carey Library, 2009.

Patai, Raphael. *The Arab Mind*, rev. ed. New York: Hatherleigh, 1983.

Peel, John D. Y., and Charles Cameron Stewart, eds. *'Popular Islam' South of the Sahara*. Manchester: Manchester University Press, 1985.

Petterson, Don. *Inside Sudan: Political Islam, Conflict, and Catastrophe.* Boulder, CO: Westview, 1999.

Pikkert, Peter. *Protestant Missionaries to the Middle East: Ambassadors of Christ or Culture?* Ancaster, ON: Alev Books, 2008.

Qaradawi, Yusuf al-. *The Lawful and the Prohibited in Islam (Al-Halal Wal-Haram Fil Islam).* Translated by Kamal El-Helbawy, M. Moinuddin Siddiqui, and Syed Shukry. Indianapolis: American Trust Publications, 1960.

Qushayri, Abu 'L-Qasim al-. *Sufi Book of Spiritual Ascent.* Translated by Rabia Harris. Edited by Laleh Bakhtiar. Chicago: KAZI Publications, 1997.

Rawandi, Ibin al-. *Islamic Mysticism: A Secular Perspective.* Amherst, NY: Prometheus Books, 2000.

Reynolds, Gabriel Said, *The Emergence of Islam: Classical Traditions in Contemporary Perspective.* Minneapolis: Fortress, 2012.

Richardson, Don. *Eternity in Their Hearts,* 3rd ed. Ventura, CA: Regal Books, 2005.

———. *Peace Child,* 4th ed. Ventura, CA: Regal Books, 2005.

———. "Redemptive Analogy." In *Perspectives on the World Christian Movement,* 4th ed., edited by Ralph D. Winter and Steven C. Hawthorne, 430–36. Pasadena: William Carey Library, 2009.

Rippin, Andrew. *Muslims: Their Religious Beliefs and Practices,* 3rd ed. New York: Routledge, 2005.

Ruthven, Malise. *Islam in the World,* 3rd ed. New York: Oxford University Press, 2006.

Saal, William J. *Reaching Muslims for Christ.* Chicago: Moody, 1991.

Sandars, G. E. R. "The Amarar." *Sudan Notes and Records* 18, no. 2 (1935): 195–220.

———. "The Bisharin." *Sudan Notes and Records* 16, no. 2 (1933): 119–45.

Schlorff, Samuel P. *Missiological Models in Ministry to Muslims.* Upper Darby, PA: Middle East Resources, 2006.

Shah, Idries. *The Way of the Sufi.* London: Penguin Books, 1968.

Silva, Ken. *Global Jihad.* McLean, VA: Isaac, 2007.

———. "Share Your Faith," Evangelism Explosion. Accessed February 10, 2021. https://evangelismexplosion.org/ministries/share-your-faith/.

"'Sorcerer' Awaits Beheading by Saudi Officials." *Kansas City Star*, April 25, 2010. A26.

Steps to Peace with God. Minneapolis: Billy Graham Evangelistic Association, 2005.

Stewart, Charles Cameron. "Introduction: Popular Islam in Twentieth-Century Africa." In *'Popular Islam' South of the Sahara*, edited by J. D. Y. Peel and Charles C. Stewart, 363–69. Manchester: Manchester University Press, 1985.

"Sukuma-nyamwezi languages," last modified May 2, 2019, https://it.wikipedia.org/wiki/Lingue_sukuma-nyamwezi.

Talman, Harley, and John Jay Travis, eds. *Understanding Insider Movements: Disciples of Jesus Within Diverse Religious Communities.* Pasadena: William Carey Library, 2015.

Tennent, Timothy C. "Followers of Jesus ('Isa) in Islamic Mosques: A Closer Examination of C-5 'High Spectrum' Contextualization." *International Journal of Frontier Missions* 23, no. 3 (2006): 101–17.

Travis, John J. "The C-Spectrum: A Practical Tool for Defining Six Types of 'Christ-Centered Communities' Found in Muslim Contexts." In *Perspectives on the World Christian Movement*, 4th ed., edited by Ralph D. Winter and Steven C. Hawthorne, 664–65. Pasadena: William Carey Library, 2009.

———. Response One in "Four Responses to Timothy C. Tennent's 'Followers of Jesus ('Isa) in Islamic Mosques: A Closer Examination of C-5 "High Spectrum" Contextualiation.'" *International Journal of Frontier Missions* 23, no. 3 (2006): 124–25.

———. "Must All Muslims Leave 'Islam' To Follow Jesus?" In *Perspectives on the World Christian Movement*, 4th ed., edited by Ralph D. Winter and Steven C. Hawthorne, 668–72. Pasadena, CA: William Carey Library, 2009.

Trofimov, Yaroslav. *The Siege of Mecca: The Forgotten Uprising in Islam's Holiest Shrine and the birth of Al Qaeda*. New York: Anchor Books, 2007.

Understanding Islam and the Muslims. Islamic Affairs Department. Washington, DC: The Embassy of Saudi Arabia, 1989.

Van Pelt, Piet. *Bantu Customs in Mainland Tanzania*, rev. ed. Tabora, Tanzania: T. M. P. Book Department, 1984.

Van Rheenen, Gailyn. *Communicating Christ in Animistic Contexts*. Pasadena, CA: William Carey Library, 1991.

———. *Missions: Biblical Foundations and Contemporary Strategies*. Grand Rapids: Zondervan, 1996.

Watt, Montgomery. *Bell's Introduction to the Quran*. Edinburgh: University of Edinburgh University Press, 1970.

Weekes, Richard V., ed. *Muslim Peoples: A World Ethnographic Survey*. Vol 1. Westport, CT: Greenwood Press, 1984.

Wehr, Hans. *Arabic-English Dictionary: A Dictionary of Modern Written Arabic (Arabic-English)*, 3rd ed. Edited by J. Milton Cowan. Ithaca, NY: Spoken Language Services, 1976.

Welch, Evie Adams. "Life and Literature of the Sukuma in Tanzania, East Africa." PhD diss. Howard University, 1974.

Wheatcroft, Andrew. *Infidels: A History of the Conflict between Christendom and Islam*. New York: Random House, 2004.

Wijsen, Frans, and Ralph Tanner. *I Am Just a Sukuma: Globalization and Identity Construction in Northwest Tanzania*. Amsterdam: Rodopi, 2002.

Winter, Ralph D. "Going Far Enough?" In *Perspectives on the World Christian Movement*, 4th ed., edited by Ralph D. Winter and Steven C. Hawthorne, 670–671. Pasadena: William Carey Library, 2009.

———, and Steven C. Hawthorne, eds. *Perspectives on the World Christian Movement*, 3rd ed. Pasadena: William Carey Library, 1999.

———, eds. *Perspectives on the World Christian Movement*, 4th ed. Pasadena: William Carey Library, 2009.

Zebiri, Kate. *Muslims and Christians Face to Face.* Oxford: OneWorld, 1997.

Zwemer, Samuel M. *The Influence of Animism on Islam.* New York: Macmillan, 1920.

BIBLIOGRAPHY (COMPREHENSIVE)

Abd al-Salam, S. *A Study of Contemporary Sudanese Muslim Saints' Legends in Sociocultural Contexts*. PhD diss., Indiana University, 1983.

Abrahams, R. G. *The Nyamwezi Today: A Tanzanian People in the 1970s*. Cambridge: Cambridge University Press, 1981.

Abu, S., and H. Abdul. "Dissertations and Theses on Islam and Muslims." *American Journal of Islamic Social Sciences* 17, no. 3 (2000): 140–48.

Abun-Nasr, Jamil M. *The Tijaniyya: A Sufi Order in the Modern World*. London: Oxford University Press, 1965.

Ahmad, H. M. G. "Essence of Islam: Evidence for the Truthfulness of the Holy Quran, Its Comprehensive Nature and Its Superiority over Revealed Books." *The Review of Religions* 101, no. 11 (2006): 4–22.

Akin, Daniel, David Nelson, and Bruce Ashford. "An Assessment of *The Camel*." Unpublished paper. Southeastern Baptist Theological Seminary, 2008.

Alford, Deann. "Unapologetic Apologist: Jay Smith Confronts Muslim Fundamentalist Fervor." *Christianity Today*, June 2008. https://www.christianitytoday.com/ct/2008/june/21.34.html.

Al-Jazairi, Abu Bakr. *See* Jazairi, Abu Bakr al-.

Allen, J. M., III. "An Evaluation of the Christology of the *Camel Training Manual*." Master of Theology thesis. Dallas Theological Seminary, 2007.

Anderson, Justice. "The Great Century and Beyond (1792–1910)." In *Missiology: An Introduction to the Foundations, History, and Strategies of World Missions*, edited by John Mark Terry, Ebbie Smith, and Justice Anderson, 199–218. Nashville: B&H Academic, 1998.

Andrzejewski, B. W. "The Study of the Bedauye Language: The Present Position and Prospects." African Studies Seminar Paper no. 4. Sudan Research Unit, Faculty of Arts. University of Khartoum, 1968.

Arkell, A. J. *A History of the Sudan: From the Earliest Times to 1821*. London: Athlone, 1955.

Armstrong, Karen. *Muhammad: A Prophet for Our Time*. New York: HarperCollins, 2006.

Atterbury, Anson Phelps. *Islam in Africa*. 1899. Reprint rev. ed. London: Darf, 1987.

Atyeo, Henry C. "Fuzzy Wuzzy Learns to Vote." *American Mercury* 82, no. 4 (1956): 129–34.

Barclay, Harold B. "Sudan (North): On the Frontier of Islam." In *Religions and Societies: Asia and the Middle East*, edited by Carlo Caldarola, 147–70. Berlin: Walter De Gruyter, 1982.

Basilov, V. N. "Popular Islam in Central Asia and Kazakhstan." *Institute of Muslim Minority Affairs* (Jan. 8, 1987): 7–17.

Bauer, Walter, Wilhelm F. Arndt, and Felix W. Gingrich. *A Greek-English Lexicon of the New Testament and Other Early Christian Literature*. Chicago: University of Chicago Press, 1957.

Beaton, A. C. "Tigri Folk Tales (Digam)." *Sudan Notes and Records* 28 (1947): 146–50.

"Beja." In *The Family of Man: The Peoples of Africa*, 281–83. Tarrytown, NY: Marshall Cavendish, 1979.

Berger, Morroe. *Islam in Egypt Today: Social and Political Aspects of Popular Religion*. Cambridge: Cambridge University Press, 1970.

Bishai, Wilson B. *Humanities in the Arabic-Islamic World*. Dubuque, IA: William C. Brown, 1973.

Bosch, David J. *Transforming Mission: Paradigm Shifts in Theology of Mission.* Maryknoll, NY: Orbis Books, 1991.

Bravmanv, R. A. *African Islam.* Washington, DC: Smithsonian Institute Press, 1983.

Brelvi, M. *Islam in Africa.* Lahore, Pakistan: Institute of Islamic Culture, 1964.

Burton, Sir Richard Francis. *First Footsteps in East Africa, or An Exploration of Harar.* 1856. Illustrated reprint rev. ed. New York: Dover Publications, 1987.

Collins, Roland O. *A History of Modern Sudan.* New York: Cambridge University Press, 2008.

Cooper, Anne. *Ishmael, My Brother: A Biblical Course on Islam.* Monrovia: MARC Europe.

Cooper, M. C. "Two Fighting Tribes of the Sudan." *National Geographic* 56 (October 1929): 165.

Corduan, Winfried. *Neighboring Faiths: A Christian Introduction to World Religions.* Downer's Grove, IL: InterVarsity Press, 1998.

Cory, Hans. *The Ntemi: The Traditional Rites in Connection with the Burial, Election, Enthronement and Magic Powers of a Sukuma Chief.* London: Macmillan, 1951.

———. *Sukuma Law and Custom.* Oxford: Oxford University Press, 1953.

Daniel, E. L. "Theology and Mysticism in the Writings of Ziya Gökalp." *Muslim World* 67, no. 3 (1977): 175–84.

Davidson, Basil. *Africa: History of a Continent.* London: Spring Books, 1972.

Delany, F. "Graves in the Langeb-Baraka Area." *Sudan Notes and Records* 33, no. 1 (1982): 58–59.

De Waal, Alex, ed. *Islamism and Its Enemies in the Horn of Africa.* London: Hurst, 2004.

Eitel, Keith E. "'To Be or Not to Be?': The Indigenous Church Question." In *Missiology: An Introduction to the Foundations, History, and Strategies of World Missions,* edited by John Mark Terry, Ebbie Smith, and Justice Anderson, 301–17. Nashville: B&H Academic, 1998.

Elton, Lord Godfrey. *General Gordon*. London: Collins, 1954.

Esack, Farid. *On Being a Muslim*. Oxford: OneWorld, 2010.

Esposito, John, ed. *Islam in Asia: Religion, Politics and Society*. New York: Oxford University Press, 1987.

Filbeck, D. *Social Context and Proclamation: A Socio-Cognitive Study in Proclaiming the Gospel Cross-Culturally*. Pasadena, CA: William Carey Library, 1985.

Fleming, G. J. "Kassala." *Sudan Notes and Records* 5, no. 2 (1922): 65–77.

Foxall, George. "Folk Islam: The Case of the Hausa of Northern Nigeria." *Africa Journal of Evangelical Theology* 11, no. 1 (1992): 24–33.

Fradin, Murray S. *Jihad: The Mahdi Rebellion in the Sudan*. Lincoln, NE: IUniverse, 2003.

"'Fuzzy Wuzzy' Will End His Days a Free Man." *The Literary Digest* 84 (February 21, 1925): 55.

Gaffney, Patrick D. "Popular Islam." *Annals of the American Academy of Political and Social Science* 524 (November 1992): 38–51.

Gilliland, Dean. "Contextualization." In *Evangelical Dictionary of World Missions*, edited by A. Scott Moreau et al, 225–27. Grand Rapids: Baker, 2000.

Gmelch, G. "Baseball Magic." In *Magic, Witchcraft, and Religion*, 2nd ed., edited by Arthur C. Lehmann and James E. Myers, 295–301. Mountain View, CA: Mayfield, 1989.

Goldschmidt, A., Jr. *A Brief History of Egypt*. New York: Checkmark Books, 2008.

Green, Denis. "Guidelines from Hebrews for Contextualization." In *Muslims and Christians on the Emmaus Road*, edited by J. Dudley Woodberry, 233–50. Monrovia: MARC, 1989.

Greenlee, David H., ed. *From the Straight Path to the Narrow Way*. Waynesboro, GA: Authentic Media, 2006.

Grudem, Wayne. *Systematic Theology: An Introduction to Biblical Doctrine*. Grand Rapids: InterVarsity Press, 1994.

Gunn, T. Jeremy. "Shaping an Islamic Identity: Religion, Islamism, and the State in Central Asia." *Sociology of Religion* 64, no. 3 (Autumn 2003): 389–410.

Hadaway, Robin Dale. "A Church Planting and Discipleship Training Project for Mwanza, Tanzania, East Africa." PhD diss., Golden Gate Baptist Theological Seminary, 1986.

Hand, W. D. "Folk Medical Magic and Symbolism in the West." In *Magic, Witchcraft, and Religion*, 2nd ed., edited by Arthur C. Lehmann and James E. Myers, 192–98. Mountain View, CA: Mayfield, 1989.

Hassan, Riaz. "Religion, Society, and the State in Pakistan: Pirs and Politics." *Asian Survey* 27, no. 5 (1987): 552–65.

Hassan, Yusuf Fadl. "The Penetration of Islam in the Eastern Sudan." In *Islam in Tropical Africa*, 2nd illus. ed., edited by I. M. Lewis, 112–13. Bloomington, IN: International African Institute, 1980.

Hatfield, C. R., Jr. "The Nfumu in Tradition and Change: A Study of the Position on Religious Practitioners among the Sukuma of Tanzania, E. Africa." PhD diss., Catholic University of America, 1968.

Hiebert, Paul G. *Anthropological Reflections on Missiological Issues*. Grand Rapids: Baker, 1994.

———. "Power Encounter and Folk Islam." In *Muslims and Christians on the Emmaus Road*, edited by J. Dudley Woodberry, 45–61. Monrovia: MARC, 1989.

Hile, P. "Communicating the Gospel in Terms of Felt Needs." *Missiology, An International Review* 5, no. 4 (1977): 499–506.

Hoffman, Valerie J. *Sufism, Mystics, and Saints in Modern Egypt*. Columbia: University of South Carolina Press, 1995.

Holt, Peter M. *A Modern History of the Sudan: From the Funj Sultanate to the Present Day*. London: Weidenfeld and Nicolson, 1961.

———., and M. W. Daly. *A History of the Sudan: From the Coming of Islam to the Present Day*, 4th ed. London: Longman, 1988.

Hunter, George G., III. "Evangelizing Pre-Christian People: A Thematic Perspective." *Journal of the American Society for Church Growth* 20 (2009): 5–36.

Hyatt, Erik. "Christian Witness in Muslim Settings." *Evangelical Missions Quarterly* (January 2009): 84–92.

Ibrahim, Abdullah Ali. "Popular Islam: The Religion of the Barbarous Throng." *Northeast African Studies* 11, no. 2 (1989): 21–40.

Jazairi, Abu Bakr al-. *Islamic Etiquette*, 2nd. ed. Translated by Jamal Al-Din M. Zarabozo. Houston: Darussalam, 2004.

Jenkins, Orville Boyd. "Beja People Summary." Unpublished working paper. Nairobi: Interfaith Research Centre, 1996.

Jennings-Bramly, W. E. "Notes: Northern Sudan: 'Bisharin Fables,' 'Stories of the Gerarish,' and 'The Soothsayer.'" *Sudan Notes and Records* 8 (1925): 177–80.

Jok, Madut Jok. *Sudan: Race, Religion, and Violence*. Oxford: Oneworld, 2008.

Katz, Marion Holmes. "Women's *Mawlid* Performances in Sanaa and the Construction of 'Popular Islam.'" *International Journal of Middle East Studies* 40, no. 3 (2008): 467–84.

Kerr, D. A. "Christianity in Muslim Society: Towards a Contextualization of Theology." *Studies in World Christianity* 3, no. 2 (1997): 121–239.

———. "Muhammad: Prophet of Liberation: A Christian Perspective from Political Theology." *Studies in World Christianity* 6, no. 2 (2000): 139–75.

Kirwan, L. P. "A Survey of Nubian Origins." *Sudan Notes and Records* 20, no. 1 (1937): 47–62.

Kraft, Charles H. "Three Encounters in Christian Witness." In *Perspectives on the World Christian Movement*, 4th ed., edited by Ralph D. Winter and Steven C. Hawthorne, 445–50. Pasadena: William Carey Library, 2009.

Kraft, Marguerite G. *Understanding Spiritual Power: A Forgotten Dimension of Cross-Cultural Mission and Ministry*. Maryknoll, NY: Orbis, 1995.

Lawless, Chuck. "Spiritual Warfare and Missions." *The Southern Baptist Journal of Theology* 9, no. 4 (2005): 34–48.

Lewis, Bernard. *What Went Wrong? The Clash Between Islam and Modernity in the Middle East.* New York: HarperCollins, 2002.

Lewis, I. M. *Islam in Tropical Africa*, 2nd ed. Bergvlei, South Africa: Hutchinson Group, 1980.

———. *Saints and Somalis: Popular Islam in a Clan-Based Society.* Lawrenceville, NJ: Red Sea Press, 1998.

Livingstone, Greg. *Planting Churches in Muslim Cities.* Grand Rapids: Baker, 1993.

Loewen, Jacob A. *Culture and Human Values: Christian Intervention in Anthropological Perspective.* Pasadena: William Carey Library, 1975.

Louw, Maria Elisabeth. *Everyday Islam in Post-Soviet Central Asia.* New York: Routledge, 2007.

Madearis, Carl. *Muslims, Christians, and Jesus.* Minneapolis: Bethany House, 2008.

Martin, Richard C., Mark R. Woodward, and Dwi S. Atmaja. *Defenders of Reason in Islam: Mu'tazilism from Medieval School to Modern Symbol.* Oxford: Oneworld, 1997.

Massey, Joshua. "Editorial: Muslim Contextualization." *International Journal of Frontier Missions* 17, no. 1 (2000): 1–4.

McDowall, David. *A Modern History of the Kurds*, 3rd ed. London: I. B. Tauris, 2004.

McGavran, Donald A. *Understanding Church Growth*, 3rd ed. Revised and edited by C. Peter Wagner. Grand Rapids: Eerdmans, 1990.

Moorehead, Alan. *The Blue Nile.* New York: Harper & Row, 1962.

———. *The White Nile.* New York: Harper & Row, 1960.

Moreau, Scott. "Contextualization, Syncretism, and Spiritual Warfare." In *Contextualization and Syncretism: Navigating Cultural Currents*, edited by Gailyn Van Rheenen, 47–69. Pasadena: William Carey Library, 2006.

Morton, John. "Ethnicity and Politics in Red Sea Province, Sudan." *African Affairs* 88 (1989): 63–76.

Moulton, James Hope and George Milligan. *The Vocabulary of the Greek New Testament*. 1930. Grand Rapids: Eerdmans, 1974.

Muhajiri, Masih. *Islamic Revolution: Future Path of the Nations*. Tehran: External Liaison Section of the Central Office of *Jihad-e-Sazaandegi*, Islamic Republic of Iran, 1982.

Musk, Bill A. "Encounter with Jesus in Popular Islam." *Evangelical Review of Theology* 10, no. 3 (1986): 247–57.

———. "Popular Islam: The Hunger of the Heart." In *The Gospel and Islam*, edited by Don M. McCurry, 208–21. Monrovia: MARC, 1979.

Nachtwey, J. "The Tragedy of Sudan." *Time* 164, no. 14 (2004): 44–46.

Nasr, Ahmad A. "Popular Islam in al-Tayyib Salih." *Journal of Arabic Literature* 11 (1980): 88–104.

Neibuhr, H. Richard. *Christ and Culture*. New York: Harper & Row, 1951.

Nevius, John Livingston. *The Planting and Development of Missionary Churches*. 1886. Hancock, NH: Monadnock, 2003.

O'Brien, Donal B. Cruise. "Satan Steps Out from the Shadows: Religion and Politics in Africa." *Africa: Journal of the International African Institute* 70, no. 3 (2000): 520–26.

Özdalga, Elisabeth. *The Veiling Issue: Official Secularism and Popular Islam in Modern Turkey*. London: RoutledgeCurzon, 1998.

Paul, A. "Ancient Tombs in Kassala Province." *Sudan Notes and Records* 33, no. 1 (1952): 54–57.

Parshall, Phil. "Lessons Learned in Contextualization." In *Muslims and Christians on the Emmaus Road*, edited by J. Dudley Woodberry, 251–65. Monrovia: MARC, 1989.

———. *Muslim Evangelism*, 2nd ed. Waynesboro, GA: Gabriel, 2003.

Perkins, Kenneth J. *Port Sudan: The Evolution of a Colonial City*. Boulder, CO: Westview, 1983.

Pocock, Michael, Gailyn Van Rheenen, and Douglas McConnell. *The Changing Face of World Missions: Engaging Contemporary Issues and Trends*. Grand Rapids: Baker Academic, 2005.

Pratt, T. D. "The Need to Dialog: A Review of the Debate on the Controversy of Signs, Wonders, Miracles and Spiritual Warfare Raised in the Literature of the Third Wave Movement." *Pneuma: The Journal of the Society for Pentecostal Studies* 13, no. 1 (1991): 7–32.

Richardson, Don. *Secrets of the Koran.* Ventura, CA: Regal Books, 2003.

Richardson, Irvine. *The Role of Tone in the Structure of Sukuma.* London: School of Oriental and African Studies, University of London, 1959.

Richter, Julius. *History of Protestant Missions in the Near East.* New York: Fleming H. Revell Co., 1910.

Riddell, Peter G., and Peter Cotterell. *Islam in Context: Past, Present, and Future.* Grand Rapids: Baker Academic, 2003.

Robinson, Andrew. *Lost Languages: The Enigma of the World's Undeciphered Scripts.* New York: McGraw-Hill, 2002.

Roden, David. "The Twentieth Century Decline of Suakin." *Sudan Notes and Records* 51 (1970): 1–22.

Roper, E. M. "Poetry of the Hadendiwa." *Sudan Notes and Records* 10 (1927): 147–58.

Salih, Hassan Mohammed. "Hadanduwa Traditional Territorial Rights and Inter-Population Relations Within the Context of the Native Administration System (1927–1970)." *Sudan Notes and Records* 61 (1980): 118–33.

Samatar, Said S., ed. *In the Shadow of Conquest: Islam in Colonial Northeast Africa.* Trenton, NJ: Red Sea Press, 1992.

Sauma, Rabban. "Ancestor Practices in the Muslim World: A Problem of Contextualization from Central Asia." *Missiology* 30, no. 3 (2002): 323–45.

Schilder, Kees. *Popular Islam in Tunisia: A Regional Cults Analysis.* Leiden, Netherlands: African Studies Centre, 1990.

Schlorff, Samuel P. "The Catholic Program for Dialogue with Islam: An Evangelical Evaluation with Special Reference to Contextualization." *Missiology* 11, no. 2 (1983): 131–48.

Shaw, Mark. *The Kingdom of God in Africa.* Grand Rapids: Baker, 1996.

Smith, Charles D. *Islam and the Search for Social Order in Modern Egypt: A Biography of Muhammad Husayn Haykal.* Albany: State University of New York Press, 1983.

Smith, R. Marvin. "Folk Islam in East Africa." *Africa Journal of Evangelical Theology* 18, no. 2 (1999): 83–106.

Spiers, Edward M., ed. *Sudan: The Reconquest Reappraised.* London: Frank Cass, 1998.

Steffen, Tom A. "Why Communicate the Gospel through Stories?" In *Perspectives on the World Christian Movement*, 4th ed., edited by Ralph D. Winter and Steven C. Hawthorne, 440–44. Pasadena: William Carey Library, 2009.

Steinbronn, Anthony J. *Worldviews: A Christian Response to Religious Pluralism.* St. Louis: Concordia, 2007.

Talman, Harley. "Comprehensive Contextualization." *International Journal of Frontier Missions* 21, no. 1 (2004): 6–12.

Tanner, Ralph E. S. *Transition in African Beliefs: Traditional Religion and Christian Change; A Study in Sukumaland, Tanzania, East Africa.* Maryknoll, NY: Maryknoll Publications, 1967.

Taylor, William D., ed. *Global Missiology for the 21st century: The Iguassu Dialogue.* Grand Rapids: Baker Academic, 2000.

Terry, John Mark, Ebbie Smith, and Justice Anderson, eds. *Missiology: An Introduction to the Foundations, History, and Strategies of World Missions.* Nashville: B&H Academic, 1998.

Theobald, A. B. *The Mahdiya: A History of the Anglo-Egyptian Sudan 1881–1899.* London: Longmans, Green, 1951.

Thomas, Douglas E. *African Traditional Religion in the Modern World.* Jefferson, NC: McFarland, 2005.

Tippitt, Alan. "The Evangelization of Animists." In *Perspectives on the World Christian Movement*, 3rd ed., edited by Ralph D. Winter and Steven C. Hawthorne, 623–31. Pasadena: William Carey Library, 1998.

Trimingham, J. Spencer. *Islam in Ethiopia.* New York: Routledge, 1959.

———. *Islam in the Sudan.* London: Oxford University Press, 1965.

————. *Islam in West Africa*. London: Oxford University Press, 1959.

Tritton, Arthur S. *Islam: Beliefs and Practices*. London: Hutchinson's University Library, 1951.

Van Rheenen, Gailyn, ed. *Contextualization and Syncretism: Navigating Cultural Currents*. Pasadena, CA: William Carey Library, 2006.

————. "Syncretism and Contextualization: The Church on a Journey Defining Itself." In *Contextualization and Syncretism: Navigating Cultural Currents*, edited by Gailyn Van Rheenen, 1–29. Pasadena: William Carey Library, 2006.

————. "A Theology of Power." *Evangelical Missions Quarterly* (January 2005). http://www.emqonline.com/emq_article_read.php? ArticleID=575.

Voll, John Obert. "The Effects of Islamic Structures on Modern Islamic Expansion in the Eastern Sudan." *International Journal of African Historical Studies* 7, no. 1 (1974): 85–98.

————. *Historical Dictionary of the Sudan*. London: Scarecrow, 1978.

Wagner, C. Peter. *The Third Wave of the Holy Spirit: Encountering the Power of Signs and Wonders Today*. Ann Arbor, MI: Vine Books, 1988.

————. *Confronting the Powers*. Ventura, CA: Regal, 1996.

Watt, W. Montgomery. *Islamic Philosophy and Theology: An Extended Survey*. Edinburgh: Edinburgh University Press, 1985.

————. *Mohammad: Prophet and Statesman*. Oxford: Oxford University Press, 1961.

Wedekind, Klaus. *Beja Narrative: Pursuit of Participants and Analysis of Aspects*. Berlin and New York: Mouton de Grutyr, 1990.

Weerstra, Hans M., ed. "Islam III." *International Journal of Frontier Missions* 13, no. 4 (1996): 161–216.

Woodberry, J. Dudley. "Contextualization Among Muslims: Reusing Common Pillars." In *The Word Among Us*, edited by Dean Gilliland, 282–312. Dallas: Word, 1989.

————, ed. *Muslims and Christians on the Emmaus Road*. Monrovia: MARC, 1989.

NAME INDEX

SUBJECT INDEX

SCRIPTURE INDEX